Teacher's

Total English

ELEMENTARY

Teacher's Book with Resource Disc

Fiona Gallagher

Contents

What's new about *New Total English*?

What makes *New Total English* different from – and better than – the first edition? Firstly, don't worry – we haven't thrown the baby out with the bathwater! We haven't changed everything. We've listened to what you said you liked about the first edition and have kept the most popular features. You'll certainly recognise the look, the format and some integral features from the first edition: the Lead-in pages, the easy-to-use lessons, the comprehensive Reference and Review and practice sections, the popular video clips. Changing to the new edition won't mean that you have to get to grips with a completely new course.

Real solutions to real needs

Some things <u>are</u> different, however. We've looked at every aspect of the course and tried to find solutions for some of your real needs. We've improved the flow of many of the lessons in the Students' Book, integrating more Can do statements and making sure that they all have clear 'outcomes'. We've also given more space to important aspects of language learning such as vocabulary, writing and listening. There's a free online Vocabulary Trainer with each level to help learners memorise new words and phrases; a complete Writing bank at the back of the Students' Book, covering different text types and writing sub-skills as well as new semi-authentic listening extracts to help students gain confidence in dealing with features such as redundancy, hesitation and ungrammatical speech. And, as you'd expect with a new edition, we've given the grammar, vocabulary and pronunciation syllabus a complete overhaul as well as updating much of the content.

New digital components

We've also included new digital components in the course package. The ActiveBook component features the Students' Book pages in digital format and includes integrated audio and video as well as interactive exercises for students to do in class or at home. The ActiveTeach component will help you get the most out of the course with its range of interactive whiteboard software tools and *MyTotalEnglishLab* will help students get better results with its range of interactive practice exercises, progress tests and automatic gradebook.

To sum up, we've kept all the best ingredients of the first edition, improved other features and added exciting new digital components to make *New Total English* an even better package. We hope you and your students will continue to enjoy using it.

The *New Total English* author team

Course package

Students' Book with ActiveBook and DVD

The *New Total English* Students' Books with ActiveBook and DVD are divided into 10–12 units that contain approximately 80–120 hours of teaching material. Each unit contains a balanced mix of grammar, vocabulary, pronunciation and skills:

- clear aims and objectives linked to the CEFR (Common European Framework of Reference)
- revised grammar, vocabulary and pronunciation syllabus
- new reading, listening and video material
- new Writing bank with model texts and focus on sub-skills
- revised and extended Pronunciation bank

ActiveBook:

- digital version of Students' Book with interactive activites and integrated audio and video
- video clips can be selected when you use the ActiveBook in your computer, or play it in a DVD player

Students' Book with ActiveBook, DVD and MyLab

Packaged with the *New Total English* Students' Book with ActiveBook and DVD, *MyTotalEnglishLab* provides students with everything they need to make real progress both in class and at home:

MyTotalEnglishLab:

- interactive exercises with feedback
- regular progress and achievement tests
- automatic marking and gradebook

Class CDs

The *New Total English* Class CDs contain all the recorded material from the Students' Books.

Workbook and Audio CD

The *New Total English* Workbooks contain further practice of language areas covered in the corresponding units of the Students' Books:

- extra grammar, vocabulary, skills and pronunciation exercises
- regular Review and Consolidation sections
- audioscripts and accompanying Audio CD
- with and without key versions available

Teacher's Book with Resource Disc

The *New Total English* Teacher's Books provide all the
support teachers need to get the most out of the course:

- background notes and instructions on how to exploit
  each unit
- suggestions for warm-up and extension activities

Resource Disc:

- extensive bank of photocopiable and printable
  classroom activities
- editable and printable progress and achievement tests
- audio and video scripts

ActiveTeach and DVD

The *New Total English* Teacher's Books will be further
enhanced by the ActiveTeach component which features:

- Students' Book in digital format with all the material
  from the ActiveBook
- all the material from the Resource Disc
- interactive whiteboard software tools
- video clips can be selected when you use the
  ActiveTeach in your computer, or play it in a DVD player

Vocabulary Trainer

The *New Total English* Vocabulary Trainer is a new online
learning tool designed to help students revise and
memorise key vocabulary from the course.
Check this exciting new component out on
www.newtotalenglish.vocabtrainer.net

Website

New Total English has its own dedicated website. In
addition to background information about the course and
authors, the website features teaching tips, downloadable
worksheets, links to other useful websites as well as
special offers and competitions. Join us online at
www.pearsonlongman.com/newtotalenglish

Each unit of the *New Total English* Students' Books has the same structure:

- **Lead-in page**
  - acts as a springboard into the topic of the unit and engages learners' interest.
  - introduces essential vocabulary related to the topic so that learners start with the same basic grounding.

- **Input lessons**
  - three input lessons, thematically linked, offering interesting angles on the unit topic. Lessons are double-page at lower levels and triple-page at Intermediate and above.
  - each input lesson leads towards a Can do learning objective in line with the CEFR Can do statements.
  - each 90-minute lesson focuses on a specific grammar area and includes vocabulary and skills work.
  - each unit usually contains at least two reading texts, a substantial listening element (including semi-authentic listenings) and pronunciation work.
  - How to... boxes develop students' competence in using language, in line with the CEFR.
  - Lifelong learning boxes offer tips and strategies for developing learners' study skills.

- **Communication page**
  - revises language taught in the previous three lessons in a freer, more communicative context.
  - each communication task practises a range of skills and has a measurable goal or outcome.

- **Vocabulary page (Intermediate and above)**
  - focuses on vocabulary systems and word-building.
  - helps learners to expand and develop their vocabulary.

- **Reference page**
  - summarises the main grammar points covered in each unit and provides a list of key vocabulary.
  - helps learners to catch up if they miss lessons and is an essential revision tool.

- **Review and practice page**
  - provides a range of exercises to consolidate key grammar and vocabulary covered in the unit.
  - can be used to check progress, enabling teachers to identify areas that need further practice.

- **Writing bank**
  - provides models and tips on how to deal with different types of writing (letters, emails and so on).
  - provides guidance on different writing sub-skills such as punctuation, spelling and paragraph construction.

- **Pronunciation bank**
  - provides a list of English phonemes, guidance on sound-spelling correspondences and weak forms.
  - summarises the pronunciation points covered in each unit of the Students' Book.

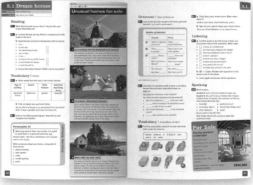

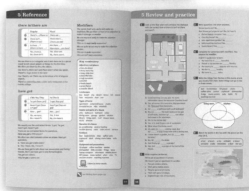
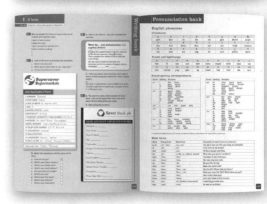

Structure of support components

A range of support components help you get the most out of each unit:

- **Students' Book with ActiveBook and DVD**
  - digital version of Students' Book with interactive activites.
  - integrated audio and video for Students' Book listening activities (including Reference pages and pronunciation activities).
  - wide variety of video clips (including drama, documentary and comedy) which can be selected when you use the ActiveBook in your computer, or play it in a DVD player.
  - interactive video activities.

- **Workbook with Audio CD**
  - consolidation of work covered in the Students' Book.
  - extensive practice of grammar, vocabulary and skills, including pronunciation.
  - regular Review and consolidation sections.
  - can be used in class or for self-study.

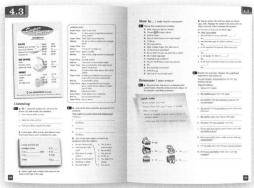

- **Students' Book with ActiveBook and MyLab**
  - interactive Workbook with instant feedback and automatic marking.
  - progress and achievement tests with automatic marking and gradebook.

- **Teacher's Book with Resource Disc**
  - provides step by step teaching notes including ideas for warmers and extension activities.
  - includes background notes and tips for dealing with particularly difficult language points.
  - Resource Disc features an extensive bank of photocopiable and printable classroom activities as well as editable and printable progress and achievement tests.

- **ActiveTeach**
  - digital version of the Students' Book to be used in class.
  - video clips that can be selected when you use the ActiveTeach in your computer, or play it in a DVD player.
  - all the material from the Teacher's Book Resource Disc.
  - a range of interactive whiteboard software tools.

- **Vocabulary Trainer**
  www.newtotalenglish.vocabtrainer.net
  - new online learning tool designed to help students revise and memorise key vocabulary from each unit of the course.

- **Website**
  www.pearsonlongman.com/newtotalenglish
  - features background information about the course and authors as well as teaching tips, downloadable worksheets and links to other useful websites.

Teaching approaches

Grammar

New Total English places a lot of emphasis on providing learners with the grammar 'building blocks' they need to communicate confidently. It aims to give learners a thorough foundation in grammar and, at the same time, provides plenty of structured and free practice. Each unit deals with grammar in a broadly similar way:

• Clear presentation and analysis

Each lesson has a clear grammar aim which is stated at the top of the page. Lessons are double-page at lower levels and triple-page at Intermediate and above. New language items are presented in context via reading and/or listening texts and grammar rules are then analysed and explained via the Active grammar boxes, which are a key feature of each lesson. *New Total English* takes a 'guided discovery' approach to grammar and learners are actively invited to think about grammar and work out the rules for themselves.

Active grammar

Regular verbs		Irregular verbs	
Infinitive	Past participle	Infinitive	Past participle
climb	climbed	take	taken
row	_____	do	_____
cycle	_____	win	_____
walk	_____	run	_____
sail	_____	hear	_____

1 In the Present Perfect, we use *have/has* + past participle with *he*, *she* and *it*. (We use *have/has* + past participle with *I*, *you*, *we* and *they*.)

2 *Regular/Irregular* past participles have the same form as the regular Past Simple.

• Varied, regular practice

Once learners have grasped the important rules, all new language is then practised in a variety of different ways so that learners are able to use the grammar with confidence. Practice activities include form-based exercises designed to help learners manipulate the new structures as well as more meaningful, personalised practice. Additional grammar practice exercises can be found in the Review and practice sections at the end of each unit as well as in the Workbooks and *MyTotalEnglishLab*. This component, which features the Workbook exercises in digital format, also provides learners with extra guidance, tips and feedback. The Teacher's Book provides a lot of guidance on how to deal with tricky grammar points. It also contains a Resource Disc with an extensive bank of printable and photocopiable classroom grammar activities which are designed to practise the language in freer, more communicative contexts.

• Easily accessible reference material

In addition to the explanations contained in the Active grammar boxes, there is a Reference section at the end of each unit which provides a summary of the grammar rules as well as extra language notes and examples. Audio recordings of the rules and examples are available on the ActiveBook and ActiveTeach components.

Vocabulary

New Total English recognises the central role that vocabulary plays in successful communication. The emphasis is on providing learners with high-frequency, useful vocabulary which is regularly practised and revised. New vocabulary is presented and practised in a variety of different ways.

• Lead-in pages

Each unit starts with a Lead-in page which provides a springboard into the topic of each unit. Featuring a variety of attractive picture prompts and related exercises, the Lead-in pages are designed to help teachers elicit vocabulary that learners already know as well as pre-teach essential vocabulary for the rest of the unit.

• Topic-based vocabulary

Each unit focuses on useful vocabulary relating to the topic of the lessons as well as vocabulary arising from the listening and reading texts. Items are generally presented in context and practised through a variety of exercises.

Vocabulary | containers

1 **a** Look at the picture and match A–H with the containers in the box.

bag ☐ bottle ☐ box ☐ can ☐
carton ☐ jar ☐ packet *A* tube ☐

b Now match the containers (1–8) with the things they can contain (a–h).

1	bag	a	juice
2	bottle	b	eggs
3	box	c	water
4	can	d	coffee
5	carton	e	toothpaste
6	jar	f	crisps
7	packet	g	rice
8	tube	h	cola

c What other things can you buy in these containers in your country?

Additional vocabulary practice is provided in the Review and practice sections of the Students' Book and in the practice exercises in the Workbook. Photocopiable vocabulary activities are also available on the ActiveTeach and on the Resource Disc which accompanies the Teacher's Book.

• Vocabulary pages (Intermediate and above)

At the lower levels there is a lot of emphasis on building learners' knowledge of high-frequency words and phrases as well as common lexical sets. Learners are introduced to collocation work at a very early stage and from intermediate level onwards, there is a greater emphasis on vocabulary systems and word-building.

• Vocabulary Trainer

Each level of *New Total English* is accompanied by a Vocabulary Trainer. This unique online learning tool focuses on the key vocabulary in each unit and helps learners memorise new words and phrases.

Speaking

The key aim for most learners is spoken fluency. However, most learners find it difficult to talk about topics which hold no interest for them and many cannot express themselves easily without support. *New Total English* develops spoken fluency in a number of ways – by giving learners discussion topics they want to talk about; by setting up situations where they are motivated to communicate in order to complete a specific task; by providing clear models and examples of how to structure discourse and by encouraging them, wherever possible, to express their own ideas and opinions.

• Fresh angles on familiar topics

Topics in *New Total English* have been chosen for their intrinsic interest and relevance. Obscure topics, i.e. those which are only likely to appeal to a minority audience, have been avoided and discussion questions have been deliberately chosen to encourage learners to draw on their own lives and experience. Inevitably, many of the topics have been covered in other ELT coursebooks but wherever possible, we have tried to find a fresh angle on them.

• Structured speaking activities

Many of the lessons in *New Total English* culminate in a structured final speaking activity in the form of a survey, roleplay etc. Learners are given time to prepare what they are going to say and prompts to help them. The activities often involve pair and group work to maximise learners' opportunities to speak in class. Many of the structured speaking activities are linked to the CEFR Can do statements.

• How to... boxes

There are regular How to... boxes throughout the course which focus on the words and expressions learners need to carry out specific functions. e.g ordering food in a restaurant.

How to... order food in a restaurant

Ask about the menu	(1) _____ you have salads?
Say what you want	I'd (2) _____ a cheese sandwich, please. I'll have a coffee.
Ask about prices	How (3) _____ is that?
Ask about payment	(4) _____ I pay by credit card?

• Communication pages

Communication pages feature at the end of each unit and engage learners in a variety of problem-solving tasks and activities. These give learners practice in a number of different skills including speaking.

• Photocopiable class activities

The photocopiable activities on the ActiveTeach and on the Resource Disc are also specifically designed to promote speaking practice.

Pronunciation

New Total English pays particular attention to pronunciation, which is integrated into lessons which present new language. The pronunciation syllabus includes word and sentence stress, weak forms, intonation and difficult sounds. The Pronunciation bank at the back of the Students' Books provides a summary of all pronunciation points in the book as well as a list of English phonemes, guidance on sound-spelling correspondences and weak forms. The ActiveTeach includes audio to accompany the Pronunciation bank. There is additional pronunciation practice in the Workbooks and Workbook Audio CD.

Listening

Listening is one of the most difficult skills to master and *New Total English* places particular emphasis on developing learners' confidence in this area. Listening texts include short scripted dialogues as well as longer, unscripted semi-authentic listenings. There is additional listening practice in the Workbooks and the video clips on the ActiveBook and ActiveTeach components further enhance learners' confidence in understanding the spoken word.

• Scripted listening activities

Scripted listening activities include short dialogues as well as longer extracts including conversations, interviews and stories. There are lots of simple 'Listen and check your answer' exercises as well as longer, more challenging extracts where learners have to listen for specific information.

• Semi-authentic listening activities

As well as the more traditional scripted listening activities, *New Total English* also includes a range of semi-authentic listening texts, i.e. recordings of one or more people speaking in an unprepared, unscripted way, although they are aware of the relevant level and therefore have adapted their own language to a certain extent accordingly. Learners benefit from listening to a semi-authentic recording because the spontaneity of spoken English means that it is full of false starts, hesitations, redundancy and 'ungrammatical' sentences. Learners need to be aware of these features and they need to develop confidence in dealing with them in order to cope with listening in the 'real world'.

• Video clips

New Total English provides a video clip to accompany each unit of the Students' Book. The videos feature a range of authentic material from a variety of different sources including short films and clips from TV documentaries and drama. The video clips expose learners to real English and are designed to motivate learners to 'raise their game' in terms of developing their listening skills.

To make the material more accessible to learners, photocopiable activities for each video clip are available on the ActiveTeach and on the Resource Disc. There are additional interactive video exercises on the ActiveBook and ActiveTeach which students can complete in class or at home.

The video clips are available on the ActiveBook which accompanies each Students' Book and on the ActiveTeach. You can select the video clips when you use the discs in your computer, or you can play them in a DVD player.

Teaching approaches

Reading

Many learners need to be able to read texts in English – for their studies, for work or simply for pleasure – and *New Total English* recognises that reading is an extremely important skill that can have a beneficial effect on all aspects of language learning including vocabulary, spelling and writing.

New Total English encourages learners to read as much as possible – in most units there are at least two substantial reading texts – and care has been taken to introduce students to as wide a range of text types as possible, from simple forms and advertisements to short texts from newspapers and magazines.

Reading texts are accompanied by a range of activities that are designed to check comprehension as well as develop key reading skills such as reading for gist, reading for specific information, guessing the meaning of words from the context and so on.

• Choice of texts

As with the listening material in *New Total English*, texts have been chosen for their intrinsic interest as well as for their usefulness in providing a vehicle for the particular grammar and vocabulary points in focus. Many of the texts have been adapted from authentic, real-life sources such as magazines and websites, and where texts have been adapted or graded, every effort has been made to remain faithful to the orignal text type in terms of content and style.

• Exploitation of texts

Each reading text in *New Total English* is accompanied by a number of exploitation exercises that have been carefully selected to develop learners' reading skills. Activities include comprehension and vocabulary work as well as practice in dealing with different reading sub-skills such as reading for gist. There are also a number of jigsaw readings where learners work together and share information.

Unit 6 Lesson 1 Exercise 9

Student A

Read this text and then give Student B the information (just tell him/her the facts).

Hostal de los Reyes Catolicos

The Hostal de los Reyes Catolicos is a luxury hotel in the city of Santiago de Compostela in the north of Spain, and is very beautiful both inside and outside. It started life in the fifteenth century as a hospital and a hostel for poor travellers, and doctors and nurses worked there. But it changed use many times and finally changed to a luxury hotel in 1953.

• Length and complexity

The length and complexity of the reading texts in *New Total English* get more challenging as the course progresses. At lower levels, the texts are very short and the emphasis is on training learners to read for specific information. At higher levels, learners are introduced to a a greater range and variety text types and more emphasis is placed on textual analysis.

Writing

In these days of electronic media, it is easy to forget that writing is not simply speech written down – effective writing has all sorts of conventions that differ from speech and that are necessary to learn in one's own language as well as in a foreign language.

New Total English pays particular attention to the important skill of writing. One of the most important new features of the revised edition is the Writing bank at the back of each Students' Book which contains 10 – 12 lessons that focus on different types of writing – emails, postcards, formal and informal letters and so on. Each lesson also provides additional advice and guidance on different writing sub-skills such as punctuation, spelling and paragraph construction.

• Model text types

Each Writing bank lesson has a Can do statement which refers to the written output that students complete at the end of the lesson. The lesson usually starts with a warmer that engages students in the topic. Learners then go on to focus on a model of the text type and in most cases, there is some comprehension work to ensure that students are familiar with the content before they start working on the format and related sub-skills. The lesson always finishes with a contextualised written output.

• Writing sub-skills

One of the most important aspects of the Writing bank is that it examines the sub-skills of writing in detail. This is important as it helps learners to build on and develop their writing skills, rather than simply providing practice in writing. Among the sub-skills covered are punctuation, grammatical cohesion, paragraphing and features such as varying the vocabulary used to both enhance interest and ensure lexical cohesion.

• How to... boxes

How to... boxes are a particular feature of the Writing bank. They usually focus on a particular sub-skill of writing and in some cases on written conventions, such as email or letter layout, appropriate formality of language for the text type or order of presentation of the content (such as in a review).

How to... use paragraphs

Look at the text and choose the correct answer.

We use paragraphs in our writing to group *different/similar* ideas together.

Look at the biography of Russell Crowe and match each paragraph with these parts of his life.

a his first acting jobs ☐

b his famous films ☐

c his early life ☐

d his personal life ☐

Learner training

New Total English places a strong emphasis on learner training and good study habits are encouraged and developed via the Lifelong learning boxes which are featured in many lessons. The Lifelong learning boxes provide useful tips and suggestions on how to continue learning outside the classroom.

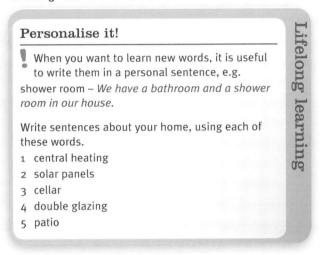

Personalise it!

❗ When you want to learn new words, it is useful to write them in a personal sentence, e.g.
shower room – *We have a bathroom and a shower room in our house.*

Write sentences about your home, using each of these words.
1 central heating
2 solar panels
3 cellar
4 double glazing
5 patio

Lifelong learning

Revision and testing

There are plenty of opportunities for revision in *New Total English* and language is constantly recycled throughout the course. At the end of every unit, there are special Review and practice pages which take the form of mini-progress checks, enabling learners to identify areas where they might need further practice. Interactive versions of the activities on these pages are available on the ActiveBook and ActiveTeach. The Workbook and accompanying Audio CD provide further practice in grammar, vocabulary and skills covered in the corresponding Students' Book. The Workbook is available in with key and without key versions.

For learners who are really serious about making rapid progress in English, *MyTotalEnglishLab* provides the perfect solution. This exciting component features the Workbook exercises in digital format as well as tips and feedback on common errors.

Regular progress and achievement tests are provided on the ActiveTeach, Resource Disc and *MyTotalEnglishLab*. *MyTotalEnglishLab* also includes automatic marking and a gradebook.

New Total English and exams

The table below shows how the different levels of *New Total English* relate to the University of Cambridge ESOL main suite examinations in terms of the language taught and the topics covered.

Starter	Builds foundation for KET
Elementary	**Useful for KET**
Pre-Intermediate	Useful for PET
Intermediate	Useful for FCE
Upper Intermediate	Useful for FCE
Advanced	Useful for CAE

While *New Total English* is not an examination preparation course, a student who has, for example, completed the Upper-intermediate level would have sufficient language to attempt the Cambridge ESOL FCE (First Certificate in English) examination. Many of the exercises in the *New Total English* Students' Books and other components are similar in format to those found in the Cambridge ESOL main suite examinations but specific training is required for all EFL examinations and we would strongly recommend this.

New Total English and the CEFR

New Total English is correlated to the CEFR (Common European Framework of Reference). Please see the *New Total English* website:
www.pearsonlongman.com/newtotalenglish for details of CEFR Can do statements for each level of the course.

CEFR	
A1	Starter
A2	**Elementary**
B1	Pre-intermediate
B1+	Intermediate
B2	Upper Intermediate
C1	Advanced

Students' Book Contents

Vocabulary	Speaking and Pronunciation	Listening and Reading
Countries and nationalities	Word stress	L Countries and nationalities
Families	Guessing game	L My family
Jobs	*a/an*: /ə/	L Jobs
		Reference p 17, **Review and Practice** p 18
Holidays	**How to...** talk about your daily routine	R Just an ordinary day
Verbs	Present Simple -*s* endings Information gap: routines	R Special jobs
Adjectives (1): colour, opinion	/ɪ/ and /iː/	L Hell's Kitchen
		Reference p 27, **Review and Practice** p 28
Activities	Activities questionnaire	L What people do in their lunch break R An online message board
Sports and games	*can/can't*	R Live the dream!
Numbers	Word stress **How to...** use the phone; take and leave a message	R Mobile Crazy! L Phone messages
		Reference p 37, **Review and Practice** p 38
Food		L and R Eating around the world
Containers Adjectives (2): feelings	/æ/ and /ʌ/ Diet quiz	L A television programme about rubbish
	How to... order food in a restaurant Roleplay: ordering a meal	L Ordering a meal in a restaurant
		Reference p 47, **Review and Practice** p 48
Homes Prepositions of place	Information gap: homes	R Unusual homes for sale L Asking for details about a house
Furniture and equipment	/æ/ and /ɒ/	L A call about insurance
Adjectives (3): places	Main stress **How to...** talk about where you come from/live	L and R A gap year destination L My country
		Reference p 57, **Review and Practice** p 58
	Past Simple endings Information gap: buildings	L and R Changing buildings
Places in a city, shops		R City break reviews
Time expressions	Contrastive stress	L and R Modern cities
		Reference p 67, **Review and Practice** p 68

Students' Book Contents

1 Your life

Overview

Lead-in	Revision: Introductions
1.1	**Can do:** Say where people and things are from **Grammar:** *to be*: positive **Vocabulary:** Countries and nationalities **Speaking and Pronunciation:** Word stress **Listening:** Countries and nationalities
1.2	**Can do:** Exchange information about your family **Grammar:** Possessive *'s*; possessive adjectives; *to be*: questions **Vocabulary:** Families **Speaking and Pronunciation:** Guessing game **Listening:** My family
1.3	**Can do:** Talk about jobs **Grammar:** *a/an*; *to be*: negative **Vocabulary:** Jobs **Speaking and Pronunciation:** *a/an*: /ə/ **Listening:** Jobs
Communication	Start and finish a basic conversation **How to...** start and finish a basic conversation
Reference	
Review and Practice	
Writing bank	Complete a form with personal information **How to...** use punctuation (1): capital letters

CEFR Can do objectives
1.1 Say where people and things are from
1.2 Exchange information about your family
1.3 Talk about jobs
Communication Start and finish a basic conversation
Writing bank Complete a form with personal information

CEFR Portfolio ideas
a) Pairwork. Find a local news magazine/website. Ask and answer questions about people in the photographs. Record your conversation.
b) Write a text about your family like Exercise 3 page 14.
c) Video. One student mimes a job. Other students try to guess the job.
d) Pairwork. Record a conversation with a partner. Ask questions to complete the Saver Bank application form on page 135.

Lead-in

In English-speaking countries (i.e. where the majority of the population are native-English speakers), people often shake hands when they meet for the first time, especially in more formal situations or in business contexts. They do not usually shake hands each time they meet after that.

OPTIONAL WARMER

Ask Ss: *How many languages can you say 'hello' in?* Ss work with a partner to make a list of greetings in as many different languages as they can (e.g. *bonjour* – French, *ni hao* – Chinese, etc.).

1a ▶ ◉ 1.07 Ss look at the dialogues and choose the correct answer to complete the sentences. Ss check answers in pairs and then listen to recording 1.07.

Answers		2	What's	3	My name's
1	your		It's		I'm; you
	My name's		How		

b ▶ Ss do the matching with a partner.

Answers		2	A
1	C	3	B

c ▶ Ss practise acting out the dialogues with each other. Emphasise the importance of using contracted forms (*My name's, What's, It's, I'm*) in order to sound natural and start using English speech patterns and rhythms.

2a ▶ ◉ 1.08 Ask Ss: *How many phone numbers do you know? Do you try to remember phone numbers when you enter them in your mobile phone?* Ss listen to recording 1.08 and repeat the phone number. Draw Ss' attention to the diphthong sound in *phone*, /əʊ/.

b ▶ ◉ 1.09 Ss listen to recording 1.09 and write down the phone numbers they hear. They check answers in pairs, then as a whole class.

Answers			
2	02096 659 248	4	02096 639 247
3	951 327 946	5	01542 984 731

c ▶ Ss circulate and practise asking for and giving phone numbers with each other. Explain to Ss that they do not have to give their real phone number.

EXTEND THE LEAD-IN

Ss circulate and find out how each student got their name (e.g. *It was my father's name*) and how they like to be called in their English class (e.g. shortened versions of their name, nicknames, by their surname, etc.).

1.1 People and places

In this lesson, Ss learn how to talk about where people and things are from and to describe countries and nationalities.

OPTIONAL WARMER

Ss look at the map in pairs. If the group is multicultural, each student shows their partner where they are from. In monolingual groups, each student can show their partner where they were born, and which countries they have visited.

Vocabulary | countries and nationalities

1 ▶ Ss look at the map in pairs and find the countries.

Answers	
Argentina	D
Australia	B
Brazil	E
China	Q
Czech Republic	K
England	G
France	H
Germany	I
Greece	M
Iran	O
Italy	J
Japan	A
Poland	L
Russia	P
Spain	F
Turkey	N

▶ Help Ss with the pronunciation and word stress of the countries. Write each country on the board. Say the name and have Ss identify which syllable is stressed for each one. (E.g. T: *Italy* – Ss: *syllable one*). Ss say the countries aloud.

OPTIONAL EXTENSION

Game: Ss close their books. For large classes, divide Ss into groups of ten or so. Ss sit in a circle. One student says a country, the next student must say another country which begins with the last letter of the previous country and so on (e.g. England, Denmark, Kenya, etc.). If a student can't think of a country, he or she drops out and the next student begins a new list of countries. The game continues until only one student is left in each group. As you monitor, help Ss with the names and pronunciation of unfamiliar countries.

2a ▶ Ask Ss if they know the name of anyone famous (not necessarily from modern times) or a famous product from the list of countries in ex. 1. Elicit a few suggestions. Use this as an opportunity to review the pronouns *he/she/it* (singular) and *they* (plural).

▶ Ask Ss to look at the four questions. Ask: *What is the difference between* Who *and* What*? (*Who *is for people.* What *is for things.) Help with the* Wh *sound /h/ in* Who and /w/ in *What*.

▶ Ss then look at the pictures with a partner. In pairs, they identify the people from the names in the box by asking and answering the questions. Ss take it in turns to ask the questions.

Answers
1   Jet Li; Daniel Craig
2   Penelope Cruz; Donatella Versace; Nicole Kidman
3   an iPod; a Mercedes car; a Panasonic Blu-ray Disc™ player
4   Dinara Safina and Marat Safin; Michelle, Malia and Sasha Obama

b ▶ Ss match the person to the country in pairs.

Answers
1   Ronaldo – Brazil; Jet Li – China; Daniel Craig – England
2   Penelope Cruz – Spain; Donatella Versace – Italy; Nicole Kidman – Australia
3   an iPod – United States of America; a Mercedes car – Germany; a Panasonic Blu-ray Disc™ player – Japan
4   Dinara Safina and Marat Safin – Russia; Michelle, Malia and Sasha Obama – United States of America

3a ▶ Ss close their books. Say: *Nicole Kidman is from Australia. She's Australian.* Ask Ss: *Are the words* Australia *and* Australian *the same?* (No.) Ss open their books and look at the table in ex. 3. Ss work in pairs to complete the table. Direct Ss to the ending section of the table to help them.

b ▶ 🔊 1.10 Play recording 1.10. Ss listen and write in the missing words. Ss check answers in pairs, then as a whole class.

Answers	
2	Argentinian
3	Brazilian
4	Italian
5	Germany
6	Iranian
7	Spain
8	Polish
9	English
10	Chinese
11	France
12	Greece

Pronunciation | word stress

4 ▶ 🔊 1.11 Play recording 1.11. Ss listen and repeat the country and nationality words. Pay particular attention to *Italian, Chinese* and *Japanese* as the word stress changes in the adjective form for these.

5 ▶ Write *Australian* on the board. Say: *Australian*, enunciating each syllable clearly (*Aus-tra-lian*). Ask: *How many syllables are there?* (three) *Where is the stress?* (*tra*, syllable two). Underline the stressed syllable on the board.

▶ Ss read the Lifelong learning box.

▶ Play recording 1.11 again. Ss listen and write the words, underlining the stressed syllable as they do so.

Answers	
Argen<u>ti</u>na	Argen<u>ti</u>nian
United States of A<u>me</u>rica	A<u>me</u>rican
Bra<u>zil</u>	Bra<u>zi</u>lian
<u>I</u>taly	I<u>ta</u>lian
<u>Ger</u>many	<u>Ger</u>man
I<u>ran</u>	I<u>ra</u>nian
<u>Ru</u>ssia	<u>Ru</u>ssian
Spain	<u>Spa</u>nish
<u>Po</u>land	<u>Po</u>lish
<u>Eng</u>land	<u>Eng</u>lish
<u>Tur</u>key	<u>Tur</u>kish
<u>Chi</u>na	Chi<u>nese</u>
Ja<u>pan</u>	Japa<u>nese</u>
France	French
Czech Re<u>pub</u>lic	Czech
Greece	Greek

Grammar | *to be*: positive

6a ▶ Ask Ss to look at the statements in ex. 2a again. Write on the board: *He's Ronaldo; They're Dinara Safina and Marat Safin*. Underline <u>*He's*</u> and <u>*They're*</u>.

▶ Ask Ss: *Which is singular and which is plural?* (*He's* is singular and *They're* is plural.) Focus on the apostrophe. Ask: *What does this mean?* (A letter is missed out and the two words are pronounced as if they were one word, the way we say it).

▶ Ss complete the Active grammar box by writing in the second word of the contractions listed (*am/is/are*). Ss check answers in pairs, then as a whole class.

Active grammar

(He) is
(She) is
(It) is
(They) are

▶ Direct Ss to the Reference section on page 17.

b ▶ 🌐 1.12 Ss complete the exercise in pairs.

Answers	
1	is; She
2	re; We
3	m
4	it; s
5	they; re; re

7 ▶ Model the examples in ex. 7 to Ss. Ss repeat the examples. Ask Ss to model another example as a whole class. (E.g. Student A: *Nicole Kidman* – Student B: *She's from Australia. She's Australian*). Ss continue the exercise in pairs. Monitor and correct any pronunciation or grammatical errors you hear.

8 ▶ Ss work in pairs. They guess where the items might come from.

Answers
A Italy
B Japan
C Australia
D Mexico
E Russia
F France
G Turkey
H United States of America
I China
J United States of America

OPTIONAL EXTENSION

Ss think of a famous person and write that person's name on a piece of paper. If they can't think of anyone, they can use the names of people mentioned in the lesson. Emphasise that it must be someone whom all the other Ss would know. Gather up the names and mix them up in a bag. Each student chooses a piece of paper with a name on it and sticks it on the back of another student with sticky tape so that each student has the name of someone famous on their back, but they don't know who it is. Ss work in small groups of four or five. Ss take it in turns to ask one question at a time about 'themselves' (e.g. *Am I American?, Am I a man?, Am I old?*, etc.) and in this way try to guess who they are. Do not worry if Ss have the same names on their back, as this can be amusing for the others in the group who see it.

1.2 Family ties

Words for family members vary between English-speaking cultures. *Grandpa* is used extensively in North America and Canada as an informal term for *grandfather*. The term *Grandad* would be more common in the UK. Likewise, *Grandma* is used in familiar contexts in North American English-speaking countries whereas *Gran*, *Granny*, *Nan* or *Nan(n)a* would be more common terms in the UK. North American English speakers often address their mothers as *Mom* (or *Mommy* for very young children) whereas *Mum* (or *Mummy* for very young children) is more typical in the UK. *Dad* is used extensively in both contexts.

In this lesson, Ss listen to two people describing a family photograph and describe their own families.

OPTIONAL WARMER

Ask all the Ss to stand up. Label the four corners of the room in the following way: oldest child in the family; youngest child in the family; middle child in the family; only child (explain only child, no brothers or sisters). Ask Ss to go to the corner of the room which corresponds to their position in their own family. In the four groups, Ss have to think of one good thing and one bad thing about being in that position in the family. (E.g. youngest child; good: having an older brother or sister to help with a problem; bad: old (hand-me-down) clothes from older brother or sister). Do not worry about Ss making mistakes during this activity. Ss will only be able to express their ideas in very basic language.

Listening

1 ▶ Ss look at the wedding photo and elicit possible answers to the two questions.

2a ▶ 🔘 1.13 Explain that you will play the recording twice. Ss must focus on the questions from ex. 2a during the first listening and on the task in ex. 2b during the second listening. Ss look at the three questions. Play recording 1.13. Ss listen and choose the correct word.

Answers
2 husband
3 Brazil

b ▶ Ss look at the family tree. Play the recording a second time. Ss listen and label the people in the photos. Ss check answers with a partner, then as a whole class.

Answers
1 Nilza
2 Nathalia
3 Eileen
4 Steve
5 Connor

3 ▶ Ss work in pairs. They use the completed family tree to decide on the relationship between the two people in each question.

Answers
1 brother and sister
2 father and son
3 husband and wife
4 father and daughter
5 sisters

Grammar | possessive 's

4a ▶ Ss look at the two sentences and choose the correct one. Ss check answers in pairs, then as a whole class.

▶ Ask: *What does the 's mean?* It shows possession. Here it is used to indicate the relationship of Nilza to Rafael. *Rafael is Nilza's son* shows the relationship of Rafael to Nilza. With more than two people, the 's goes after the second name (e.g. *Steve is Amber and Connor's father*, not *Amber's and Connor's father*).

Answer
Sentence 2

b ▶ Ss make eight sentences about Amber and Rafael's family. Ss compare their answers in pairs first, then as a whole class.

5 ▶ Ss look at the pictures and complete the phrases.

Answer
2 Rafael's phone
3 Almir's jacket
4 Kim's wedding ring
5 Nathalia's sunglasses
6 Eileen's handbag

OPTIONAL EXTENSION

Ask Ss to give you something which belongs to them (e.g. pencil, key ring, etc.). Try to have about 15 or more items if possible. At a later stage in the lesson, put the items on the desk. Alternatively, ask for these items earlier in the lesson and put them on the desk now. The idea is that Ss will not remember easily who gave you what. Ss work in pairs to make a list of the items on the desk (e.g. *X's pencil, Y's key ring*). The winners are the pair who remember correctly who the items belong to.

Vocabulary | families

6a ▶ Ss match the family words to the meanings. Ss check answers in pairs, then as a whole class.

Answers

2 g
3 a
4 e
5 b
6 h
7 c
8 f

b ▶ Ss find the meanings of the words in their dictionaries. Ss check answers in pairs, then as a whole class.

7 ▶ Ss write sentences about their own family. They compare sentences with a partner, then as a whole class.

Grammar | possessive adjectives

8a ▶ ● 1.14 Explain to Ss that they are going to hear someone else describe a photo, similar to the photo in ex. 1. Ss read the text first, ignoring the underlined words for now. Tell Ss that there are five mistakes in the written text. Play recording 1.14. Ss listen to identify the mistakes. Ss check answers with a partner, then as a whole class.

Answers

~~sister~~ brother
~~sons~~ daughters
~~aunt~~ grandmother
~~daughter~~ sister
~~brother~~ uncle
~~grandmother~~ wife

b ▶ Ss read the text again, focusing on the underlined words in order to complete the Active grammar box.

▶ Ask: *Which words are used when there is one ' owner' ?* (*my, his, her, your*) *Which words are used when there is more than one ' owner' ?* (*our, your, their*)

▶ Write on the board:

This is Heather. This is Heather' s brother.

This is Ben. This is Ben' s wife.

▶ Underline the words *Heather' s* and *Ben' s*. Ask Ss: *Which words could we use instead of Heather' s and Ben' s?* (*her* and *his*). Establish that in English what matters is the gender of the 'owner'. We say *This is his wife. Wife* refers to a woman, but it is still *his* wife because Ben is a man.

▶ Direct Ss to the Reference section on page 17.

Active grammar

my
his
her
their

9 ▶ Ss complete the gaps by using possessive adjectives. Ss check answers in pairs, then as a whole class.

Answers

1 My
2 their
3 our
4 your
5 her
6 your
7 his

Grammar | *to be*: questions

10a ▶ Ss focus on the completed questions in ex. 9 and use them to complete the Active grammar box using either *is* or *are* in the spaces provided. Ask: *Is is singular or plural?* (singular) *What about are?* (Plural, but remember *you* can be both singular and plural.)

▶ Direct Ss to the Reference section on page 17.

Active grammar

Is is
Are are

b ▶ Ss focus on the dialogue between Mike and Heather, who described her family in ex. 8. Mike is asking Heather questions about the photograph. Ss complete the dialogue with *she, he, my, your, is* or *are*.

Answers

1 she
2 is
3 is
4 he
5 my
6 is
7 is
8 your
9 are

OPTIONAL EXTENSION

Draw your immediate family tree on the board. Tell Ss one or two things about your family. (E.g. *My mother is 65. Her name is Rita. She' s from Ireland*, etc.) Ss draw their own family tree. In pairs, they tell each other about their families.

Speaking

11 ▶ Ss write down five names of people in their family. In pairs, they ask and answer about who the people are. Do not worry about Ss making mistakes during this activity. Monitor and note down any errors you hear to deal with later.

▶ It might be useful to have Ss work with someone new for this activity, especially if they have already discussed their families in pairs.

1.3 Working for a living

In English-speaking countries, the traditional working week consists of a 9 a.m. to 5 p.m. working day with an hour off for lunch (35 hours a week). However, with more and more people working from home, working freelance, working part-time or working more flexible hours, the traditional model is changing. Achieving a healthy 'work/ life balance' (time devoted to work and to one's personal life) is becoming more important although for many workers, there is increasing pressure to work longer and longer hours in order to perform to the maximum. Most people in Britain have between 20 and 28 paid days as holiday each year whereas in the US and Canada, between ten and 20 is the norm. In the US, there are ten public holidays each year. In England and Wales, there are eight, known as Bank Holidays.

In this lesson, Ss listen and read about different people's jobs and talk about their own jobs.

OPTIONAL WARMER
Elicit all the names of jobs Ss can think of. Put them on the board. Ss work in pairs. They take it in turns to mime one of the jobs on the board to their partner, who tries to guess which job it is.

Vocabulary | jobs

1 ▶ Ss look at the photos with a partner and match the job to the correct photo. Help Ss with the pronunciation of these words. Focus in particular on the word stress in the names of the different jobs and the /ə/ sound in the *-er* and *-or* word endings. Ask Ss: *Which of the jobs do you like best?* See which is the most popular job in the class.

> **Answers**
> B   a chef
> C   a computer programmer
> D   a sea captain
> E   a dentist
> F   a farmer
> G   a shop assistant
> H   a TV producer
> I   an engineer
> J   a doctor
> K   an architect
> L   an actor

2a ▶ 🔘 1.15 Ss should have their books closed for the first listening. Preteach *retired*, *director* and *landlord*. Play recording 1.15 through. Ss listen and identify which jobs are mentioned.

> **Answers**
> marketing director, television producer, lawyer, farmer, landlord, chef, engineer, computer programmer, teacher, sea captain

b ▶ Play the recording again. Ss listen to complete the sentences in their books. If Ss find the listening very difficult, you might like to pause the recording and give feedback between the first and second speaker.

> **Answers**
> 2   brother-in-law
> 3   lawyer
> 4   uncle
> 5   chef
> 6   brother
> 7   computing; computer programmer
> 8   uncle

3a ▶ Ss look at the question, then read the text to find the answer. During feedback, check the meaning of *unemployed*. Ss should have been able to guess the meaning from the context.

> **Answers**
> four (Cheryl's mother is retired but works part-time.)

b ▶ Ss complete the sentences with a partner.

> **Answers**
> 1   happy at work
> 2   retired
> 3   63 years old
> 4   in work
> 5   unemployed

OPTIONAL EXTENSION
Ss look at the list of jobs in ex. 1 and categorise them into jobs where you have to wear special clothes/uniform to work (e.g. a chef, a sea captain) and jobs where you can wear whatever you like (a computer programmer, a TV producer). There will be some overlap.

Grammar | a/an

4a ▶ Direct Ss to the jobs in ex. 1 again. Ask Ss to focus on the article (the first word). Ask: *Is it always a?* (No, sometimes *an*.) Ask Ss to decide when it is *a* and when *an* and to complete the Active grammar box.

▶ Write on board: *They are ___ artists.* Ask: *What goes in the space?* (Nothing, no article.) *Why?* (A and an are only used with singular nouns.) Point out that *unemployed* doesn't have *a* or *an* either – *unemployed* is an adjective.

▶ Direct Ss to the Reference section on page 17.

Active grammar

an
an
a
a

b ▶ Ss write *a* or *an* beside the words. Ss check answers in pairs, then as a whole class. Draw Ss' attention to the initial /h/ sound in *handbag*. Some Ss may be inclined to see it as a silent letter and use *an*.

Answers
1 a
2 an
3 a
4 a
5 an
6 an
7 a

Pronunciation | /ə/

5a ▶ 🌐 1.16 Focus on the pronunciation of the articles. Demonstrate how the use of *an* can affect the pronunciation of the next word. It sounds like *a nanswer* /nɑːnsə/, *a nuncle* /nʌŋkl/.

b ▶ 🌐 1.17 Ss listen and repeat the jobs.

▶ Direct Ss to the Pronunciation bank on page 148.

Listening

6 ▶ 🌐 1.18 Ss listen to the four speakers and decide what each job is. Direct Ss to the language suggested in the Students' Book before they start. Check answers together.

Answers
1 dentist
2 farmer
3 architect
4 chef

Grammar | *to be*: negative

7 ▶ Ss look at the text about Cheryl in ex. 3 again. Write on the board *I'm a teacher. I'm not a dentist.* Ask: *Is the second sentence positive or negative?* (Negative.) *What word shows you it's negative?* (*Not*.) Explain to Ss that we use the contracted forms in spoken English and informal writing.

▶ Ss use the text about Cheryl in ex. 3 in order to complete the Active grammar box. Ss check answers in pairs, then as a whole class. Help Ss with the /z/ sound in *isn't*.

▶ Direct Ss to the Reference section on page 17.

Active grammar

'm not
isn't
isn't
aren't

8 ▶ Ss complete the sentences using the correct negative forms. Ss check answers in pairs, then as a whole class.

Answers
1 isn't
2 'm not
3 aren't
4 isn't
5 aren't
6 'm not
7 'm not
8 aren't

▶ Ss practise saying the sentences. Correct any pronunciation errors, especially non-use of the contracted forms.

Speaking

9a ▶ Ss work with someone they don't know well in the class. Each student thinks of a job and writes it down on a piece of paper. Ss then try to guess each other's jobs. Limit the questions to ten guesses. Ss can give the initial letter of their job if their partner is finding it hard to guess.

b ▶ Extend the activity to ask about the jobs of other members of the family.

OPTIONAL EXTENSION

Ss sit in a large circle. Ss can use their real job or an imaginary job for this activity.
Student 1 says: *I'm a X* (names their job). Student 2 says *A* (names Student 1) *is a X and I'm a Y* (names their job). Student 3 says: *A* (names Student 1) *is an X, B* (names Student 2) *is a Y and I'm a Z.* Student 4 continues and so on. Ss who cannot remember the correct sequence of jobs are 'out'. The winner is the person who correctly remembers all the names and jobs.
With very small groups (fewer than six), Ss can say *I'm an X and my mother/father is a Y* instead of just naming one job.

1 Communication

In this lesson, Ss introduce themselves, start and finish conversations and exchange personal information with each other.

OPTIONAL WARMER

With multicultural classes, Ss can tell others the typical way of greeting and saying goodbye in their cultures. Is it different for formal and informal situations? With monolingual groups, Ss can tell others how they greet family members, friends, colleagues, a stranger, etc. (kiss on cheek, hug, handshake, nothing, etc.).

1a ▶ 🌐 1.19 Elicit from Ss all the ways they know of saying *hello* and *goodbye* in English. Ss quickly read through the expressions and then listen to recording 1.19. They tick the expressions which they hear. Ss check answers in pairs. Do not give feedback yet until Ss have completed the *How to...* box.

Answers
Excuse me ...
See you later
Bye
Hello
Hi
Good evening
(Good morning)
Goodbye
See you soon

b ▶ Ss listen again and complete the *How to...* box.

Answers
Start: Excuse me, Hi, Good evening, Good morning
Finish: See you later, Bye, Good night, See you tomorrow, Goodbye, See you soon

▶ Ask Ss to categorise the words into three groups: informal, formal and both. Discuss the different categories. You may need to draw their attention to the /h/ sound in *hello* and *hi*.

2a ▶ Ss match the questions with the answers. Explain *single* (not married). Ss check answers with a partner.

Answers
2 e
3 a
4 d
5 b

b ▶ Ss use the questions in ex. 2a to write answers about themselves.

3a ▶ Ss complete the dialogues using the suggestions in the box.

b ▶ 🌐 1.20 Ss listen to recording 1.20 to see if they were correct.

Answers
1
I'm from Alicante.
2
Excuse me, are you Krystof?
Yes, I am. I'm from Warsaw.
I'm a teacher.

4 ▶ Ss practise asking and answering the questions in ex. 3a with their partner, using real information about themselves.

5a ▶ Elicit different ways of asking questions to find out this information, e.g. *Are you married/Are you single? How do you spell your name? Is there a Y in your name? Spell your name, please. What do you do? Where are you from?* etc. Most of these questions were covered in ex. 2 and 3 and can be taught as fixed expressions without explaining the grammar at this point. Tell Ss not to worry about making mistakes during this activity.

▶ Ss mingle and ask and answer each other's questions.

b ▶ Try to keep the feedback short. Ask: *Who is married?* Encourage Ss to shout out the answers about the others they have spoken to. They cannot answer about themselves.

OPTIONAL EXTENSION

Put the following headings on the board: *Age*; *Job*; *Income/salary*; *Parents' job*; *Hobbies*; *Marital status*; *Qualifications*.
Ss discuss which topics they would ask a stranger questions about if they were at a party.
Note: What is polite to ask questions about varies from culture to culture and it can be useful for Ss to know what is appropriate in an English-speaking environment, e.g. it would not be considered polite to ask a stranger questions about their age, income, qualifications or about their parents' job.

1 Review and practice

1 ▶

Answers
1 his
2 my
3 their
4 Our
5 her
6 Her
7 my
8 Tessa's
9 his

2 ▶

Answers
1 Elizabeth is from the United States. She is American.
2 Ivan and Katia are from Russia. They are Russian.
3 I am from France. I am French.
4 You are from England. You are English.
5 Pavlos is from Greece. He is Greek.
6 His camera is from Japan. It is Japanese.
7 I am from Poland. I am Polish.

3 ▶

Answers		7	Russia	11	Is
4	Are	8	Is	12	No
5	aren't	9	from	13	isn't
6	are	10	is		

5 ▶

Answers
1 Where are you from?
2 How old are you?
3 What do you do?
4 Are they your brother and sister?
5 Are they German?

6 ▶

Answers					
1	an	4	a	7	an
2	an	5	a	8	an
3	a	6	a		

7 ▶

Answers
Jobs: retired, dentist, television producer, engineer, shop assistant
Family: grandparents, son, niece, cousin

8 ▶

Answers
1 son
2 aunt
3 actor
4 wife's
5 student

1 Writing bank

1 ▶ Ss' own answers

2a ▶

Answers
1 a job application
2 your name (first name and surname)
3 no

b ▶

Answers
b 10
c 1
d 9
e 5
f 11
g 2
h 8
i 6

3a ▶

Answers
Thomson
Steve
March
British
Hart Road
Birmingham
English, Italian
Mr Alfred Thomson
Steve Thomson

nationalities, months

b ▶

Answers
Carol, Wilson, I, English, Arabic, I'm, British, I, Manchester, My, February

4a/b ▶ Ss complete the application form.
Ss' own answers

Overview

Lead-in	Revision: Daily routine; telling the time
2.1	Can do: Describe what you do every day Grammar: Present Simple: I/you/we Vocabulary: Holidays Speaking and Pronunciation: How to... talk about your daily routine Reading: Just an ordinary day
2.2	Can do: Describe other people's routines Grammar: Present Simple: he/she/it/they Vocabulary: Verbs Speaking and Pronunciation: Present Simple -s endings; Information gap: routines Reading: Special jobs
2.3	Can do: Talk about everyday objects Grammar: Noun plurals this, that, these, those Vocabulary: Adjectives (1): colour, opinion Speaking and Pronunciation: /ɪ/ and /iː/ Listening: Hell's Kitchen
Communication	Talk about what you do on holiday
Reference	
Review and Practice	
Writing bank	Write about your routine How to... join sentences (1): and, then, after that

CEFR Can do objectives
2.1 Describe what you do everyday
2.2 Describe other people's routines
2.3 Talk about everyday objects
Communication Talk about what you do on holiday
Writing bank Write about your routine

CEFR Portfolio ideas
a) Ask a friend about his/her routine. Write an article.
b) Ask your partner to open the book at any page and choose a picture. Don't look at your partner's book. Ask questions about the photo and find it in your book. Record your conversation.
c) Video. One student mimes an everyday action or object. Other students try to guess the action or object.
d) Write your diary for one day. Write your activities.

Lead-in

OPTIONAL WARMER
Ask Ss: *What time of day do you prefer to do these things: study, read the paper, go to a film, phone friends, go to the gym ... ?* etc. In feedback, establish whether most of the class are morning, afternoon, evening or night people.

1a ▶ Ask Ss to cover the names of the activities in the box. Ask them to look at the pictures and discuss with a partner what the people are doing. Do not worry if they don't know the exact words/phrases for the activities at this point. Then, Ss look at the verbs in the box and match them to the pictures. Check answers as a whole class.

Answers		
A leave work	B get up	D get home
	C have dinner	

b ▶ Ss match the activities to the time of day.

Answers
1 have breakfast, leave home, go to work
2 have lunch
3 leave work, get home, have dinner
4 go to bed

2a ▶ 🔘 1.21 Ss listen to the recording and write the correct times in the spaces provided. They then match the times to the clocks. Ss check answers with a partner and then as a whole class.

Answers	
2 two – f	5 seven – e
3 eight – a	6 two – b
4 three – h	7 four – g
	8 five – d

b ▶ 🔘 1.22 Ss listen and identify the speaker.

Answers		
1 D	2 A	4 C
	3 B	

EXTEND THE LEAD-IN
In pairs. Ss think of their favourite period of day and write down the time this period usually starts and when it usually ends, e.g. *quarter past seven till eight o' clock – the morning when I get up and before I leave home and go to work*. The other student asks when their favourite time of day is and why (*I have the house to myself; I listen to the news on the radio; I feel great after a shower*, etc.). Ss will only be able to express their ideas in very basic English. Encourage them to express their views as best they can and do not worry about mistakes during this activity.

2.1 Fun Club

A package holiday is a holiday organised by a tour operator which combines flight and accommodation and sometimes food and entertainment in the cost of the holiday. This traditionally has appealed to people who wanted to travel to a sunny climate, often Spain, Italy or Greece, for two weeks holiday in the summer. These holidays tend to be relatively cheap and before the advent of cheaper airfares, often offered the only affordable way of travelling abroad for many people. Holiday-makers would typically travel in chartered airplanes and stay in custom-built apartment complexes situated near the sea. In more recent years, the concept has expanded to include activity holidays like skiing or other themed holidays such as cooking or photography holidays. Package holidays are now often aimed at specific target groups, e.g. young and single people, senior citizens, etc. The range of destinations has also widened considerably and now people can take package holidays at any time of the year.

In this lesson, Ss read about the typical daily routine of Penny, a holiday rep working for Fun Club, and then describe their own daily routines.

OPTIONAL WARMER

Give Ss two minutes to make a list in pairs of all the different types of holidays they can think of, e.g. *skiing*, *camping*, *beach*, *bus tour*, etc. Find out which pair had the most ideas. Elicit their suggestions and put them on the board. Ask which type of holiday they like best.

Reading

1a ▶ Ss look at the pictures. Teach *package holiday* (a holiday where everything is arranged for you; Club Med is a good example and is fairly well known internationally) and *holiday rep* (someone who works for this kind of company and helps the clients on holiday).

Answers
She's a holiday rep.

b ▶ Ss match the pictures A–D to the labels. Ss compare answers in pairs and then as a whole class.

Answers
entertainment C
nightclub D
games at the swimming pool B

2a ▶ Ensure Ss understand what Penny's job is. Elicit some of the things a holiday rep does. Ss then look at the list of activities. They read the text and put the activities in the correct order.

Answers
1 (Get up)
2 Go to the hotels
3 Tell clients about parties
4 Have lunch
5 Organise games at the pool
6 Take clients to a restaurant
7 Go to a nightclub
8 Get home

b ▶ Ss read the text again in order to complete the chart with the correct times. Teach *about two* to give an approximate time and *two in the morning/two in the afternoon*.

Answers
2 11 – go to the hotels
3 11.15 – tell clients about parties
4 2 o'clock – have lunch
5 3.30 – organise games at the pool
6 7.45 – take clients to a restaurant
7 10.30 – go to a nightclub
8 1.45 in the morning – get home

3 ▶ Ss discuss if they would like this kind of holiday or this kind of job in pairs. Elicit reasons for their preferences in feedback.

Vocabulary | holidays

4a ▶ Ss match the verbs to the nouns, then check their answers in the text.

Answers
2 c
3 a
4 e/a
5 b

b ▶ Ss find five different *have* + noun collocations in the text, then use the expressions to complete the sentences. Ss check answers with a partner, then as a whole class.

Answers
1 have dinner
2 have problems
3 have fun
4 have lunch

Grammar | Present Simple: *I/you/we*

> **OPTIONAL GRAMMAR LEAD-IN**
>
> Write out a selection of questions and answers from the reading text on strips of paper, one question or answer for every student. Include varied questions (*Yes/No* questions and *Wh-* questions). Ss mingle, those with question cards ask the question and try to find the student with the matching answer. With small classes, this can be done with the whole class. With larger classes, divide them into groups.

5 ▶ Ss look at the reading text and complete the Active grammar box.

> **Active grammar**
>
> | | |
> |---|---|
> | have | do |
> | don't | don't |
> | Do you | you finish |

▶ Make sure Ss are clear about the two types of questions. Put up some questions and answers on the board. Ask Ss: *What do you notice about the different answers to the questions?* (Some are *Yes/No* answers and some provide more information.) *Which questions go with which type of answer?* (*Do you* questions and question-word questions.)

▶ Direct Ss to the Reference section on page 27.

6 ▶ Ss match the questions to the answers. Do the first one as a whole class. Ss work alone, then check answers with a partner before checking answers as a whole class.

▶ Point out *What do you do?* as a way of finding out about a person's job rather than *What is your job?*

> **Answers**
>
> 2 e
> 3 d
> 4 b
> 5 a

▶ Help Ss with the pronunciation of the questions, especially the weak /ə/ sound of the auxiliary verb *do*. Ss practise asking and answering these questions in pairs. Monitor closely and correct mistakes.

7a ▶ Ss work in pairs and complete the dialogue.

> **Answers**
>
> 2 Yes
> 3 do
> 4 I
> 5 When
> 6 have
> 7 you
> 8 don't
> 9 do
> 10 work
> doctor

b ▶ 🔊 1.23 Ss listen to recording 1.23 to check if their answers were correct. Ask two Ss to say the dialogue for whole class feedback. Correct as necessary. Then Ss practise acting out the dialogue in pairs.

> **OPTIONAL EXTENSION**
>
> Ss play a 'What's my job?' game. Before Ss start the game, elicit all the different types of jobs they know. Refer Ss to ex. 1 in Lesson 1.3 for a list of jobs. Put the suggestions on the board. Ss work in small groups of four or so. One student thinks of a job. The other Ss take turns to ask ten *Yes/No* questions to try to guess what the job is. (Some examples of questions are contained in ex. 6 but you may want to elicit other types of questions they might ask first, e.g. *Do you work alone?*, *Do you wear special clothes?*, etc.)

8 ▶ Ss complete the *How to…* box, using the language and information they completed in ex. 7.

> **Answers**
>
> 1 When
> 2 do (you) go
> 3 At
> 4 Where
> 5 in a hospital

Speaking

9a ▶ Ss look at the chart in ex. 2b. They create their own entries under the 'You' heading, focusing on their daily routine. Ss write short sentences. Don't conduct feedback yet, as Ss will use their entries for ex. 9b.

b ▶ Ss discuss their entries with a partner. Encourage Ss to ask lots of questions about their partner's list, focusing particularly on routines, times and places as in the *How to…* box. Do not worry about Ss making mistakes during this activity. Encourage them to use all the language they have. Make a note of obvious errors to deal with later.

▶ **Tip:** It is a good idea to vary the student pairings regularly to add variety to exercises. Ss have already discussed aspects of their routines with other Ss in the class, so make sure they are working with someone new. If it is difficult to move around in the classroom, this can be achieved by moving one student from the end of each row to the other end.

c ▶ In pairs, Ss discuss how their routines differ on holiday. Put headings on the board (e.g. *Morning, Afternoon, Evening, Bedtime*) to help focus the discussion, especially if Ss are reluctant to speak.

2.2 A very special job

Madame Tussaud (1761–1850) was a French wax sculptor who exhibited wax sculptures of famous people. Her permanent collection of wax sculptures opened in London in 1836. The original display contained 400 figures. Today, the museum has become a major tourist attraction in London with branches in many other major cities. The sculptures range from historical political figures to contemporary rock stars and athletes and one of the most famous sections of the museum is the 'Chamber of Horrors', which includes wax sculptures of famous murderers and their victims.

In this lesson, Ss read about what is involved in the jobs of three people: a wax model hairdresser at Madame Tussaud's, a theme park ride inventor and a shark tank cleaner in a zoo. Ss ask and answer questions about other people's habits and routines.

OPTIONAL WARMER

Ss work in small groups of three or four. They describe to the others in the group an activity they enjoy doing in their job/studies and secondly, an activity they don't enjoy doing in their job/studies.

Reading

1a ▶ Ss look at the people in the photos and discuss what the jobs are with a partner. Do not give the names of the jobs yet as Ss will find out in the reading.

b ▶ Scanning: Explain to Ss that they will read the three texts twice, the first time very quickly just to find out what the people's jobs are and the second time much more slowly in order to understand more fully. Explain that they do not need to understand the text fully after the first reading. Stop the activity after a minute. Ss compare answers in pairs and then as a whole class.

Answers
Jo Kinsey: wax model hairdresser
Jeanette Ewart: shark tank cleaner
John Wardley: theme park ride inventor

c ▶ Ss read the texts more slowly, this time focusing on the underlined words. First teach *theme park* (e.g. Disneyworld, in Florida) and *zoo* (a place where exotic animals are kept, not a farm). Ask Ss to try to guess the meanings of the underlined words from the surrounding words and to match the words to the labels in the pictures. Ss check answers in pairs and then as a whole class.

Answers
B hairdresser
C shark tank
D sharks
E inventor
F rides

2 ▶ Ss read the text again to find out which of the three people does the five activities.

Answers
1 Jo
2 John
3 Jo
4 John
5 Jeanette

OPTIONAL EXTENSION

Ss discuss with a partner which of the three jobs they would like most and which least. They must explain why, e.g. *I like Jeanette's job best. I love animals and I think sharks are very interesting* or *I don't like Jeanette's job. I think sharks are very scary. I hate their big teeth*, etc.

Vocabulary | verbs

3 ▶ Ss work in pairs. They choose the correct verb from the texts to complete the sentences. Check answers as a whole class.

Answers				
1 works	3	have	6	goes
2 talk	4	watches	7	cleans
	5	dries	8	checks

Grammar | Present Simple: *he/she/it/they*

4 ▶ Ss complete the Active grammar box with their partner.

Active grammar

Affirmative	Negative
has/have	doesn't invent
invents	don't leave
talk	doesn't work
watches/watch	
works	

▶ Write these sentences on the board: *The diver watches her. The visitors watch her.* Ask why the verb forms are different (third person singular and plural). Write: *John has an interesting job. The visitors have fun.* Again, ask students about the verb forms (irregular third person singular and plural). Elicit the negative for third person singular and plural forms (e.g. *She doesn't clean the tank. They don't clean the tank.*).

▶ Direct Ss to the Reference section on page 27.

5a ▶ Ss complete the sentences using the verbs in the box. They check answers in pairs, and then as a whole class.

Answers				
1 talks	3	likes	6	plays
2 washes	4	goes	7	have
	5	watches	8	leave

b ▶ Ss change the sentences to make them negative.

Answers

1	doesn't talk	5	doesn't watch
2	doesn't wash	6	doesn't play
3	doesn't like	7	don't have
4	doesn't go	8	don't leave

Pronunciation | Present Simple
-s endings

6a ▶ 🔘 1.24 Ss close books and listen to the three verbs in recording 1.24. Ask them to focus on the endings of the words. They should be able to hear the different endings. Ss then repeat the words.

b ▶ 🔘 1.25 Ss put each verb into the correct column as they listen. Check answers, then ask Ss to repeat the verbs.

Answers
/s/ talks, likes
/z/ cleans, goes
/ɪz/ washes, watches

c ▶ 🔘 1.26 Direct Ss to the first six completed sentences in ex. 5a. Play recording 1.26. Ss repeat the sentences, paying particular attention to the verb endings. Ss should be able to see which verbs take the /ɪz/ sound fairly easily as it corresponds to the spelling. It is more difficult for them to pick up on the voiced and unvoiced sounds.

▶ Direct Ss to the Pronunciation bank on page 148.

OPTIONAL EXTENSION
Put all the verbs from this lesson on the board. Add a few more, e.g. *begin*, *help*, *speak*, *finish*, *wear*, etc.
Ss work in pairs. Call out the names of jobs. Ss have two minutes to think of sentences about the daily routine of a person with that job, using the verbs on the board.
E.g. *A teacher: He/She listens to students*; *He/She works in a school*. The pair with the most sentences gets a point – but only if they get the grammar and pronunciation of the verbs right. Ss who use a verb no one else thought of also get a point. The pair with the most points wins.

Grammar | Present Simple: questions

7a ▶ In pairs, Ss look at the dialogue and guess what the missing words might be. Do not give feedback yet as they will get the information from the recording.

Answers

Does	don't
does, feeds	Does
Do	doesn't, works

b ▶ 🔘 1.27 Ss listen to recording 1.27 to see if they were right.

8 ▶ Tell Ss to use the information from the completed dialogue in ex. 7 to choose the correct form in the questions. They cross out the incorrect words in the questions.

▶ Focus on the use of the auxiliary verb *do/does* and point out that you drop the -s after the verb (not *Does she feeds the sharks?*).

▶ Direct Ss to the Reference section on page 27.

Active grammar
1 Do, eat, don't
2 Does, clean, doesn't
3 Does, like, does

9a ▶ Ss complete the questions using the correct form of the verbs.

Answers

1	Does, like	3	Does, invent
2	Do, watch	4	Do, talk
		5	Does, have

b ▶ Ss change the questions and ask their partner direct questions about themselves. Ss practise asking and answering the questions, giving true information in their answers.

Answers
1 Do you like your work?
2 Do you watch DVDs?
3 Do you invent computer games?
4 Do you talk in your sleep?
5 Do you have children?
Ss' own answers

c ▶ Ss make new questions, this time asking and answering about their families and friends.

Suggested answers
Does your mother work every day?
1 Does your brother like his work?
2 Do your grandparents watch DVDs?
3 Does your friend invent computer games?
4 Does your sister talk in her sleep?
5 Do your friends have children?
Ss' own answers

Speaking

10 ▶ Ss work in pairs. Student A's information is on page 129 and Student B's information is on page 133. Give Ss a minute or two to read their information. Ss can use their dictionaries. They should not look at their partner's information. Ss follow the instructions and ask and answer questions about Doug's routine. Do not worry if Ss make mistakes during this activity.

OPTIONAL EXTENSION
Ss interview each other about their jobs and daily routine and write up a 'A Day in the Life'-type article about their partner.

2.3 Hell's Kitchen, NYC

Shopping habits have changed dramatically in recent years, especially in relation to second-hand goods. Nowadays, ordinary people are getting more involved in selling these items as well as buying them in places other than the more well-established flea markets. A popular phenomenon in the UK is the car boot sale: people fill their cars with all kinds of objects they no longer want and drive to a designated field or car park where they try to sell the objects. A similar phenomenon in the US and Australia is known as a yard sale, or garage sale, where people sell from their gardens or garages. Second-hand book and clothes shops are common and nowadays many people use eBay and other Internet sites to buy and sell second-hand items. The Freecycle Network (TFN) is a popular Internet site where people can donate goods to re-use and recycle, rather than throwing them away.

In this lesson, Ss listen to people at Hell's Kitchen flea market in New York, then describe everyday items.

OPTIONAL WARMER

Write *local shop*, *supermarket*, *department store*, *butcher' s*, *pharmacy*, *market*, *baker' s* on the board. Elicit what kind of things people buy in each type of place.

Listening

1a ▶ Ss think about their shopping habits and complete the table individually.

b ▶ Ss compare their shopping habits with a partner. Direct Ss to the suggested language in the example dialogue in their books.

2a ▶ 🔘 1.28 Teach *second hand* (not brand new). Elicit the kind of things and places where you can buy things second hand (eBay; second-hand bookstores or clothing shops; jumble sales in schools; special magazines, etc.). Play recording 1.28. Ss listen to find out what a flea market is (a big market, usually outdoors, where second-hand goods are bought and sold).

b ▶ Ss read the questions. Play recording 1.28 again. Ss listen and choose the correct word.

Answers
1	US	3	clothes and shoes
2	two days a week	4	like

c ▶ Put the following headings on the board: *Clothes*, *Jewellery*, *Shoes*, *Furniture*. Ss discuss the kind of things that they might buy at a flea market.

Grammar | noun plurals

3a ▶ Ss look at the picture and see if they know the names for any of the items. They then work in pairs to label the objects. Check answers.

Answers
1	scarves	7	mobile phones
2	books	8	laptops
4	shoes	9	MP3 players
5	watches	10	cameras
6	diaries	11	DVD players

b ▶ 🔘 1.29 Ss listen to recording 1.29 and tick the items they hear. Ss check answers in pairs, then as a whole class.

Answers
bags	scarves	mobile phones
shoes	watches	laptops
	books	

OPTIONAL EXTENSION

Ss categorise the objects into things they would be happy to buy second hand and things they would not. Ss compare categories with a partner.

4 ▶ Ss use the list of words in ex. 3a to complete the rules about plural forms in the Active grammar box.

Active grammar

-es, watches
-ies, diaries
-f, scarves

▶ Direct Ss to the Reference section on page 27.

5 ▶ Ask Ss if they know any other irregular nouns like *person – people*. They probably know a few already, e.g. *foot – feet*. Explain they are going to learn how to use the dictionary to find the plurals of nouns. Teach the abbreviation *pl* which is sometimes found in dictionaries.

▶ Ss look at the dictionary entry for *person*. In pairs, they find the plurals of the other words. Ask Ss to identify the irregular plurals.

Answers
addresses	classes	nieces
buses	dictionaries	wives
children	families	women
	men	

Vocabulary | adjectives (1): colour, opinion

6a ▶ Ask Ss how many colours they can see in the picture in ex. 3a. Then, they find and circle the eight colour adjectives in the box.

Answers
blue	green	white
brown	grey	yellow
	red	

OPTIONAL EXTENSION

Ss discuss in pairs what their favourite colour is for a car, for a phone and for a winter coat.

b ▶ Show Ss two things which are the complete opposite of each other (e.g. two money notes – one brand new and the other old and worn; or two books – one very large and the other very small). Ask Ss: *What is the difference between these two notes/books?* The difference should be immediately obvious to them.

▶ Ss look at the remaining words in the box and make pairs of opposites. Encourage Ss to use a dictionary for the words they don't know. Ss check answers in pairs, then as a whole class.

Answers
big – small
horrible – nice
modern – old-fashioned
old – young
pretty – ugly
useful – useless

OPTIONAL EXTENSION

Ss practise making sentences to describe the items in the picture in ex. 3a (e.g. *The bag is yellow*, *The shoes are old-fashioned*, etc.).

Grammar | *this, that, these, those*

7a ▶ ⏺ 1.30 Ss look at the pictures of Karl and Jodie at a market stall in ex. 8a. Ask: *Where are they? What are they doing? What are they looking at?* Ss listen to the recording to find out what Jodie and Karl are looking at.

Answers	
a belt	scarves
a coat	shoes
	a bag

b ▶ Ss listen again to identify the adjectives from ex. 6a.

Answers	
horrible	pretty
ugly	old-fashioned
nice	useful

c ▶ Ss discuss the questions in pairs.

Answers		
		3 yes
1	no	4 no
2	no	5 yes

8a ▶ Ss listen again to recording 1.30 and fill in the missing words.

Answers			
1	horrible	3	pretty
2	ugly	4	old-fashioned

b ▶ Ask Ss to look at the pictures and the completed sentences in ex. 8a and then to complete the Active grammar box.

▶ As part of the feedback, explain that *this* (singular) and *these* (plural) are for things near to us; *that* (singular) and *those* (plural) are for things farther away. Use gestures to demonstrate the point to Ss. Help Ss with the pronunciation of the four words.

▶ Direct Ss to the Reference section on page 27.

Active grammar
singular: this; that
plural: these; those

c ▶ Ss correct the underlined words. Ss check answers in pairs, then as a whole class.

▶ Emphasise to Ss that *those* and *these* are plural and take *are*, e.g. Those/These *are cars*. *This* and *That* are singular and take *is*, e.g. That/This *is a car*.

Answers			
1	that	3	Is
2	This	4	aren't

Pronunciation | /ɪ/ and /iː/

9a ▶ ⏺ 1.31 Put the /ɪ/ and /iː/ vowel sounds on the board. Play recording 1.31 and write *this* and *these* under the correct sound. Ss listen and repeat.

b ▶ ⏺ 1.32 Play recording 1.32. Ss put the words in the correct column of the table. Ss listen again and repeat the words.

▶ Direct Ss to the Pronunciation bank on page 147.

Answers
/ɪ/ this – big, listen, sister, swim, think
/iː/ these – clean, green, niece, read, teacher

OPTIONAL EXTENSION

Dictate further words to Ss (e.g. *sheep, bit, dinner, invent, film, people, sleep, keep, lip, sit, meet*). Ss add them to the table.

Speaking

10 ▶ Ss work in pairs to produce sentences including *this/that/these/those* plus the adjectives from ex. 6a, as in the example. Help Ss with the sentence stress and intonation, exaggerating it a little to make the point.

2 Communication

In this lesson, Ss listen to people describing their holidays and ask and answer questions about their own holiday routines.

1 ▸ Ss look at the photos showing different holiday destinations. In pairs, they match the captions to the photos.

Answers
1 C
2 A
3 B

2a ▸ ◉ 1.33 Ss listen to the people describing holidays and match the speakers to the photos.

Answers
Matt – C
Wendy – B
Gareth – A

b ▸ Ensure Ss understand the vocabulary in the questions before playing the recording a second time. Ss listen again to find out what each speaker brings with them on holiday.

Answers
1 Wendy
2 Matt
3 Gareth
4 Matt
5 Gareth

c ▸ Ss listen and match the activity to the speaker or speakers.

Answers
1 Gareth
2 Matt
3 Wendy
4 Gareth
5 Wendy and Gareth

3 ▸ Ss work with a partner to decide which item corresponds to which type of holiday.

Suggested answers
All: camera, guidebook, magazine, passport, suitcase, sunscreen
Beach: sunbathe
City: go sightseeing, museum
Mountains: go skiing

4a ▸ Ss look at the words in the box. In pairs, they complete the questions using one of the words for each gap. In feedback, help Ss with the *Wh* sounds in the questions.

Answers
2 Who
3 you
4 do
5 When
6 do
7 What
8 time, go

b ▸ Ss match the answers to the questions in ex. 4a. Ss check answers in pairs, then as a whole class.

Answers
b 1
c 5
d 6
e 8
f 7
g 2
h 3

5a ▸ Ss work in pairs and ask each other about their holiday routines using the questions from ex. 4a. Encourage Ss to answer at length, without worrying about making mistakes. As you monitor, note down any obvious errors, which you can deal with later.

b ▸ Ask a number of Ss to describe their partner's holiday routines to others in the class. With large classes, Ss can work in groups.

2 Review and practice

1 ▶

> **Answers**
> B He reads his emails at half past nine.
> C He eats a sandwich at quarter to one.
> D He finishes work at half past six.
> E He watches television at ten o'clock.
> F He goes to bed at half past eleven.

2 ▶

> **Answers**
> 1 get up
> 2 has
> 3 go
> 4 cleans
> 5 play

3 ▶

> **Answers**
> 1 don't get up
> 2 doesn't have
> 3 don't go
> 4 doesn't clean
> 5 don't play

4 ▶

> **Answers**
> 1 What does she do in the afternoon?
> 2 Where does he have lunch?
> 3 Do you work in an office?
> 4 When does he finish work?
> 5 What do you do in the evening?

5 ▶

> **Answers**
> 1 holidays   6 sharks
> 3 parties   8 scarves
> 5 watches

6 ▶

> **Answers**
> 2 these, bags, horrible
> 3 that, suitcase, old
> 4 What's this? It's an MP3 player. It's modern.
> 5 What are those? They're scarves. They're pretty.

7a ▶

> **Possible answers**
> **Personal/Clothes:** bag, belt, book, clothes, coat, scarf, shoe, watch, laptop computer, mobile phone, MP3 player
> **House/Home:** magazine, DVD player, laptop computer
> **Equipment:** digital camera, laptop computer, mobile phone, MP3 player

b ▶
Ss' own answers

2 Writing bank

1 ▶

> **Answers**
> 1 She's a police officer.
> 2 no
> 3 a sandwich
> 4 no, in the morning
> 5 5.30
> 6 watch TV or read a book

2a ▶

> **Answers**
> 1 get up
> 2 work
> 3 town centre
> 4 check
> 5 sandwich
> 6 meetings
> 7 finish
> 8 friends
> 9 park
> 10 watch

b ▶

> **Answer**
> the pronoun

3a ▶

> **Answers**
> 1 and
> 2 after that
> 3 then

b ▶

> **Answers**
> 1 then
> 2 and
> 3 Then
> 4 After that

4 ▶ Ss' own answers

5 ▶ Ss write about their routines.

3 Activities

Overview

CEFR Can do objectives
3.1 Talk about what you do in your free time
3.2 Talk about your abilities
3.3 Take and leave a simple phone message
Communication Talk about other people's abilities
Writing bank Write a short message

CEFR Portfolio ideas
a) Pair recording. A friend leaves a message on your phone about a party at his/her house. Phone back and record your answer.
b) Write an article about your friend. Write about what he/she can do or can't do.
c) An elderly member of your family sends you a note. He/She needs your help. Read the note and write your reply message.

Lead-in

OPTIONAL WARMER
Ss work in pairs and tell their partner what they would do on their day off, e.g. *read the paper*, *go for a walk*, *stay in bed*, etc. Write their suggestions on the board.

1a ▶ Ss look at the photos and choose six verbs and verb phrases in the box that describe them.

Answers
A swim   C listen to music;
B go shopping;   read a book
   meet friends   D play the guitar

▶ Ask Ss to check the words they don't know with a partner. Draw their attention to the use of the definite and indefinite article: *go to* a *concert/go to* the *gym*; *play football/play* the *guitar*; *watch TV/watch* a *DVD*; *surf* the *Internet/read* a *book*.

b ▶ Elicit answers to the questions as a whole class. Ask Ss which of the activities they enjoy doing.

Possible answers
1   go to a concert, meet friends, play football
2   go for a walk, go shopping, go to a concert, go to the gym, play football, sunbathe, swim
3   cook, listen to music, play games online, play the guitar, surf the Internet, watch TV/a DVD

c ▶ Ss organise the words according to the table in pairs. There will be some overlap between the categories. Encourage Ss to discuss these.

Possible answers
At home: cook, listen to music, meet friends, play games online, play the guitar, read a book or magazine, sunbathe, surf the Internet, text friends, watch TV/a DVD
In the park: go for a walk, go to a concert, listen to music, meet friends, play the guitar, play football, read a book or magazine, sunbathe, text friends
At the shops: go shopping, meet friends, text friends
At a club/nightclub: go to a concert, listen to music, meet friends, text friends
At a sports centre/swimming pool: go to the gym, meet friends, play football, sunbathe, swim

2a ▶ Encourage Ss to add as many activities as they can.

b ▶ In pairs, Ss ask and answer questions about their free time. Draw Ss' attention to the use of prepositions: *in the morning/evening*, *at the weekend*, *on Mondays*.

c ▶ Ss tell the class about their partner. With larger groups ask: *Who else plays the guitar? Who else likes reading?* to speed up the feedback.

3.1 Lunchtime leisure

It is common for workers in English-speaking countries in Europe or America to have a lunch break during the working day. Typically, the time given for this is one hour and indeed traditionally this break was commonly referred to as the 'lunch hour'. However, as people are working in increasingly pressurised jobs, the concept of lunch hour is changing and many people are taking shorter breaks at lunchtime and even eating at their work station. A typical lunch consists of a sandwich and a drink, often eaten in parks or coffee shops. A large lunch in a restaurant during the working day is not very common except for important business meetings or on special occasions.

In this lesson, Ss focus on what people do in their free time. They listen to and read about what people do in their lunch break. Ss talk and write about their own free-time activities.

Listening

1 ▶ 🔵 1.34 Ask Ss to focus on the photos. Elicit ideas about the kind of things people do in their lunch break (*listen to their iPods/the radio*, *go for a walk*, *meet friends*, *check emails*, etc.). Put suggestions on the board. Try to elicit some of the key vocabulary from the listening text during feedback (e.g. *canteen*, *go for a walk*, *go shopping*, *carry on working*, *check emails*, *go to the gym*, etc.).

▶ Tell Ss they are going to listen to four people talking about what they do in their lunch break. Explain you will play the recording twice. They must do ex. 1 as they listen the first time and ex. 2 as they listen a second time.

▶ Ss listen and match the speaker to the correct photo.

> **Answers**
> Stig: photo D
> Amber: photo C
> Matt: photo A
> Ailsa: photo B

2a ▶ Ss look at the activities in the table, then listen and tick which activities are mentioned by whom. Ss check answers with a partner, then as a whole class.

> **Answers**
> Stig: 3, 4, 6, 8
> Amber: 7, 8
> Matt: 3, 5, 6, 7
> Ailsa: 1, 2, 8

b ▶ Ss read the five sentences. Play recording 1.34 again. Ss listen to see if the statements are true or false. After listening, Ss check answers with a partner and then as a whole class.

> **Answers**
> 1 F
> 2 T
> 3 T
> 4 F
> 5 F

Grammar | adverbs of frequency

> **OPTIONAL GRAMMAR LEAD-IN**
> Focus on the false statements 1 and 5 from ex. 2b:
> *Stig sometimes stays at his desk in the lunch hour.* Ask: *Why is this false? What is the right answer?* (*Stig* usually *has lunch at his desk; he* always *leaves his desk at lunchtime.*)
> *Ailsa goes to the gym in her lunch break.* Ask: *Why is this false? What is the right answer?* (*Ailsa* never *goes to the gym at lunchtime.*)

3a ▶ Ss complete the sentences with a partner, then use the audioscript to check their answers.

> **Answers**
> 1 take
> 2 leaves, goes
> 3 takes, goes
> 4 goes, has

b ▶ Ss complete the first part of the Active grammar box. Draw the scale on the board and ask Ss to come up and fill in the correct frequency words during feedback.

▶ Write on board: *Amber is* <u>often</u> *at her desk. He* <u>usually</u> *goes for a walk. She doesn't* <u>always</u> *take a lunch break. She* <u>never</u> *goes to the gym.* Underline the adverbs of frequency. Ss complete the second part of the Active grammar box.

> **Active grammar**
> (always), usually, (often), sometimes, (occasionally), never
> after the verb to be
> before other verbs

▶ Negative sentences: Explain how the adverbs go between the auxiliary *don't/doesn't* and the main verb in negative sentences. Ask: *Where is the negative in* She never goes to the gym*?* (It is contained in the word *never*. *She doesn't never go/She never go to the gym* are both incorrect.)

▶ Direct Ss to the Reference section on page 37.

4a ▶ Ss order the words to make sentences. Ss check answers with a partner, then as a whole class. Help Ss with the word order: *in the morning, on Sundays, at the weekend*, etc. go at the end of the sentence.

Answers
1 We often go to concerts.
2 Lara occasionally cooks Chinese food.
3 Jason usually plays football in the evening.
4 My parents never read in bed.
5 I always go shopping at the weekend.
6 Dan sometimes goes to the gym in the morning.

b ▶ Ss rewrite the sentences to make them true about themselves. Ss compare sentences with a partner. Elicit three or four sentences during feedback.

OPTIONAL VARIATION

In pairs Ss make sentences about themselves. Give them a few minutes to prepare their sentences. Each pair reads out their sentences and the others have to guess whether the sentences are true or false, e.g. *I never eat chocolate. X usually gets up early on Saturdays. Y sometimes sings in the shower*, etc.

c ▶ Ss discuss what they/their colleagues do during their lunch break. Ss can use the vocabulary in ex. 2a and the diagram in ex. 3b to help them.

Reading

5 ▶ Ss make sentences about Shane based on the text. Ss should read the text silently.

Answers
1 never sleeps
2 always leaves the office
3 always uses the computer
4 sometimes listens to music
5 occasionally goes shopping

6 ▶ Ss first complete the words and then use the text to order the days of the week. Focus on the pronunciation of the words, especially *Tuesday, Wednesday* and *Thursday*. Ask: *What day is today? What day is tomorrow?* Teach the expressions *the day after tomorrow* and *the day before yesterday*.

Answers
Tuesday
Wednesday
Thursday
Friday
Saturday
Sunday

Vocabulary | activities

7a ▶ Ss work with a partner. They read through the lesson in order to find the activities to complete the word forks.

Answers
go to the gym, go to the park, go to an evening class, go to a concert, go to the cinema
go on the Internet, go on Facebook
go for a walk, go for a long lunch
go shopping, go running

b ▶ Ss add expressions to the word forks. Ss compare answers with a partner, then as a whole class.

Suggested answers
go to sleep, go to work, go to town
go on a picnic, go on holiday, go on a trip
go for a swim, go for a cycle, go for a drive
go hiking, go jogging, go cycling

c ▶ Divide the board into three sections. Write blank word forks for *have, do* and *read* in each section. Invite Ss to come to the board and add expressions to the word forks.

Suggested answers
have an idea, have fun, have dinner, have a bath
do the shopping, do my homework, do yoga
read a book, read a magazine, read the news

Speaking and writing

8a ▶ Direct Ss to the questionnaire. Ask them to read through the activities and tick the ones that apply to them, then write in when they do this activity, e.g. *on Sunday mornings, on Saturday evenings, at night, in the morning, at the weekend*. They then add activities to the chart.

b ▶ Ss interview each other about what they do in their free time and complete the questionnaire for their partner.

9a ▶ Ss work alone and brainstorm ideas about their free time. Ss compare lists with a partner.

b ▶ Model one or two example sentences on the board, e.g. *I watch TV on Monday evenings. I read the newspapers on Saturdays.* Ss write a short paragraph based on their notes for ex. 9a.

OPTIONAL VARIATION

Class survey. Put the following headings on the board: *usually, sometimes, occasionally, never.* (If Ss are confident, you can increase the number of headings, e.g. *rarely, often, once a week.*). Elicit *How many of us watch TV every day?, How many never go to the gym?*, etc. Collate the information under the different headings. You can use the list of activities in ex. 8a and 2a for this. Find out the most popular activities in the class. With larger classes, Ss can work in groups. Ss write the results of the survey, e.g. *70 percent of us go for walks once a week*, etc.

3.2 Can you do it?

Rebecca Romero is an English athlete from Surrey. Her first sport was rowing and she won a silver medal in the Athens 2004 Olympics and a gold medal in the World Championships in 2005. However, she suffered from back pain and she gave up rowing in 2006. Instead, she took up track cycling and she won a gold medal for cycling in the Beijing 2008 Olympics. She is the second woman ever to win medals in the Olympics for two different sports. Roswitha Krause of East Germany was the first woman to do this, winning medals in swimming (1968) and handball (1976 and 1980). Individual track cycling is no longer an event in the Olympic programme which means that Rebecca Romero will not be able to defend her title at future Olympic games. See http://www.rebeccaromero.co.uk/ for further information.

In this lesson, Ss read about Olympic medallist Rebecca Romero. They learn how to describe their own and other people's abilities.

Vocabulary | sports and games

1a ▶ Ss focus on the pictures and match them to an activity.

Answers
aerobics D
basketball J
chess H
judo I
rowing G
running F
skiing B
tennis A
windsurfing C
yoga E

OPTIONAL EXTENSION
Ask Ss to categorise the words into (1) indoor/outdoor activities and (2) activities which we do alone/in teams.

b ▶ Ss complete the table and check answers with a partner, and then as a whole class.

Answers
do: judo, yoga
go: rowing, skiing, windsurfing
play: basketball, tennis

▶ Draw Ss' attention to the fact that *play* is usually used with activities done in teams or games. *Do* is usually used with non-game activities, for instance those we do alone. Ask Ss what they notice about what is usually used with *go* (the *-ing* form of the verb).

c ▶ Ss ask and answer questions about the activities in pairs. Review the phrases *on Mondays*, *at the weekend*, *in the morning* to help them.

OPTIONAL EXTENSION
Ss close their books. They take it in turns to mime one of the activities to another student, who must guess what it is and give the whole expression: *go skiing, play basketball, do yoga*, etc.

Reading

2a ▶ Direct Ss to the photos of Rebecca Romero and discuss the question as a whole class.

Answers
rowing, track cycling

b ▶ Tell Ss they are going to read the first part of a newspaper article about Rebecca Romero. Preteach *degree* and *medal*.

▶ Ss look at the table first and then read the short text. Ss complete the table. Elicit answers as a whole class.

Answers
Age: 29
Nationality: British
Qualifications: degree in sports science and English
Achievements: two Olympic medals in two different sports

3 ▶ Direct Ss to the longer text about Rebecca Romero. Put the word *ceremony* on the board and encourage Ss to guess the meaning as they read. Ss read the text and answer the questions. Ss compare answers in pairs before whole-class feedback.

Answers
1　rowing
2　has a bad back
3　doesn't remember
4　skiing

Grammar | can/can't

4a ▶ Ss cover the text on the previous page and with a partner try to remember what Rebecca can and can't do. They look at four activities in ex. 4a and in pairs put a ✓ against what she can do and an ✗ against what she can't do. Ss check their answers in the text.

Answers
✓ cycle fast
✗ row, run, play tennis

b ▶ Ss complete the sentences using *can* and *can't* and the question form. Put *can* and *can't* on the board and point to the correct answer during feedback.

> **Answers**
> can
> can
> Can
> can't

▶ Ask Ss if they notice anything different about the verb *can*. Elicit the following: it never changes (no *s* after *he/she can*). It doesn't need another verb to make it negative or to ask a question (*I can't swim*, not *I don't can swim. Can you swim?* not *Do you can swim?*). It almost always has another verb with it (*I can swim*).

▶ Ss complete the Active grammar box.

> **Active grammar**
> can
> can't
> Can
> can't
> 1   No
> 2   No

▶ Direct Ss to the Reference section on page 37.

c ▶ Ss note which of the activities listed they can and can't do. Ask Ss to write short sentences about their abilities, e.g. *I can play chess, I can't play football*, etc.

> **OPTIONAL EXTENSION**
> Ss work in pairs to make sentences and the other Ss guess who or what they are describing, e.g.
> *It can fly. It can talk. It can't sing.* (a parrot)
> *He can fly. He can lift heavy objects. He can't do magic.*
> (Superman)

Pronunciation | /æ/, /ə/, /ɑː/

5 ▶ 🔵 1.35 Tell Ss they are going to listen to two mothers describing what their children can and can't do. Ss look at the list of activities. Play recording 1.35 once. Ss check answers with a partner, then check with the whole class.

> **Answers**
> play the piano – S
> sing – J, S
> dance – S
> play football – J
> play tennis – J, S
> ski – S
> speak French – J, S
> speak Spanish – S
> ride a bike – J
> drive a car – S

6a ▶ 🔵 1.36 Play recording 1.36. Ss note how *can* and *can't* are pronounced. Put the phonetic symbols on the board and say the sentences for the Ss, emphasising the different vowel sounds. Ss repeat the sentences after the recording. Draw Ss' attention to the final /t/ ending in *can't*.

b ▶ Direct Ss to ex. 5 again. Model a few questions about what Jonny and Susie can do with the whole class. Ask: *Can Susie speak Spanish?* Ss answer *Yes, she can*, or *No, she can't*. Ss continue the exercise in pairs.

▶ Direct Ss to the Pronunciation bank on page 148.

7a/b ▶ Ss work in pairs and ask and answer questions about themselves based on the activities listed in ex. 4c. Ss then go on to ask each other questions about other abilities, similar to the ones listed in ex. 5. Monitor and correct any errors you hear.

Speaking

8a ▶ Ss work in small groups. They look through the various activities and discuss their own abilities in relation to them. Encourage Ss to respond to what others can and can't do, e.g.

S1: I can play the saxophone.

S2: Oh, when did you learn? Is it difficult? etc.

It is not important if they make mistakes during this activity.

b ▶ One student from each group describes their overall findings to the rest of the class.

> **OPTIONAL VARIATION**
> Give each student one of the abilities from the *can* column in ex. 8a. They circulate and ask other Ss if they have that ability. If the answer is 'No', they move on, but if the answer is 'Yes', they have to find out two more things about that ability and that person.
> E.g. *Can you speak three languages? Yes. Which languages? Where did you learn French?*, etc.

3.3 Phone fun

Spelling conventions for text messages are often different from those in 'regular' writing. Single digits and single letters often replace words in text messages and informal emails. Some common abbreviations used in text messaging are *C u l8r* (See you later), *Txt b4 u go* (Text me before you go) and *R u coming 2nite?* (Are you coming tonight?). Other abbreviations include *OMG* (oh my God!), *LOL* (laugh out loud), *ASAP* (as soon as possible) and *FYI* (for your information). However, these spellings and abbreviations are only acceptable in informal settings and should never be used in other contexts, especially exams or more formal emails.

In this lesson, Ss read about texting and phone throwing competitions and listen to phone messages. They practise making short telephone calls where they take and leave simple phone messages.

Reading

> **OPTIONAL WARMER**
>
> Ss discuss in pairs when they would text rather than phone someone. Put these headings on the board to guide the discussion: *Who?/Why?* (reason for the call) *When?* (time of day), etc. Don't worry about Ss making mistakes during this activity, but encourage them to express their views as best they can.

1 ▶ Ss answer the questions in pairs. Establish whether Ss make more 'social calls' or 'work calls' on their mobiles during class feedback.

2a ▶ Tell Ss they are going to read about two different mobile phone competitions. Elicit suggestions as to the kind of activities which might happen at these events.

▶ Explain to Ss that they will read the text twice, the first time very quickly and the second time much more slowly. Direct them to the questions and tell them they have one minute to find this information in the text as quickly as possible. Teach *throw* (mime throwing a ball). Explain that they do not need to understand the text fully at this point. Stop the activity after a minute and have Ss call out the answers.

> **Answers**
> a 2
> b 3
> c 1

b ▶ Ss look at the columns and predict what the answers will be with a partner. Do not give feedback as they will find the answers in the text. Preteach *fan, the average phone user* and *champion*.

▶ Ss read the text again silently and complete the matching exercise as they read. Ss check answers in pairs, then as a whole class.

> **Answers**
> 2 d
> 3 h
> 4 f
> 5 g
> 6 c
> 7 b
> 8 a

c ▶ Elicit reactions to the numbers from Ss as a whole class.

3a ▶ Ss close their books. Ask: *What else do you use your mobile phone for?* Elicit suggestions (e.g. take photos, play games, etc.).

▶ Ss open their books and look at the list in ex. 3a. They tick the features they use on their mobile.

b ▶ Ss compare lists with a partner. Review the adverbs of frequency from Lesson 3.1 (*sometimes, occasionally, never*, etc.). In feedback, ask Ss how often they use each feature.

Vocabulary | numbers

4 ▶ ◯ 1.37 In pairs, Ss match the figures to the written number in the box. Then they listen to recording 1.37 to see if they were right.

> **Answers**
> | | |
> |---|---|
> | 16 | sixteen |
> | 60 | sixty |
> | 600 | six hundred |
> | 601 | six hundred and one |
> | 660 | six hundred and sixty |
> | 6,000 | six thousand |
> | 6616 | six thousand, six hundred and sixteen |
> | 60,000 | sixty thousand |
> | 600,000 | six hundred thousand |
> | 6,000,000 | six million |
> | 6,000,000,000 | six billion |

Pronunciation | word stress

5a ▶ ◯ 1.38 Play recording 1.38. Ss listen and underline the strong sounds, the main stress in the numbers.

▶ Revise the phonetic symbols /ɪ/ and /iː/ to help emphasise the point. Ss repeat the words after you.

> **Answers**
> four<u>teen</u> <u>for</u>ty

b ▶ ◯ 1.39 Ss listen to recording 1.39 and tick the number they hear. They check answers with a partner, then as a whole class.

Answers
1 forty
2 eighty
3 seventeen
4 thirteen
5 ninety
6 sixteen

c ► Ss test each other.

► Direct Ss to the Pronunciation bank on page 148.

OPTIONAL EXTENSION

Ask Ss if these numbers have any significance as ages in their country (e.g. driver's licence at 16, voting at 18, women retiring at 60, etc.).

Listening

OPTIONAL LEAD-IN

Ss work in small groups to discuss the following questions: *How many phones do you have in your house? Which rooms are they in? Are there times when you don't answer the phone (e.g. during dinner, etc.)?* In whole-class feedback, establish who uses the phone the most in each group.

6a ► 1.40 Tell Ss they are going to listen to five different phone messages. Ss read the five names first. Play recording 1.40 once and Ss listen to find out which name relates to which message.

Answers
Damian 4
Mary Wilde 5
Benson Cameras 3
Steve Henshaw 2

b ► Ss read through the written messages in their books. Play the recording again. Ss complete the texts with the missing words. They check answers in pairs and then as a whole class.

Answers
1 Jane, cinema
2 call, 0752
3 Brown, camera, week, 6.30
4 dinner, office
5 David, 391, call

► Play message 5 again. Ss listen to how we say *88*.

Answers
double eight

7a ► 1.41 Ss work in pairs to put the sentences into the correct order.

Answers
2 Hello, can I speak to Laura, please?
3 She isn't here right now. Can I take a message?
4 Yes, please ask her to phone Jeffrey.
5 OK. What's your number?
6 It's 011 908 5561.
7 OK. Bye.

b ► Ss practise the dialogue in pairs. Monitor Ss, correcting any obvious mispronunciation you hear.

8 ► Ask Ss: *Is the dialogue in exercise 7 a formal or informal call?* (formal) Elicit when we make formal calls (e.g. to make an appointment, to find out information about opening/closing times, to make a complaint, etc.). Ask: *Who do we make informal calls to?* (friends, family)

► Ss complete the *How to...* box in pairs. The dialogue in ex. 7a will help them for some of the answers.

Answers
1 take
2 ask
3 number
4 It's
5 This
6 message

Speaking

9 ► Ss practise making phone calls in pairs. Give Ss time to read their individual briefs. Student A's brief is on page 129. When Ss have finished, ask a different pair to model each of the phone calls to the others.

OPTIONAL EXTENSION

Ask Ss: *What are the good things about having a mobile phone?* (can always be reached, texting, etc.). Ask: *Are there any bad things about them?* (can extend the working day, interruptions, etc.) Ss work in small groups. They make a list of four advantages and four disadvantages of mobile phones. Do not worry about Ss making mistakes during this activity.

3 Communication

A skills exchange is where one person offers a particular skill or service in exchange for another skill or service from someone else. It is like a 'swap shop' for skills/ services. People post their skills and what they are looking for onto a skills exchange noticeboard or website.

In this lesson, Ss discuss other people's abilities and needs in the context of a Skills Exchange service.

OPTIONAL WARMER

Ss look at the jobs column in ex. 1a. They work in small groups and decide which of the jobs they consider
(1) most interesting, (2) most difficult, (3) most boring,
(4) most stressful.

1a ▶ Ss work in pairs to match the abilities to the jobs.

Answers
1 g
2 i
3 a
4 b
5 j
6 h
7 c
8 e
9 f
10 d

b ▶ Ss extend the list of jobs and abilities. Give them a few prompts to get started (e.g. doctor, Prime Minister).

2 ▶ Elicit ways of looking for an electrician or a plumber to do something in your house (e.g. ads in the *Yellow Pages* phone book, ads in local newspapers, word-of-mouth).

▶ Ss read the advert for Barton Skills Exchange. Elicit what a Skills Exchange is.

3a ▶ Ss read about Carmen and Brian and complete the Barton Skills Exchange cards for them. They check answers in pairs and then as a whole class.

Answers
Carmen
What she can do: speak Spanish and German, paint and draw, take digital photos and change them on the computer
What she needs: a driver
Brian
Phone number: 577 894 505
What he can do: repair cars and engines, repair houses, make furniture in wood and metal, repair computers
What he needs: a cleaner

b ▶ 🔘 1.42 Ss listen to recording 1.42 and complete the skills exchange cards for the other two people. Ss check answers with a partner after the first listening. Play the recording a second time then check answers.

Answers
Dario
Phone number: 887 715 992
What he can do: play the piano and guitar, drive, play computer games
What he needs: a photographer
Lizzie
Phone number: 0777 334 898
What she can do: play football, basketball and tennis, cook, clean and do housework
What she needs: someone to repair her laptop

4 ▶ Ss work in pairs and match skills for the four people. Before they start, remind Ss to use *can't* as well as *can*. Ask them to give as many justifications for their pairings as they can.

Suggested answers
Dario and Carmen
Brian and Lizzie

5a ▶ Give Ss a minute or two to think about their own skills and what skill or service they need. Direct Ss to the suggested language in the example dialogue before they start. Each student interviews two other Ss and completes a skills exchange card for them.

b ▶ Ss reform into small groups. Try to ensure that the Ss in this group have not spoken to the same students during ex. 5a. Each student should have two skills exchange cards. Ss compare cards and match.

▶ Encourage Ss to explain and justify their views. It is not important if Ss make mistakes during this activity. During monitoring, note down any obvious errors and deal with them in a general way when the activity has finished.

3 Review and practice

1 ▶

Answers
1 Malcolm doesn't have a job.
2 Malcolm doesn't have an address.
3 Malcolm never goes to work in the morning.
4 Malcolm never eats in restaurants.
5 Malcolm occasionally has lunch in a café.
6 Malcolm sometimes meets friends in the park.
7 Malcolm's days are always boring.
8 Malcolm doesn't like his life.

2 ▶ Ss' own answers

3 ▶

Possible answers
1 Computers can check spellings/can't play football.
2 Sharks can swim/can't drive.
3 Mobile phones can send picture messages/can't think.
4 Dogs can run/can't send text messages.

4 ▶

Answers
he can play basketball   he plays the guitar
he can't play tennis   he sings too
he doesn't like tennis   he doesn't dance
                                he can't play the piano

5 ▶

Answers

			W	E	E	K	E	N	D
		T	U	E	S	D	A	Y	
	M	O	N	D	A	Y			
		S	U	N	D	A	Y		
			E						
	T	H	U	R	S	D	A	Y	
S	A	T	U	R	D	A	Y		
	F	R	I	D	A	Y			
			Y						

6 ▶

Answers
1 go   4 go   8 do
2 meet   5 send, go   9 go
3 go   6 show   10 go
           7 buy   11 watch

7 ▶

Answers
2 a nightclub   4 running   7 the Internet
3 a DVD   5 reading   8 swimming
                 6 music

3 Writing bank

1 ▶

Answers
1 C
2 A
3 D
4 B

2 ▶

Answers
A to Louisa, from Ben – Can you call him before then?
B to Steve, from Dave – Can you come and watch it at my house?
C to Sally, from Suze – Can you get some (bread)?
D to Mr Owens, from Michael Thomas – Can you get to the meeting at 8.30?

3 ▶

Answers
1 ? (question mark)
2 . (full stop)

4 ▶

Answers
1 full stop, full stop, question mark
2 full stop, question mark, full stop
3 full stop, question mark, full stop

5 ▶ Ss' own answers

6 ▶ Ss write three messages.

Overview

Lead-in	Revision: Food; measures; money
4.1	**Can do:** Talk about quantities **Grammar:** Countable and uncountable nouns *much/many/a lot of* **Vocabulary:** Food **Listening and Reading:** Eating around the world
4.2	**Can do:** Talk about your diet and lifestyle **Grammar:** *a/an*, *some* and *any* **Vocabulary:** Containers Adjectives (2): feelings **Speaking and Pronunciation:** /æ/ and /ʌ/ Diet quiz **Listening:** A television programme about rubbish
4.3	**Can do:** Order food in a restaurant **Grammar:** Object pronouns **How to...** order food in a restaurant Roleplay: ordering a meal **Listening:** Ordering a meal in a restaurant
Communication	Ask people for things and give people things **How to...** go shopping at a market
Reference	
Review and Practice	
Writing bank	Describe yourself and other people **How to...** use pronouns (1)

CEFR Can do objectives
4.1 Talk about quantities
4.2 Talk about your diet and lifestyle
4.3 Order food in a restaurant
Communication Ask people for things and give people things
Writing bank Describe yourself and other people

CEFR Portfolio ideas
a) Recording. You cannot go to the supermarket today. Telephone the supermarket and ask for the things you need. (Your partner should be the supermarket assistant.)
b) Video. Mime eating different kinds of food. Can your friends guess what you are eating?
c) Write your personal profile for Peoplenet.com.

Lead-in

The US, Canada, Australia and New Zealand each have their own currencies, all called dollars and cents. In the UK, the pound sterling and pence are used. The Republic of Ireland is part of the eurozone and uses euros and cents, while South Africa uses the rand and cents.

OPTIONAL WARMER

Ss work in small groups of three or four. They tell each other what their favourite food is in these situations: (1) in bed when you're not feeling well, (2) at the beach on a hot day, (3) served with a drink in a bar.

1a ▶ Ss look at the photos. They match the words in the box to the food in the pictures. They check answers in pairs, then as a whole class.

> **Answers**
> A apples, beef, cheese, chicken, eggs, fish, milk, tomatoes
> B tea
> C apples, strawberries, tomatoes, watermelon
> D bread, pasta, rice

b ▶ Ss match other words they know to the pictures.

2a ▶ Elicit how often Ss shop for food (once a week, every day, twice a week, etc.). Ask: *Do you buy a lot of milk? Do you buy a lot of fruit?* etc.

▶ Ss put the words into the correct column. Check answers as a whole class.

> **Answers**
> Food: grammes, kilos
> Drink: litres
> Money: dollars, euros, cents

b ▶ Ss work with a partner to find other words.

3a ▶ Ss match the words in the box to the pictures. Elicit answers as a whole class.

> **Answers**
> A credit card
> B coin
> C note
> D cash machine
> E receipt

b ▶ Ss work in pairs to ask and answer questions. Ss talk about the different places they buy their food (supermarket, market, local shop, etc.). Then they discuss how they pay (cash, cheque, credit card).

> **Answers**
> Pictures B and C show cash.

4.1 A world of food

Most families in English-speaking countries value eating dinner together as often as possible. However, as people lead increasingly busy lives, this often takes place only at the weekend, if at all. Surveys show that eating dinner in front of the TV is becoming more and more common in many Anglophone countries. People's busier schedules also explain the rising popularity of fast-food restaurants and convenience foods like frozen and ready-made dinners. These are sometimes referred to as 'TV dinners'. In Australia, a family barbecue (or 'barbie') is very common, especially at weekends in summer, and these often take place in public parks or on beaches where special barbecues are provided by the Council. A large Sunday lunch continues to be a popular family get-together in the UK and Ireland although it is unlikely to take place every week for most families nowadays. Roast meat and potatoes are key ingredients and indeed the meal is often referred to as the 'Sunday roast'.

In this lesson, Ss read about and listen to eating habits of people from different parts of the world. Ss talk about their own eating and shopping habits.

OPTIONAL WARMER

Put some or all of the questions from ex. 2b on the board (except for *has a ration book?*). In pairs, Ss discuss the questions in relation to their own families' eating habits.

Reading

1a ▶ Ss look at the family in the picture. Ask: *Where do you think this family is from?* Tell Ss they will read about this family in a minute. First they look at the three small pictures and match them to the words.

Answers
rice C
bananas A
hot dogs B

b ▶ Discuss this as a whole class.

Answers
All three foods, especially rice and bananas, are eaten in many different countries. Rice is particularly associated with Asian cultures; bananas are often associated with Caribbean cultures; hot dogs are associated with the US.

2a ▶ Scanning: Explain to Ss that they will read the text twice, the first time very quickly and the second time much more slowly. Direct them to the first instruction and tell them they have one minute to find this information in the text. Explain that they do not need to understand the text fully at this point. Stop the activity after a minute and have Ss call out the answers.

Answers
A   bananas – the Esteban family from Cuba
B   hot dogs – the Merton family from the United States
C   rice – the Toros from Japan

b ▶ Ss look at the questions. Explain *ration book* (the government decides how much of a particular item you can buy, not the shopper, due to shortages, e.g. during a war) and *fast food restaurants* (McDonald's or Burger King).

▶ Put the words *convenience food* and *tropical* on the board before Ss read the text, and encourage them to guess the meaning of these words if they don't know them rather than look them up in the dictionary. Ss compare answers in pairs before whole-class feedback.

▶ Ss read the text again, this time at their own pace. Explain that they do not need to understand every word in the text.

Answers
1   Toro
2   Esteban
3   Esteban
4   Merton
5   Merton
6   Toro and Merton (only once a week)

Listening

3a ▶ 🔵 1.43 Play recording 1.43 through. Ss listen and tick the countries they hear.

Answers
Brazil, Canada, Iran

b ▶ Play recording 1.43 again, this time stopping after each speaker. Ss listen and tick the foods mentioned by each speaker. Ss compare answers after each speaker. Give whole-class feedback at the end.

Answers
Speaker 1: black beans, rice, seafood
Speaker 2: lamb, seafood
Speaker 3: dried fruit, rice, seafood

4 ▶ Ss discuss the questions in pairs. If working with a multicultural group, try to ensure Ss are working with a partner from a different cultural background. Make a list of favourite foods from the class during feedback.

Answers   Ss' own answers

Grammar | countable and uncountable nouns

5a ▶ Direct Ss to the three pictures at the top of page 40. Ss decide which of the items they can count (the bananas, the hot dogs) and which they cannot (the rice). Count the bananas and the hot dogs for the Ss (*one, two, three bananas*; *one, two hot dogs*). Put the words *countable* and *uncountable* on the board.

Answers
1 bananas, hot dogs   2 rice

OPTIONAL GRAMMAR LEAD-IN

Ask: *What do you usually have for breakfast?* Elicit various suggestions and put them on the board. Put two headings on the board, *countable* and *uncountable*. Ask Ss which column the suggestions should go under, e.g. coffee, bread, tea, orange juice, etc., for uncountable; pancakes, apples, etc., for countable. Try to elicit details: *how many cups of coffee*, *how many pieces of toast*, etc. Put *2 cups of coffee*, *3 pieces of toast*, etc., in the countable column.

b ▶ Direct Ss to the shopping list. Ss decide whether the red and blue words are countable or uncountable. They check answers in pairs.

Answers
1 countable   b uncountable

c ▶ Ss complete the Active grammar box.

Active grammar
1 Countable   2 Uncountable

▶ Point out that uncountable nouns have no plural forms but we can say *two cups of coffee* or *two litres of milk*. We rarely say *one banana* or *one apple* when speaking of a singular noun. We usually say *a banana* or *an apple* instead.

▶ Direct Ss to the Reference section on page 47.

OPTIONAL EXTENSION

Ss close their books. Dictate food words to Ss. Ss decide whether the words are countable or uncountable and write the words in the correct column in their exercise books. To make it a little more challenging, dictate the countable words in the singular (e.g. *egg* rather than *eggs*).

6 ▶ Ss find and correct the mistakes with a partner.

Answers
1 I don't like rice.   4 I drink orange juice ...
2 Do you eat bread?   5 Do you like milk ... ?

Vocabulary | food

7a ▶ Ss read through audioscript 1.43 and underline all the food words they see. They use these words to complete the table.

Answers
Meat: pork, ham, lamb, duck   Vegetables: beans
Seafood: lobster, scallops   Others: nuts, spices

b ▶ Ss work with a partner or use dictionaries to add words to the columns. Give them a time limit of three minutes for this to add an element of fun to the list-making. See which pair has the longest list for each column.

Grammar | much/many/a lot of

8a ▶ Ss focus on the four extracts and decide whether the underlined words are countable or uncountable.

Answers
seafood, fast food – uncountable
takeaways, burgers – countable

b ▶ Ss focus on the red words in the extracts and then complete the Active grammar box. Ss compare answers with a partner, then as a whole class.

Active grammar
(how) much + uncountable noun
(how) many + countable noun
(not) a lot of + both

▶ Direct Ss to the Reference section on page 47.

9a ▶ Ss choose the correct option(s) in each sentence. Sometimes more than one option is correct.

Answers
1 much   4 much/a lot of
2 much/a lot of   5 many/a lot of
3 many   6 a lot of

b ▶ Ss complete the dialogue in pairs using the words and phrases from the box.

Answers
1 much   4 six
2 a lot   5 coffee
3 tomatoes   6 many

10 ▶ Ask Ss about (1) where and (2) when they usually do their weekly shopping (e.g. supermarket, street market, small shops; Thursday nights, Saturday mornings, etc.). For multicultural groups ask about typical opening and closing times in their countries (Lunch hour breaks? Late opening nights? 24-hour shops? Open on Sundays? etc.).

▶ Ss work in pairs and find out about each other's weekly shopping. They ask each other questions similar to those in ex. 9b.

Big supermarkets and giant out-of-town shopping malls have become more and more popular in English-speaking countries in Europe, America and Australia, and these stores are often open until very late, or even 24 hours a day in some cases. Small grocer's shops and bakeries have found it hard to compete, but farmers' markets and speciality food shops are slowly beginning to gain in popularity again in some places.

4.2 Trash tales

In this lesson, Ss listen to part of a TV programme looking at people's diet and interview each other about their own diets.

> **OPTIONAL WARMER**
>
> Ss work in small groups of three or four. They decide on what they consider to be the 'Five Main Rules' for healthy living. (E.g. Drink lots of water. Eat lots of fruit and vegetables. Drink green tea. Get exercise, etc.) In feedback, elicit suggestions and put them on the board.

Vocabulary | containers

1a ▶ Ss find examples of the containers in the picture.

> **Answers**
> A   bag
> B   bottle
> C   carton
> D   jar
> E   packet
> F   tube
> G   box
> H   can

b ▶ Ss match the containers with what they contain. Ss compare answers in pairs, then as a whole class.

> **Answers**
> 1g
> 2c
> 3b
> 4h
> 5a
> 6d
> 7f
> 8e

c ▶ Ss list other things that can be bought in the various containers.

Listening

2 ▶ Ss look at the TV guide extract. Explain *rubbish* (what people throw away) and *bin* (show them in the picture). Ss discuss the three questions in pairs.

> **Answers**
> 1   what people have in their rubbish bins and what it tells us about their diet
> 2   Doctor Laurence Redburn
> 3   Ss' own opinions

▶ Use this opportunity to teach *a healthy diet*, *an unhealthy diet*, and *to be on a diet*. Ss need to know this for the listening text.

3a ▶ ⬤ 1.44 Play recording 1.44 once. Ss listen to decide which of the bins are being described. Ss check answers in pairs.

> **Answers**
> bin on the left: 2
> bin on the right: 1

b ▶ Play the recording a second time. Ss listen and write the names of the foods in the correct column. They check answers in pairs, then as a whole class.

> **Answers**
> Healthy foods: potatoes, carrots, bananas, apples, juice, milk, water, pasta, fish
> Unhealthy foods: instant coffee, biscuits, burgers, crisps
> Tea bags are mentioned but it is not clear whether Laurence considers them to be healthy or not.

4 ▶ Ss discuss the two questions in pairs.

> **Answers**
> 1   Ss' own opinions
> 2   rice, oranges, salad: generally considered healthy
>   hot dogs: generally considered unhealthy
>   chocolate, red meat: opinions vary

> **OPTIONAL VARIATION**
>
> Refer Ss back to the different types of food which they met in Lesson 4.1 (meat, fish, seafood, fruit, vegetables, nuts, fast food, drinks). Ss interview their partner about everything their partner ate yesterday. (E.g. *For breakfast? For dinner? Anything else?*). When both Ss have finished, they look at the two lists to see if they each have a balanced diet.

Grammar | a/an, *some* and *any*

5 ▶ Ss focus on the examples taken from the recording and complete the Active grammar box.

> **Active grammar**
>
> Singular countable: a/an
> Plural countable: some, any
> Uncountable: some, any

▶ Direct Ss to the Reference section on page 47.

6a ▶ Ss complete the conversation in pairs. Check answers as a whole class.

> **Answers**
> 1   any
> 2   a
> 3   some/a lot of
> 4   some/a lot of
> 5   any
> 6   any
> 7   a
> 8   any
> 9   a
> 10 a

b ▶ 🔘 1.45 Ss read the paragraph and correct the underlined mistakes. Ss check answers in pairs, then listen to see if they were right.

> **Answers**
> a pizza
> some burgers
> some coffee
> a can of cola
> any tea
> some meat
> any sweets

Pronunciation | /æ/ and /ʌ/

7a ▶ 🔘 1.46 Write the two words, *pasta* and *some*, on the board. Play recording 1.46. Ss listen to identify the two vowel sounds. Show the phonetic symbols for the two sounds.

b ▶ 🔘 1.47 Ss read the words. Play recording 1.47. Ss listen and identify the /æ/ and /ʌ/ sounds. Ss practise saying the words.

> **Answers**
> /æ/: salad, lamb, apple, carrot
> /ʌ/: butter, lunch

▶ Direct Ss to the Pronunciation bank on page 147.

> **OPTIONAL EXTENSION**
> Write the following sentence on the board: *Anne and Chuck have butter on their pasta.* Say the sentence several times at increasing speed, like a tongue twister. Ss repeat after you.

Vocabulary | adjectives (2): feelings

8a ▶ Ss look at the pictures and match the pictures to the adjectives. They check answers in pairs.

> **Answers**
> 1   unhealthy
> 2   tired
> 3   healthy
> 4   fit
> 5   thirsty
> 6   hungry

b ▶ Ss categorise the adjectives in pairs. Check answers as a whole class.

> **Answers**
> Positive: fit, healthy
> Negative: hungry, thirsty, tired, unhealthy

c ▶ Ss complete the sentences using the adjectives from ex. 8a.

> **Answers**
> 1   tired
> 2   thirsty
> 3   hungry
> 4   fit
> 5   unhealthy

Speaking

9a ▶ Elicit food preferences from Ss before they start the task. Ask: *Do you usually drink tea or coffee? Do you add milk to tea or coffee? What do you drink if you are thirsty: water, milk, cola, fruit juice? What's your favourite fruit? What would you have for a snack between meals?* etc.

▶ Ss look at the 12 food items in the quiz. Explain what the X, ? and ✓ symbols mean. Give Ss a few minutes to complete the 'you' column.

b ▶ Ss use the chart to interview each other about what they eat/drink. Direct Ss to the example dialogue to help them.

c ▶ Ss use the key on page 129 to evaluate their partner's diet.

4.3 Ready to order?

In this lesson, Ss listen to two people ordering food in a restaurant. They then read the menu for the restaurant and practise ordering food.

Listening and speaking

1 ▶ Ss look at the photo of an American diner. They discuss the questions in pairs.

2a ▶ ● 1.48 Ss listen to recording 1.48 twice, the first time to get a general understanding of the conversation for ex. 2a and the second time to listen for more detailed information for ex. 2b. Ensure Ss understand *fries* (potato chips).

▶ Play the recording once. Ss listen and mark which items are ordered by Jenny and which by Sam. Ss check answers in pairs.

> **Answers**
> cheese sandwich S
> fries S
> salad J
> coffee S
> water J

b ▶ Play the recording a second time. Ss listen and fill in the missing words in the bill. They check answers in pairs, then as a whole class.

> **Answers**
> 1 fries
> 2 medium
> 3 large
> 4 water

▶ Ask Ss what they think *mineral water* is (water bought in a bottle) and the terms *small*, *medium* and *large*.

3 ▶ ● 1.49 Play recording 1.49. Preteach *vegetarian* (no meat). Ss listen and answer the questions. They check answers in pairs, then as a whole class.

> **Answers**
> 1 vegetarian pizzas
> 2 How much is (that?)
> 3 $16.70 (sixteen dollars and seventy cents)
> 4 by credit card

4a ▶ Ss look at the menu. Ask: *Is this an expensive restaurant?* (No.) Ss look at the headings. Do not explain *side orders* to Ss yet. Ask them to work it out for themselves as they read. Ss read the menu and match the headings to A–C. They check answers in pairs, then as a whole class.

> **Answers**
> A Main dishes
> B Side orders
> C Drinks

b ▶ Teach *How much is a burger? How much are fries?* Direct Ss to the bill in ex. 2b again. Demonstrate to Ss how to say the prices in the bill, e.g. *A coffee is $2.95* (two dollars ninety-five); *A mineral water is $2.25* (two dollars twenty-five), etc.

▶ Ss work in pairs. Student A looks at the prices on page 129. Student B asks about the prices in the menu and fills in the gaps.

5a ▶ Elicit ways of ordering food in a restaurant. Ask Ss how they would get a waiter's attention in a restaurant. Establish how to do it in an English-speaking country (arm raised or a nod, not clicking fingers or calling 'Waiter').

▶ Ss look at the beginnings and endings of sentences from the recording. Elicit the answer to the first one as a whole class, then Ss work in pairs to match the sentence halves.

> **Answers**
> 1 c
> 2 d
> 3 f
> 4 e
> 5 g
> 6 a
> 7 b

b ▶ Ss check their answers by reading the audioscript on pages 152–153. They complete the *How to...* box.

> **Answers**
> 1 Do
> 2 like
> 3 much
> 4 Can

▶ Say the expressions for the Ss and ask them to repeat them. Help with the pronunciation and intonation patterns. Draw Ss' attention to the /d/ sound in *I'd like* (not *I like*).

c ▶ Ss complete the dialogue with words from ex. 5a and 5b.

> **Answers**
> 1 can
> 2 I'd
> 3 Do
> 4 want
> 5 have
> 6 much
> 7 Can

d ▶ Ss practise the dialogue in pairs. Monitor and correct any errors you hear.

Grammar | object pronouns

6a ▶ Ss look at the cartoons. Elicit what is happening in each one. Ss then match the sentences with the speech bubbles. Ss check answers in pairs, then as a whole class.

> **Answers**
> 1 D
> 2 B
> 3 C
> 4 E
> 5 A

b ▶ Ss read the speech bubbles again and complete the Active grammar box.

> **Active grammar**
> him
> her
> us
> you
> them

▶ Direct Ss to the Reference section on page 47.

7a ▶ Ss choose the correct option, then check with a partner. Give feedback.

> **Answers**
> 1 me, her
> 2 her
> 3 them
> 4 him
> 5 us

b ▶ Ss complete the sentences in pairs.

> **Answers**
> 1 me
> 2 them
> 3 us
> 4 it
> 5 you

Speaking

8 ▶ Ss work in groups. Try to ensure Ss are working with new people for this activity. One student is the waiter/waitress taking orders and the others are customers placing orders from the menu in ex. 4a. They use the language learned in ex. 5.

> **OPTIONAL EXTENSION**
> Ss imagine they have been on a desert island for the last two years and have just returned to their country again. In pairs, Ss tell each other what meal they would choose the first evening back home.

4 Communication

In this lesson, Ss buy and sell food at a market.

> **OPTIONAL WARMER**
>
> Ss talk about markets in pairs. Put the following headings on the board: *Do you like markets? Why/Why not? What do you buy/don't you buy? Prices*

1a ▶ ⬤ 1.50 Ss focus on the photo of the market. Teach *stall* (a shop at a market).

▶ Tell Ss they are going to hear a woman shopping at a market. Ss look at the food words and the three exercises. Explain that the woman goes to three different stalls.

▶ Play recording 1.50 through once. Ss listen and tick the correct blue boxes. Ss check answers in pairs.

> **Answers**
> Stall 1: apples, bananas, melon
> Stall 2: beef, chicken, fish
> Stall 3: cheese, milk

b ▶ Play the recording a second time. Ss listen and tick the red boxes. If necessary, pause the recording after each stall. Ss check answers in pairs.

> **Answers**
> Stall 1: apples, bananas
> Stall 2: beef, fish
> Stall 3: cheese, milk

c ▶ Ss answer the questions. Only play the recording a third time if they appear to be struggling. Ss check answers in pairs, then as a whole class.

> **Answers**
> apples: 1 kg
> fish: 400 g
> milk: 2 litres
> beef: 500 g
> cheese: 200 g
> Shopping total: €24.30 (twenty-four euros and thirty cents)

2 ▶ Ss do the exercise in pairs.

> **Suggested answers**
> kilos: carrots, potatoes, sugar
> grammes: coffee, lamb, sugar
> litres: cola, fruit juice, mineral water

3 ▶ Ss listen to recording 1.50 again in order to complete the *How to...* box.

> **Answers**
> 1 help
> 2 like
> 3 need
> 4 Here
> 5 How much
> 6 That's

▶ Help Ss with the intonation patterns for these expressions. Write *How much are the apples?* on the board and demonstrate the rise and fall of the intonation pattern. Draw arrows up and down to show Ss how to mark intonation. Say the other expressions and ask Ss to notice the intonation patterns for each one.

4a ▶ Ss work in groups of three. Student A is a shopper and Ss B and C are both shop assistants. Shoppers decide on their shopping lists and shop assistants decide on prices. Give Ss about five minutes to prepare.

b ▶ When Ss are ready, they start buying and selling the groceries. Shoppers cannot go over their budget of 40 euros.

▶ In feedback, Ss tell the class about what they have bought/sold. Compare prices, e.g. *Who bought the cheapest bananas?* etc. (Do not focus attention on the superlative form at this stage as this will be introduced in a later unit.)

c ▶ Ss change roles and do the roleplay again.

4 Review and practice

1 ▶

Answers					
1	d	3	f	5	a
2	e	4	c	6	b

2 ▶

Answers			
		3	two
1	many	4	much
2	water	5	much

3 ▶

Answers					
		3	some	6	some
1	some	4	any	7	a
2	a	5	any	8	any

4 ▶

Answers	
1	We, them
2	She, us
3	They, them
4	He, it
5	We, her

5 ▶

Answers					
1	I	4	they	7	her
2	He	5	them	8	She
3	him	6	me	9	me

6 ▶

Answers	
1	rice
2	burger
3	bread
4	watermelon
5	tomatoes
6	chicken
7	milk
8	pizza

7 ▶

Answers			
1	bottle	3	bin
2	packet	4	packet
		5	can

8 ▶

Answers	
2	tired
3	thirsty
4	unhealthy
5	fit
6	hungry

4 Writing bank

1 ▶ Ss' own answers

2a ▶

Answer
2

b ▶

Answers	
1	c
2	d
3	e
4	a
5	b

3a ▶

Answers	
1	he
2	she
3	it
4	they

b ▶

Answers	
1	She's Brazilian.
2	He's a professional footballer.
3	They're Russian.
4	It's a very big city.
5	It's a cold country but it's very beautiful.

4a ▶ Ss' own answers

b ▶ Ss write a personal profile for a social networking site.

5 Home

Overview

CEFR Can do objectives

5.1 Talk about your home
5.2 Talk about things you have
5.3 Describe where you live
Communication Talk about things you need to furnish a home
Writing bank Start and end an informal email

CEFR Portfolio ideas

a) Record a radio advertisement, or design a web page for renting your home to holiday visitors. Describe the location, rooms and contents. Don't forget to tell customers how to contact you.
b) Imagine you have just moved into your home. Make a video for your friends describing your home and telling your friends why you like it.
c) Choose a holiday photograph. Write an email to a friend describing the landscape in the photo.

Lead-in

OPTIONAL WARMER

Ss look at the pictures of different houses. Elicit which house they like best and why.

1a ▶ Ss look at the photos to identify the different houses.

Answers
1 C
2 A
3 D
4 B

b ▶ Ss match the house type to the description.

Answers
a 3
b 4
c 1
d 2

2 ▶ Ss look at the rooms in the box and match them to the activities. Ss check answers in pairs, then as a whole class.

Suggested answers
You can eat in the dining room.
You can have a shower in the shower room or in the bathroom.
You can keep things you don't use in the attic.
You can sleep in the bedroom.
You can watch TV in the living room or in the bedroom.
You can work in the study.

3 ▶ Direct Ss to the photos again. Ask: *Do you think all the homes are in the same area?* Teach *the same* (the opposite of *different*). Teach *landscape* (what you can see when you look out of a window or around you). Elicit different kinds of landscapes (e.g. fields, hills, mountains, etc.).

▶ Ss look at the compass. Teach *in the north/south/east/west/centre of the country*. Ss ask and answer the questions with a partner.

4a/b ▶ Ss work in small groups and discuss the questions.

EXTEND THE LEAD-IN

Elicit: *Which room do you usually spend the most/the least time in? What do you do in that room?* (E.g. *I spend most time in my kitchen. There is a big table and I study there too. When friends come, we have dinner in the kitchen.*). Ss work in pairs. They (1) tell their partner about their favourite rooms and (2) discuss what they think are the best/worst colours for different rooms. (E.g. *I don't like bright orange or red in a bedroom because it keeps me awake.*) Teach *bright*, *pale* and *dark* before Ss start.

5.1 Dream homes

Home ownership is regarded as very important in many English-speaking countries. It is estimated that the home ownership rate is 77 percent in Ireland, 70 percent in Australia, 69 percent in both the UK and the US and 67 percent in Canada. The well-known expression 'An Englishman's home is his castle' sums up many people's attitudes, suggesting that your home is your private domain, and you are truly safe and able to do whatever you like once you are inside it. Most people get a long-term mortgage from the bank in order to buy their home, which they pay back in monthly instalments. Many people then try to 'climb the property ladder' by selling their first relatively cheap home (often known as 'starter home') and taking out a larger mortgage to buy a second, more expensive home when their income gets higher. Many go on to buy larger, more expensive homes as their earnings rise.

In this lesson, Ss read about three unusual houses for sale and listen to a conversation between an estate agent and a potential buyer. They practise talking about homes and conduct an estate agent/buyer roleplay.

OPTIONAL WARMER

Write the following on the board: *The White House*; *the Starship Enterprise*; *10 Downing St*; *Buckingham Palace*; *221B Baker St*; *4 Privet Drive*. Explain that these are famous addresses. Ask: *Who lives there?* (The White House – the president of the USA; the Starship Enterprise – the crew in *Star Trek*; 10 Downing St – the British prime minister; Buckingham Palace – the Queen of England; 221B Baker St – Sherlock Holmes; 4 Privet Drive – Harry Potter) Elicit the names of other famous places where people live.

Reading

1 ▶ Ss discuss the questions with a partner. Elicit answers.

2a ▶ Ss look at the photos. Ask: *What kind of houses are these?*

▶ Scanning: Direct Ss to the text in their books. Explain that they will read the text twice, the first time very quickly and the second time much more slowly. Tell them they have one minute to find what is unusual about each home. Explain that they do not need to understand the text fully at this point. Stop the activity after a minute and have Ss call out the answers.

Answers
1 It's a windmill.
2 It has an unusual roof and small windows.
3 It's eco-friendly.

b ▶ Ss look at the questions and read the text again. Explain that they do not need to understand every word in

the text. Ss match the features to the correct house. They check answers in pairs, then as a whole class.

Answers
1 a 3; b 2; c 1
2 a 3; b 1; c 2

c ▶ Ss discuss the questions as a whole class. Elicit reasons why they would like/not like to live in any of these houses.

Vocabulary | homes

3a ▶ Ss work in pairs and complete the table with words from the texts.

Answers
Type of building: windmill, villa
Rooms: bedroom, shower room, kitchen, dining room, living room, cellar, study, attic, library, garage
Other features: patio, roof, windows, central heating, double glazing, solar panels
Adjectives describing house: luxurious, large, unusual, private, small, cool, light, sunny, lovely, eco-friendly

b ▶ Ss look at the suggested questions in their books. Elicit other questions they might ask (e.g. *Does it have an attic? Is it sunny? Is it near a park?* etc.) Ss ask and answer questions about each other's house. Ensure Ss are working with a different partner from ex. 1.

OPTIONAL VARIATION

Draw the floor plan of a house on the board to demonstrate what you want Ss to do. Ss draw a floor plan of their own house or apartment and show it to their partner, describing where each room is, who sleeps where, etc. Ss ask and answer questions about each other's house.

4 ▶ Talk to Ss about writing new words and expressions in a vocabulary journal as a useful way of remembering them. Discuss the various ways to categorise the new words (alphabetically, thematically, etc.). Direct Ss to the note on personalising new vocabulary as a useful way to learn and remember it.

▶ Ss write sentences about their homes using the words in the box. Ss compare their sentences.

Grammar | *there is/there are*

5 ▶ Ss use the text in ex. 2 to complete the Active grammar box.

Active grammar

Singular: isn't, Is, isn't
Plural: are, Are, are, are

▶ Explain that we use *there is* and *there are* to talk about what is in particular places. Help Ss with the pronunciation of the contracted forms: *there's, there isn't, there aren't*. Point out that there is no contraction for *there are* and that in short answers, there is no contraction for *Yes, there is* (not *Yes, there's*).

▶ Review *some* and *any* from the previous unit: *There are some chairs. There aren't any tables.*

▶ Direct Ss to the Reference section on page 57.

6 ▶ Ss complete the questions using *is there* or *are there*. Then, they answer the questions. Ss check answers in pairs, then as a whole class.

> **Answers**
> 1   are there? There is one bedroom in the eco-villa.
> 2   Is there? Yes, there is.
> 3   Is there? No, there isn't.
> 4   are there? There are two bathrooms in the detached house.
> 5   Are there? No, there aren't.

Vocabulary | prepositions of place

7 ▶ Ss find the eight prepositions in the text. They read the sentences containing the preposition and then match the preposition to the pictures.

> **Answers**
> in, next to, in front of, behind
> under, on, between, near

8a ▶ Elicit the different kinds of houses/homes people live in (apartment, semi-detached house, cottage, castle, villa, etc.). Elicit ideas about 'dream' homes – a home they would buy if they were very rich. Put the headings from ex. 3a on the board. Ss make notes about their 'dream home'.

b ▶ Ss work in pairs and describe their dream home.

Listening

9a ▶ Tell Ss they are going to listen to a conversation between Jon and an estate agent for the Italian house in ex. 2. Elicit some examples of the kind of questions Jon might ask (*How much is it? How big is it? How many bedrooms are there?* etc.).

▶ Ss look at the questions and see if they can answer any of them. (They should be able to answer questions c, d, e and f.)

> **Answers**
> c   five
> d   yes
> e   yes
> f   No, there are two bathrooms.

b ▶ 🔊 1.51 Play recording 1.51 once. Ss number Jon's questions in the correct order.

> **Answers**
> a   3   e   5
> b   6   f   2
> c   1   g   8
> d   4   h   7

c ▶ Play the recording again. Ss listen and answer the questions. Ss check answers in pairs, then as a whole class.

> **Answers**
> c   five bedrooms
> f   No, there are two bathrooms.
> a   no, not necessary
> d   yes, a large sunny garden
> e   yes, one kilometre away
> b   Don't know.
> h   Yes, there's a school in the village.
> g   300,000 euros

Speaking

> Property experts say that the three most important criteria when buying a house are 'Location, location, location', suggesting that the only thing that matters is where the house is located. The posher the area, or the better the schools in that area, the more valuable the house.

> **OPTIONAL LEAD-IN TO ROLEPLAY**
>
> Write the following on the board: *garden; how many bedrooms; how many bathrooms; facilities nearby; price; landscape from windows*. Ss work in small groups of three or four and discuss together which of the headings are important/not important to them when choosing where to live. (E.g. *What do you think is important? The landscape is important for me. I like to look out of the window in the evening. A garden is important for me. I enjoy gardening at weekends.*) Do not worry if Ss make mistakes during this activity. In feedback, establish what is important to most Ss when choosing where to live.

10 ▶ Ss conduct an estate agent and buyer roleplay in pairs. Student A reads the description of the house for sale on page 129. Student B has to ask questions to find out about the six items listed. Give Ss a minute or two to prepare. Ss conduct the roleplay in pairs. Do not worry about Ss making mistakes during this activity.

▶ When Ss have finished they swap roles and read the new information. Student B is now an estate agent in Manhattan and Student A is interested in buying an apartment. In feedback ask: *How many bought the villa in Spain? How many bought the apartment in Manhattan?*

5.2 To have and have not

In this lesson, Ss listen to a phone call about home insurance. They practise asking and answering questions about their possessions.

OPTIONAL WARMER

Ss look at the two different rooms. In pairs they decide who they think might live there: a large family with young children; an older couple; a single man/woman; a group of friends. They must give reasons for their opinions. (E.g. *I don't think a family with young children live in B, it's too small. I think older people live in A; the room is not very modern*, etc.)

Vocabulary | furniture and equipment

1a ▶ Ss look at the two rooms and tell their partner which room they prefer and why. (E.g. *I like A because you can see the garden from the window.*)

b ▶ Elicit some of the things Ss can see in the pictures (e.g. table, chairs, etc.) before they start. Ss match the objects with the numbered items in the pictures. They check answers in pairs, then as a whole class.

> **Answers**
> bed 9
> chair 6
> coffee table 8
> cooker 3
> cupboard 4
> dining table 7
> dishwasher 5
> fridge 2
> lamp 14
> microwave 11
> plant 12
> sofa 13
> TV 1
> washing machine 10

c ▶ Ss work in pairs to extend the list for each room. Encourage Ss to use their dictionaries. Ask: *Which pair has the longest list for Room A/Room B?* in feedback. Write *Room A* and *Room B* on the board and note Ss' answers under each heading.

> **Answers**
> Room A: curtains, stool, cushion, book, candle, rug
> Room B: picture, picture frame, armchair, laptop, mobile phone, music system, garden chairs, parasol

2 ▶ Elicit one or two general examples of equipment, furniture and personal possessions before Ss start.
Ss work in pairs. They use the words from ex. 1 to complete the word maps.

> **Possible answers**
> equipment: cooker, dishwasher, lamp, microwave, TV, washing machine
> furniture: bed, chair, coffee table, sofa, stool
> personal possessions: book, laptop

OPTIONAL EXTENSION

Quickly review *There is/There are* and the prepositions of place (*on, under, between*, etc.) from the previous lesson. Imagine a room or look at a picture of a room in a magazine.
Ss draw a large rectangle in their exercise books. Describe the furniture in the room to the Ss. (*There's a large sofa in the middle of the room. There's a chair next to the sofa on the left and a coffee table in front of the sofa.*) Ss listen to your description and draw the furniture in the correct position in the room. Teach *in the middle, on the left, on the right* before you start. Ss compare their drawings of the room.

Listening and speaking

Ensure Ss understand what is meant by home insurance (an agreement with a company; in this agreement, the customer pays a certain amount of money a year to the company and in return, if anything happens to the house – fire, burglary, etc. – the company will pay for the damage).

3a ▶ 🔘 1.52 Explain the context of the phone call to the Ss. Play recording 1.52 once. Ss listen and decide which of the two pictures is being described. They check answers in pairs.

> **Answer**
> B

b ▶ Play the recording again. Ss listen and tick the things which Pete has got and cross the things he hasn't got. They check answers in pairs, then as a whole class.

> **Answers**
> ✓: chairs, coffee table, fridge, laptop computer, microwave, mobile phone, music system, sink, sofa, studio apartment, terrace, TV
> X: cooker, dining table, garden, house

4a ▶ Elicit examples of 'valuable' possessions. Explain that a valuable possession can also be something which is very important to you but may not be valuable to anyone else. Ask: *What makes something valuable to you?* (money, memories, can't be replaced, etc.)

▶ Give Ss a minute or two to list their five most important possessions individually.

b ▶ Ss compare their lists with a partner and give justifications, as in the example.

Grammar | have got

5a ▶ ⬤ 1.53 Ss listen to the first part of recording 1.53 again. They complete the gaps in the dialogue in their books.

> **Answers**
> haven't
> 've
> Has
> hasn't
> 's

b ▶ Ss use the dialogue to complete the Active grammar box. They check answers in pairs, then as a whole class.

> **Active grammar**
> Affirmative: 've
> Negative: I/We/You/They, hasn't
> Question: Have, Has, haven't

▶ Draw a simple version of a room with a cooker, a table and chairs in it. Ask: *What room is this?* (a kitchen) Point at the table and ask: *What is this?* (a table) Write *It's got a table* and *It's a table* on the board. For each one ask: *Am I talking about the table or the kitchen?* Underline the *'s* in each sentence. Establish that *'s* is a contraction of *is* in *It's a table* and a contraction of *has* in *It's got a table*. Help Ss with the pronunciation of the contracted forms.

▶ Draw Ss' attention to the short answers at the bottom of the Active grammar chart. We don't use *got* in the short answer. *Yes, I have* is correct, not *Yes, I've got*.

▶ Direct Ss to the Reference section on page 57.

6a ▶ Ss look at the sentences about Pete. First they decide which sentences are true and which are not. They check answers with a partner and then correct the false ones. They practise saying the correct sentences in pairs, then as a whole class.

> **Answers**
> 1 He hasn't got a house.
> 5 He's got two chairs.
> 6 He hasn't got a garden.

b ▶ Ss use the prompts to write questions using *has/have got* and write true short answers.

> **Answers**
> 1 Have you got an apartment?
> 2 Has your home got a garden?
> 3 Has your home got an attic?
> 4 Have you got a dishwasher?
> 5 Have you got a big sofa?
> 6 Has your home got a garage?
> 7 Have you got a pet?
> 8 Have you got a bicycle?
> The answers to these questions are the students' own answers.

Pronunciation | /æ/ and /ɒ/

▶ Ss focus on the two sounds /æ/ and /ɒ/.

7a ▶ ⬤ 1.54 Play recording 1.54. Ss listen and identify the different sounds.

> **Answers**
> got, laptop, watch: /ɒ/
> cat: /æ/

b ▶ ⬤ 1.55 Ss listen to recording 1.55 and underline the word they hear. They check answers in pairs, then as a whole class.

> **Answers**
> 1 hat
> 2 on
> 3 top
> 4 packet

> **OPTIONAL EXTENSION**
> Ss say one of the eight words listed to their partner, who must identify which sound it is. Ss identify the difference in the sounds and practise saying them.
> Ss practise saying sentences which contain both sounds, e.g. *He's got a packet of coffee in his bag. He's got a laptop in the bottom of the sack.*

▶ Direct Ss to the Pronunciation bank on page 147 for further examples of the sounds.

Speaking and writing

8 ▶ Ensure Ss are working with a new partner. Direct Ss to the questions in ex. 6b again. Elicit other questions which could be asked about possessions and homes (e.g. *Have you got a big house? Have you got a car? Have you got any valuable possessions?*) Ss take it in turns to ask each other questions about their home and possessions, noting which items each has that the other hasn't got, and vice versa. Do not worry about Ss making mistakes during this activity.

9 ▶ Ss look at the sample paragraph in their books and write a similar paragraph about their partner, based on the information gained in ex. 8.

> **OPTIONAL EXTENSION**
> Gather up the different paragraphs. Read out a selection of the paragraphs to the Ss, but without using the name of the person being written about. The other Ss must try to guess which student it is.

5.3 World class

A 'gap year' is a period of time, usually a year, when people do something different with their lives. Typically, it refers to students who take a year off from their studies either before starting, during or immediately after university. Most people travel abroad or work at something new during the gap year, or often combine the two by working overseas. Volunteering and community service jobs are very popular activities during the gap year.

In this lesson, Ss read and listen to a variety of people saying where they are from and describing the landscape there. Ss talk about their own countries.

OPTIONAL WARMER

Ss work in pairs. They look at the photos and discuss which type of landscape they would like best and which they would like least (1) to live in and (2) for a holiday. They must give reasons for their choice.

Listening and reading

1a ▶ Ss read the list of places and match them to the photos. Ss check answers in pairs, then as a whole class.

Answers
mountains D
desert C
forest E
hills A
lake B

b ▶ In pairs, Ss try to guess which countries the pictures are from. Do not give the answers yet as the information is in the reading text and on recording 1.56.

2a ▶ Ask Ss: *What do young people do when they finish high school/secondary school in your country?* (start a job, go to university, etc.) If Ss are unfamiliar with the notion of a gap year, explain that this is when young people travel before starting a job or university. Ask: *Would you like to do this? Where would you go?*

▶ Ss look at the website entry about travel destinations for a gap year and answer the question. Ss check answers in pairs, then as a whole class.

Answers
Similarities: In both countries, lovely panoramas where the mountains/hills come down to the sea
Differences: Argentina: very high mountains, very hot and very cold; Ireland: low hills and very wet

b ▶ 🔵 1.56 Play recording 1.56 once. Ss listen and match the countries with the five photos. Note that there is no photo of Japan.

Answers
A Ireland
B Poland
C Spain
D Argentina
E Kefalonia (Greece)

3a ▶ Review *in the north/south/east/west of the country.* Students complete lines 1 and 2 using information from the reading text. Play recording 1.56 again. Ss listen and complete the table. They check answers in pairs, then as a whole class.

Answers
1 high mountains
2 low hills, west
3 Spain, south
4 Poland, east
5 lovely forest, north
6 Japan/Osaka, huge city

b ▶ Help Ss with the pronunciation of the adjectives. Ss make sentences about the six places they've heard and read about, using *There is/There are.*

Answers
There are high mountains in the south of Argentina.
There are low hills in the west of Ireland.
There are beautiful lakes in the east of Poland.
There's a lovely forest in the north of Kefalonia.
There's a huge city in the west of Japan.

Vocabulary | adjectives (3): places

4a ▶ Ss add two further adjectives from the box to describe a desert in pairs.

Suggested answers
dry, famous; beautiful and huge are also possible

b ▶ Ss make word maps for the other nouns using adjectives from the box. There will be some overlap.

▶ As an extension, Ss think of more adjectives to add to the word maps.

Suggested answers
mountain: beautiful, cold, famous, high
island: beautiful, famous, green, huge, long, popular, wide
forest: beautiful, famous, green, huge, wide
beach: beautiful, busy, famous, long, noisy, popular, wide
hill: beautiful, famous, green, low
river: beautiful, famous, long, wide
city: beautiful, busy, famous, huge, noisy, popular

Pronunciation | main stress

> **OPTIONAL PRONUNCIATION LEAD-IN**
>
> Write out the adjectives from ex. 4a on individual strips of paper, one word per strip. Ss work in groups of ten or so. Give each student a strip of paper. Try to have at least two words of one, two and three syllables for each group. Ss circulate and say the adjective to each other. They group themselves according to the sound of the words. (The connection is the number of syllables in the word.)

5 ▶ 🔊 1.57 Play recording 1.57. Ss listen and answer the questions.

> **Answers**
> 1   two syllables   2   <u>river</u> <u>desert</u>

▶ The stress is usually on the first syllable in words of two syllables.

6a ▶ Ss look at the Lifelong learning box. Ask Ss to look up the words in their dictionaries to see how the syllables are marked (dots) and how the word stress is marked.

▶ Ss look at the words. They use their dictionaries to find out which is the strong syllable. Do not give feedback yet.

> **Answers**   fam•ous   nois•y
> de•<u>tached</u>   lux•<u>ur</u>•ious   <u>pop</u>•u•lar

b ▶ 🔊 1.58 Play recording 1.58. Ss listen to check their answers.

> **OPTIONAL EXTENSION**
>
> Write the following words on the board:
> A: *apartment, competition, island, understand*
> B: *forest, important, information, remember*
> Divide Ss into As and Bs. They use their dictionaries to find the syllables and word stress for each word on their list.
> Ss work in pairs, A and B. Each student points to a word on their list and asks their partner to pronounce it. They correct any mistakes they hear.

Grammar | modifiers

7a ▶ 🔊 1.59 Ask Ss to look at the four sentences. See if they remember which place they refer to (1 desert in Spain; 2 lake area in Poland; 3 island in Greece; 4 Osaka in Japan).

▶ Play recording 1.59. Ss listen and complete the sentences with the correct word.

> **Answers**
> 1   really   3   very
> 2   quite   4   very, not very

▶ Ask: *Which are the strongest?* (*really* and *very*) *Which is the weakest?* (*not very*). Explain that the modifiers go before the adjective.

b ▶ Ss look at the different thermometer readings and complete the scale. They check answers in pairs, then as a whole class.

> **Active grammar**   20°: quite
> 40°: really, very   10°: not very

▶ Direct Ss to the Reference section on page 57.

8 ▶ Ss make sentences in pairs using the prompts given. Ss call out answers in whole-class feedback.

> **Possible answers**
> 1   Britain is not very big.
> 2   Mount Everest is very high.
> 3   The Amazon is very long.
> 4   Mexico City is really busy.
> 5   Canada is very cold.
> 6   Spain is not very cold.

9 ▶ Ss work in pairs. They make sentences about their own and other countries.

> **OPTIONAL VARIATION**
>
> Ss work in pairs. They choose a country or famous place and write sentences about it using *quite,* (*not*) *very* and *really*. Ss read out their descriptions to the rest of the class. The other Ss try to guess which country/place is being described.

Listening and speaking

▶ Explain that you will play the recording twice. The first time, Ss must try to get the general idea and answer the two questions in ex. 10a; the second time they will try to understand more details and answer the questions in 10b.

10a ▶ 🔊 1.60 Play recording 1.60. Ss listen and answer the questions.

> **Answers**
> Wales. Yes, she likes it.

b ▶ Ss read through the headings. Play the recording again. Ss listen and tick the ones she talks about.

> **Answers**
> 1, 2, 3, 5, 7

11a ▶ Ss focus on the *How to…* box and review how to (1) say where they live, (2) say what kind of place it is and where it is near, (3) describe the landscape where they live and (4) say whether they like where they live or not. Ss prepare what they will say about their country to their partner.

b ▶ Ss work in pairs. They describe where they live and their country to a partner and speak about which parts of their country they like/don't like.

5 Communication

In this lesson, Ss decide together how to furnish a new apartment and how much to pay for each item of furniture.

1 ▶ Ss look at the picture of the apartment. Ask: *Do you like this apartment? Why/Why not?* Ss discuss with a partner what the apartment has got/not got. Establish that there is a cooker and a sink but nothing else.

> **Answers**
> The apartment has got a cooker, a sink and cupboards. It hasn't got a dishwasher, fridge, washing machine, sofa, coffee table, TV, CD player, music system, dining table, chairs or beds.

2a ▶ Ss look at the list of items and choose ten things that they need to furnish the apartment. Ss should use their dictionaries to look up unknown words.

b ▶ Ss work in pairs and compare their lists. Together they agree on ten items and rank them in order of importance, e.g. *I think a bed is very important. You have to sleep at night. You can sit on a bed but you can' t sleep in a chair*, etc. Do not worry about Ss making mistakes during this activity. Encourage Ss to express their opinions as best they can.

▶ Ss then compare lists with a different pair.

3a ▶ Ss work in groups of three. Each student has different information about home furniture/equipment and prices. Student A's information is on page 129, Student B's information is on page 133 and Student C's information is on page 56. Give Ss several minutes to read about the activity and look at their individual information.

▶ Ss then discuss what they will buy, compare prices and decide how much to spend on each item. They have a maximum of 1,000 euros to spend. Explain to Ss that they must talk about their information; they cannot just show their information to the others in the group.

b ▶ Ss compare their lists with other groups.

> **OPTIONAL VARIATION**
> Cut pictures with prices shown out of a home shopping catalogue for Ss to use for this activity.

> **OPTIONAL EXTENSION**
> Ss work in pairs. They choose two things they could change or buy for the classroom to make it a nicer room (e.g. *paint the walls yellow, buy a big plant for the window*, etc.).

5 Review and practice

1 ▶

Answers
2 Is there
3 there isn't
4 there's
5 there isn't
6 there's
7 are there
8 there aren't
9 is there
10 there's

2 ▶

Answers
1 I haven't got a video camera.
2 She hasn't got a mobile phone.
3 They haven't got a lot of money.
4 Their car hasn't got a CD player.
5 England hasn't got a lot of mountains.

3 ▶

Answers
1 Has Rachel got a laptop computer? Yes, she has.
2 Have they got a big house? No, they haven't.
3 Has your apartment got a garden? No, it hasn't.
4 Has Kelly got a washing machine? Yes, she has.
5 Has Spain got a desert? Yes, it has.

4 ▶ Ss' own answers

5 ▶

Possible answers
living room: coffee table, music system, sofa
overlapping living room/kitchen/bedroom: bookshelves, CD player, chairs, table, TV
kitchen: cooker, cupboard, dishwasher, fridge, washing machine
bedroom: bed

6 ▶

Answers
A the sea
B an island
C mountains
D a city
E a forest
F a river
G a lake
H a beach
I a desert
J a bay

5 Writing bank

1 ▶

Answers
1 the Great Barrier Reef
2 in the centre of Australia
3 Yes, there's Perth in the west.
4 in the east

2a ▶

Answers
closing sentences C
ending D
greeting A
name of the sender E
opening sentence B

b ▶

Answers
1 greeting
2 opening sentence
3 closing sentences
4 ending
5 name of the sender

3 ▶

Answers
1 c
2 a
3 b

4 ▶

Answers
1 but
2 and
3 or
4 but
5 or

5a ▶ Ss' own answers

b ▶ Ss write the beginning and end of the email.

c ▶ Ss write an email to a friend.

Overview

Lead-in	Revision: Places in town
6.1	Can do: Talk about the past Grammar: Past Simple of *to be*: all forms Past Simple of regular verbs: positive Speaking and Pronunciation: Past Simple endings Information gap: buildings Listening and Reading: Changing buildings
6.2	Can do: Describe a visit to a city Grammar: Past Simple: irregular verbs Vocabulary: Places in a city, shops Reading: City break reviews
6.3	Can do: Talk about past events in your life Grammar: Past Simple: questions and negatives Vocabulary: Time expressions Speaking and Pronunciation: Contrastive stress Listening and Reading: Modern cities
Communication	Understand a store guide and ask for what you want How to... shop in a department store
Reference	
Review and Practice	
Writing bank	Describe a place How to... join sentences (3): *because, so*

CEFR Can do objectives
6.1 Talk about the past
6.2 Describe a visit to a city
6.3 Talk about past events in your life
Communication Understand a store guide and ask for what you want
Writing bank Describe a place

CEFR Portfolio ideas
a) What is the most beautiful building in your country? Get a photograph of the building. Write a short description of the building. Say where it is, explain how it is used and how it has changed.
b) Write your personal profile for a social networking site. Write paragraphs about yourself and your city, your family, your work, your hobbies and interests. Choose the topics which are most important for you and for your friends.
c) Video. Record a one or two minute video in which you introduce yourself and give a review of a city you have visited.

Lead-in

OPTIONAL WARMER
Ss think of their local town or city. In pairs, they list five reasons why their city is better/worse than the next big city in the area. If you are working with a multicultural group, Ss list five reasons why their own city is better/worse than the city/town they are in now. (E.g. *The food in x restaurant is fantastic. The mountains outside the city are really beautiful*, etc.)

1a ▶ Ss look at the photos. They see if they recognise the different places in the pictures and match them to the words in the box. They check answers in pairs, then as a whole class. Ensure Ss understand the difference between a *library* and a *bookshop*.

Answers
bar, bus station, café, factory, museum, restaurant

b ▶ Ss check the words they don't know with a partner. Encourage Ss to use dictionaries if they are stuck.

c ▶ 🔵 1.61 Play recording 1.61. Ss listen to the words and count how many syllables each word or phrase has. Play the recording a second time. Ss mark the stressed syllable. Ss check answers in pairs, then as a whole class.

▶ Ss practise saying the words. The first syllable is stressed in all except for *museum*, where the second syllable is stressed. Note that speakers sometimes 'drop' a syllable, as in *fact(o)ry*, *lib(ra)ry* or *rest(au)rant*.

Answers
art gallery 4	café 2	museum 3
bank 1	cinema 3	post office 3
bar 1	factory 2	restaurant 2
bus station 3	hospital 3	school 1
	library 2	station 2

2 ▶ In pairs, Ss ask and answer questions about what people can do in the various places. Elicit one or two suggestions for each place in feedback. Ss use their own language for this exercise and may make mistakes. Do not worry about error correction but do ensure that Ss are clear about what the words in ex. 1 mean.

3a ▶ Ss look at the list of shops in the right-hand column. Do not explain the words they don't know yet but encourage Ss to guess meanings or use their dictionaries. Ss match the items to the shops. They check answers in pairs, then as a whole class.

Answers
1	f	3	d	5	c
2	e	4	b	6	a

b ▶ Ss work in pairs and think of other items which can be bought in the various shops.

6.1 Changes

The term 'listed building' refers to a building or site which is deemed to be of great architectural and/or historical importance. In England alone, this relates to approximately half a million buildings on the statutory list. Many more buildings and private dwellings are on local council lists but these do not always have statutory protection. It is not possible to extend, demolish or alter a statutory listed building in any way without permission from the relevant governmental body and owners of listed buildings or sites can face prosecution if they carry out unauthorised alterations. They can also be compelled to maintain and repair the buildings they own.

In this lesson, Ss read about and listen to people describing the changing function of several well-known buildings in various parts of the world. Ss practise talking about how buildings have changed in recent times.

OPTIONAL WARMER

Ss decide in pairs which is (1) their favourite old building and (2) their favourite modern building in the local city/town. Ss compare answers.

Reading

1a ► Ss look at the photos in the text. Ask them if they recognise any of the buildings they see. Ss scan the text quickly to find out the names of the buildings.

Answers
1 Oxford Castle in England
2 the Musée d'Orsay in Paris
3 the Smolny Institute in St Petersburg
4 the Moshulu in Philadelphia

b ► Ss look at the table. Make sure Ss understand the two headings, *now* and *in the past*. Ss read the text again, to find out what each building is now and what it was before. Explain *century* (100 years) before they read. Ss check answers in pairs, then as a whole class.

Answers
1 a hotel – a prison
2 an art gallery – a (train) station
3 an office – a school
4 a restaurant – a sailing ship

c ► In pairs or small groups, students say whether they know the places, or other similar ones.

OPTIONAL EXTENSION

Think of several buildings in the local city/town which were built for a different purpose from their existing one (often banks, town halls, offices …). Write the current names of the buildings on the board. Ss decide what the original function of each building was.

Grammar | Past Simple of *to be*

2 ► Ss look at the text again. Ask Ss to underline all the forms of the verb *to be* in the sentences (*is/are* and *was/were*). Ss complete the Active grammar box. They check answers in pairs, then as a whole class.

Active grammar

I/He/She/It	We/You/They
wasn't	were
Was	were
wasn't	

► Help Ss with the initial /w/ sound in *was* and *were* and the weak vowel sound /ə/ in *was* in affirmative and negative sentences. Show Ss the contracted negative form on the board.

► Direct Ss to the Reference section on page 67.

3 ► Ss correct the sentences about each of the buildings following the example given.

Answers
1 No, it wasn't. It was a train station.
2 No, it was a prison. Now it's a shopping centre.
3 No, it wasn't a sailing ship in the nineteenth century. It was a sailing ship in the twentieth century.
4 No, it isn't. It's an art gallery.

OPTIONAL EXTENSION

Write: *an hour ago, at 8 o' clock last night, last Saturday evening, this time last year* on the board. Ss interview each other about where they were at these times (e.g. *An hour ago I was on the bus; At 8 o' clock last night I was in the cinema; Last Saturday evening I was at a party*, etc.).

Listening

4a ► 1.62 Ss look at the two photos on page 61. Elicit suggestions as to what the two buildings are used for now (a supermarket and an art gallery). This should be clear from the photos.

► Play recording 1.62. Ss listen and match the speaker to the building. Ss check in pairs, then as a whole class.

Answers
Jason: 1
Angeles: 2

b ▶ Ss look at the sentences in pairs and predict which sentences describe each building. Do not give feedback yet. Play the recording again. Ss listen to check if their predictions were right.

> **Answers**
> Hoover Building: 2, 3, 4
> Reina Sofia: 1

5 ▶ Ss complete the sentences with words from the box. Ss check their answers with a partner, then listen to see if they were right.

> **Answers**
> 1 factory, equipment
> 2 Reina Sofia, modern art

Grammar | Past Simple of regular verbs: positive

6 ▶ Ss read the sentences again. They find the four verbs and note the ending for each. They check answers in pairs, then as a whole class.

> **Active grammar**
> produced, studied, planned
> 1 worked
> 2 produced
> 3 studied
> 4 planned

▶ Direct Ss to the Reference section on page 67.

7a ▶ Ss find all the examples of the past simple in the audioscript on page 154 and write them in the correct column.

> **Answers**
> + -ed: worked, opened, visited, looked, started
> + -d: produced, changed, lived
> remove -y, + -ied: married, studied
> double consonant: planned, stopped

b ▶ Ss use the prompts to write sentences using the Past Simple.

> **Answers**
> 1 The Hoover Factory produced vacuum cleaners.
> 2 Alicia studied at the Sorbonne.
> 3 My brother started a new job yesterday.
> 4 My mother married my father in 1977.
> 5 The prison changed to apartments in 2002.
> 6 My father stopped work at the age of sixty.

Pronunciation | Past Simple endings

8a ▶ 🔵 1.63 Ss close their books. Write the three verbs *worked, opened, started* on the board. Play recording 1.63. Ss listen and note the different endings used for each verb.

▶ Ss look at their books to see the correct phonetic sound. They repeat the verbs.

b ▶ 🔵 1.64 Ss listen to recording 1.64 and write the verbs in the correct column.

> **Answers**
> /t/: looked, produced
> /d/: lived, changed, planned, studied
> /ɪd/: visited

▶ Say *produced*. Ask: *How many syllables do you hear?* (two, not three syllables) Say *looked, changed*. Ask: *How many syllables do you hear?* (one, not two) Ask: *When does the past tense ending sound like a new syllable* /ɪd/? (after verbs ending in /t/ and /d/)

▶ Direct Ss to the Pronunciation bank on page 148.

c ▶ Ss practise reading the sentences from ex. 7b in pairs. Ss correct each other. Monitor closely and correct any mispronunciation of past tense endings.

Speaking

9 ▶ Ss work in pairs, A and B. As look at the information on page 130 and Bs look at the information on page 133. Direct their attention to the information chart and explain that this is to be filled in about their partner's building. Student A describes their building and Student B completes their chart as they listen. Then, Ss swap roles.

10 ▶ Put the following headings on the board: *schools, shops, libraries, cinemas*. Ss work in pairs and discuss how these buildings have changed in modern times (e.g. *Schools have bright colours now; they have paintings on the walls; they have toilets inside*, etc.) Do not worry about Ss making mistakes during this activity. Encourage them to give their opinions as best they can. Note down any obvious errors to correct later.

> **OPTIONAL EXTENSION**
> Ss make notes about different houses they have lived in or spent time in in the past (e.g. grandparents' house, holiday home, etc.) Put *rooms, garden, colours, décor, location* and *when I lived there* as prompts on the board. Ss work in pairs and tell each other about the different places they have lived (e.g. *I lived in a city apartment. It was very small. It had two bedrooms and a terrace but no garden*, etc.)

6.2 City breaks

With air travel becoming less expensive and more routes opening up, flying overseas to another city for a weekend break has become popular in recent years. People travel to shop, to sightsee, for a romantic break, etc. In addition, city breaks are often linked to 'stag nights' or 'hen parties'. Groups of friends, usually of the same sex, get together for a party shortly before one of the group gets married. Combining the pre-marriage party with a city break is becoming very popular.

In this lesson, Ss read a number of 'city break' reviews and tell their partner about visits to cities they have made.

OPTIONAL LEAD-IN

Elicit places to go for a weekend break. (e.g. a big city like Paris or New York; a country hotel with walks and good food; a spa with relaxation treatments and beauty therapies, etc.). Ss work in groups of three and decide where they would like to go for a weekend break.

Reading

1a ▶ Ss look at the pictures and layout of the texts. They do not read yet. They decide what type of website the text is taken from.

> **Answer**
> a travel website

b ▶ Ss skim-read the text quickly. Make sure they read the headings too. Explain that they will have an opportunity to read more slowly in ex. 2. They match the opinions to the writers. Ss check answers in pairs, then as a whole class.

> **Answers**
> 1   Susanna Lloyd
> 2   Christiane Gautier
> 3   Alvin Parmiter
> 4   Manolo Sanchez

2 ▶ Ss read the texts more slowly and answer the questions.

> **Answers**
> 1   because it was raining
> 2   wedding rings
> 3   No. The food was awful.
> 4   Yes. He says he wants to go back there for a week.

OPTIONAL EXTENSION

Ss work in pairs and decide what each person (1) liked and (2) didn't like about the different cities.

> **Answers**
> **Dublin**
> Positives: lively, noisy, exciting city, the old streets and the park
> Negatives: a lot of tourists, the rain
> **New York**
> Positives: a lot to do, great museums and shopping, famous restaurants
> Negatives: unfriendly people, expensive shops, awful food
> **Havana**
> Positives: different from other cities, beautiful buildings, interesting cigars
> Negatives: the restaurants and shops
> **Dubai**
> Positives: great markets and shops, modern and luxurious hotel
> Negatives: expensive

3a ▶ Ss find expressions with *break* in the text. They then try and match them to the definitions given. Ss check answers in pairs, then as a whole class.

> **Answers**
> 1   a three-night break, a short break
> 2   a good break, wonderful break
> 3   city break

b ▶ Ss look at the expressions in pairs and decide what they might mean.

> **Answers**
> 1   when you stop working or studying for a short time in order to have a coffee
> 2   a short holiday in winter
> 3   when you stop working or studying for a short time in order to eat lunch
> 4   a short weekend holiday
> 5   stop working or studying for a short time

4 ▶ Ss work in pairs and decide which city break they would choose. They must give reasons for their choice.

Vocabulary | places in a city, shops

5a ▶ Ss put the words from the box into the correct column. Ss check answers in pairs, then as a whole class.

> **Answers**
> Shopping: clothes shop, department store, jeweller's, market, newsagent's, shoe shop
> Places in/near a city: airport, building, gallery, hotel, museum, park

b ▶ Ss add words to the table with a partner. Encourage them to use their dictionaries. Elicit suggestions in feedback.

6 ▶ Ss match the descriptions to the places in ex. 5a. Ss check answers with a partner, then as a whole class.

> **Answers**
> 1 department store
> 2 hotel
> 3 park
> 4 newsagent's
> 5 gallery/museum
> 6 market

Grammar | Past Simple: irregular verbs

7a ▶ Focus on the first text about Dublin. Write *We arrived at lunchtime* and *It rained all day* on the board. Ask: *What is the infinitive of these verbs?* (*arrive* and *rain*). Ss should be familiar with regular forms of the past simple from the previous lesson.

▶ Now, write *We left Dublin yesterday* and *We flew there on Friday morning* on the board. Elicit or give the infinitive forms of these verbs (*leave* and *fly*). Explain that these are irregular verbs which do not follow the same pattern of adding *-ed* to the infinitive.

▶ Ss focus on the four reviews and complete the Active grammar box. Ss check answers with a partner, then as a whole class.

> **Active grammar**
>
> spend – spent
> go – went
> take – took
> buy – bought
> meet – met
> see – saw
> eat – ate
> have – had

▶ Explain that many of the most common verbs in English are irregular and do not have an *-ed* ending. The best way to learn these past forms is to memorise them. There is no rule to learn.

b ▶ Ss complete the text with verbs from the Active grammar box.

> **Answers**
> 2 flew
> 3 took
> 4 saw
> 5 met
> 6 ate
> 7 spent
> 8 left

8a ▶ Ss find the four time expressions in the text.

> **Answers**
> yesterday: text on Dublin
> last year: text on Dubai
> last month: text on New York
> a few weeks ago: text on Havana

b ▶ Ss put the expressions in chronological order with a partner.

> **Answers**
> 1 ten minutes ago
> 2 an hour ago
> 3 six hours ago
> 4 at eight o'clock last night
> 5 yesterday at midday
> 6 last Sunday afternoon
> 7 last Saturday evening

c ▶ First, Ss write six sentences about themselves, three true sentences and three false sentences. Ss must use an irregular verb and a time expression for each sentence. Then, Ss take turns to read a sentence to their partner, who must try to guess whether the sentence is true or false. Direct Ss to the example dialogue before they start.

Speaking

9 ▶ Give Ss a few minutes to think of a city that they have visited. They make notes about (1) what they liked and (2) what they didn't like about this city. Put headings on the board to help them, e.g. *atmosphere*, *shops*, *restaurants*, *museums/galleries*, *famous sights*, *transport*.

10 ▶ Ss work in pairs. Try to ensure that they are working with a different partner from ex. 4. Ss tell their partner about what they liked/didn't like about the city. As you monitor, note down any errors which you might like to deal with afterwards but try to avoid correcting Ss during the speaking activity.

> **OPTIONAL EXTENSION**
>
> Write the following on the board: *a romantic weekend break for two*, *a short break for a family with young children*, *a short break for a family with teenage children*, *a city break for a group of friends*. Ss work in groups of three or four and decide on a suitable 'city' destination for each category.

6.3 New citizens

In this lesson, Ss read about the multicultural nature of modern cities and listen to two people describing their backgrounds and where they live. Ss interview each other about their past and write short biographies.

OPTIONAL LEAD-IN

Ask Ss about the countries they have been to. Find out if any of the students have lived in another country for longer than two months. Ask Ss: *Why do people travel to live in another country?* (E.g. their job; their partner is from a different country; to learn the language; to find work; to study, etc.) Make a list of reasons on the board. In pairs, Ss discuss which of the reasons listed are the most common reasons for travelling to live in a new country.

Reading and listening

1a ▶ Ss look at the photo and decide which city it is.

Answer
c

b ▶ Ss now identify which ethnic group is represented in the photo. Do not give feedback at this point as Ss will check their answer in the text during ex. 2a.

2a ▶ Direct Ss to the first paragraph of the text. Tell them to read it quickly to find the answer.

Answer
The photo shows members of the Indian community living in London.

b ▶ Explain to Ss that they will read the whole text twice, the first time very quickly and the second time much more slowly. Direct them to the two columns and tell them they have two minutes to match the nationalities to the cities. Explain that they do not need to understand the text fully at this point. Stop the activity after two minutes and check answers.

Answers		
2 d	3 f	5 c
	4 a	6 e

c ▶ Ss look at the questions and then read the text again, at their own pace. Explain they do not need to understand every word in the text. Ask Ss not to use their dictionary while they read. Explain that there is a vocabulary exercise on the text to follow. Ss check answers in pairs, then as a whole class.

Answers
1 The first Indian restaurant opened in London.
2 Many Portuguese and Turkish people moved to Paris and Frankfurt.
3 A lot of Chinese people moved to California.
4 Many Koreans moved to the US.

3 ▶ Ss look at the text again. They find the words in the text and try to guess what these words mean before using them in the six sentences. Ss check answers in pairs, then as a whole class.

Answers
1 culture
2 workers
3 immigrants
4 tradition
5 citizen
6 foreign

4 ▶ Ss work in small groups of three or four and discuss the questions.

OPTIONAL EXTENSION

You might like to widen the discussion by putting the heading *Your city* on the board with the following sub-headings underneath: *Food, Festivals, Clothes, Shops.* Ss talk about the different ethnic groups in their city or region in relation to the headings.

5a ▶ 🔘 1.65 Explain that Ss will listen to two people talking about where they are from. Ss look at the question. Play recording 1.65. Ss listen and decide which cities the speakers live in now.

Answers	Sean – New York	Meera – London

b ▶ Ss look at the statements. Play the recording again. Ss listen and match the speaker to the statements. They check answers in pairs, then as a whole class.

Answers	
1 and 4 – Sean	2, 3 and 5 – Meera

c ▶ Ss read the sentences and decide which are correct. They correct the mistakes in the other sentences.

Answers
2 Poor Irish people went to America in the 1840s.
4 Meera's family went to London in the 1980s.
5 Meera went to India for her cousin's wedding.

d ▶ Ss read the audioscript and check their answers.

Grammar | Past Simple: questions and negatives

6 ▶ Ss choose the correct word to complete the rule based on the negative sentences they read in the audioscript for ex. 5d.

Active grammar
infinitive
infinitive
did
didn't

▶ Write *Did you went to school in India? Did you walked to school?* on the board and then cross out the past tense form in *went* and *walked* and write *go* and *walk* to show Ss that we use the bare infinitive form of the verb to make questions. Explain that it is the same for negative sentences.

▶ Remind Ss that the verb *to be* does not need the auxiliary *didn't* to form the negative: *he wasn't there*; *they weren't there*. Help Ss with the pronunciation of *didn't*.

▶ Direct Ss to the Reference section on page 67.

7a ▶ Direct Ss to the photos of Heather and Stig. Explain that they are going to listen to these two people talking about their past. Tell Ss that they are going to write the questions for the listening exercise. Ss work in pairs and make questions using the prompts given. Check answers.

Answers
1 Did Heather go to English school in New Brunswick?
2 Did Heather leave home in 2005?
3 Did she meet her partner in Canada?
4 Did Stig go to school in Norway?
5 Did Stig study economics at university?
6 Did he become an economics teacher?

b ▶ 1.66 Teach *overseas* (another word for *abroad*). Play recording 1.66. Ss listen and answer the seven questions (including the example question) from ex. 7a. Ss check answers in pairs, then as a whole class.

Answers
0 Yes, she did.
1 No, she didn't. She went to French school.
2 Yes, she did.
3 No, she didn't. She met her partner overseas.
4 No, he didn't. He went to school in England.
5 Yes, he did.
6 No, he didn't. He became an English teacher.

c ▶ Ss correct the false statements following the example given. They check answers in pairs, then as a whole class.

Answers
1 Heather didn't go to school in London.
2 People didn't use cars in the sixteenth century.
3 Beethoven didn't paint the *Mona Lisa*.
4 Marco Polo didn't own a mobile phone.
5 I didn't watch a DVD last night.
6 My parents didn't move to Los Angeles.

Vocabulary | time expressions

8a ▶ Elicit when the 70s and 80s started (1970/1980) and finished (1979/1989). Revise how to say dates, e.g. 2002 (*two thousand and two*), 2011 (*twenty eleven*), 1862 (*eighteen sixty-two*), 1990 (*nineteen ninety*), 1905 (*nineteen oh five*), etc. Ss complete the sentences with the correct time expression. They check answers in pairs, then as a whole class.

Answers
1 in the 1960s
2 when I was five
3 in 1492
4 in those days
5 in the nineteenth century

b ▶ Ss use the expressions to make true sentences. Ss compare answers with a partner. Elicit two or three examples for each expression during feedback.

Answers
1 In 2 century 3 was 4 the

Pronunciation | contrastive stress

9a ▶ 1.67 Ss close their books. Write *I'm an English teacher* on the board. Say it for Ss, using normal stress patterns. Write *Are you a science teacher?* above the first sentence. Explain that now *I'm an English teacher* is an answer to that question. Insert *No,* at the front, e.g. *No, I'm an English teacher.* Say the sentence for the Ss, putting stress on the word *English*. Ss listen and identify the stressed word. Ask: *Why is* English *stressed?* (to give emphasis)

▶ Ss open books. They look at the two examples. Ask: *Which word do you think will be stressed?* Do not give feedback yet.

▶ Play recording 1.67. Ss listen and mark the stressed word for each. They then practise saying the sentences.

Answers
1 Mumbai 2 Rome 3 horrible

b ▶ Direct Ss to the prompts in the table. In pairs, Ss practise the dialogues using secondary stress patterns.

▶ Direct Ss to the Pronunciation bank on page 148.

Speaking and writing

10a ▶ Ss think of questions they might ask their partner about their past. They don't need to write the questions. Elicit headings on the board to ask questions about, e.g. *growing up, school, favourite subjects, jobs, study, friends*, etc.

▶ Ss work in pairs. They take turns to ask each other about their past. Encourage Ss to ask lots of questions and get further details from their partner during the conversation. Do not worry about Ss making mistakes during this activity.

b ▶ Ss write a short biography of their partner based on their interviews.

OPTIONAL EXTENSION

Direct Ss to the text *Modern Cities* again. Ask: *What is difficult about moving to a new city/country/school?* (E.g. new people, new customs, new language, new food, etc.) Elicit a list of difficulties on the board. In pairs, Ss decide which things would be the most difficult (1) when you arrive first and (2) when you are living there a longer time. Encourage Ss to draw on their own experience for this.

6 Communication

In English-speaking countries, it is considered standard behaviour to give personal items to family and close friends at Christmas and for birthdays. Children usually give their mother/father a present on Mother's Day or Father's Day. It is customary to give a present for a wedding, or when a child is born (usually baby clothes or equipment), but also when someone moves into a new house, leaves work, retires, etc. It is common for several people to group together to buy such gifts. Smaller gifts are often given as a token of thanks after someone has done something for you. People bring fruit or flowers when visiting someone in hospital, and wine, chocolate and/or flowers when invited to eat in someone's house. Couples might also give each other gifts, especially on Valentine's Day and on wedding anniversaries.

In this lesson, Ss buy and sell gifts in a department store.

OPTIONAL WARMER

Elicit special events when people buy presents for several different people at the same time (e.g. for religious festivals such as Christmas or for national celebrations such as Chinese New Year). Elicit where people get ideas for presents, e.g. Christmas markets, catalogues, speciality gift shops, strolling around the city centre. Teach *department store* if Ss don't mention this. Ss work in pairs. They compare their gift shopping habits with each other. Ask: *Where do you get ideas for presents? Where do you shop for presents?*

1 ▶ Teach *department store* (a large shop where you can buy clothes, household goods, beauty products, etc.; give examples). Discuss the four questions as a whole class. Teach *escalator* (moving stairs), as they need this for the listening exercise.

2a ▶ ⊙ 1.68 Teach *on the ground/first/second floor* and *in the basement* (draw a map of a building). Play recording 1.68. Ss listen and complete the gaps in the store guide. They check answers in pairs, then as a whole class.

Answers
Top floor: Men's shoes, Furniture
Ground floor: Music
Basement: Computers

b ▶ Ss listen to the recording again (or look at the audioscript) and complete the *How to...* box in their books. They check answers in pairs, then as a whole class.

Answers
1   can I find
2   Have you got
3   I have
4   much

c ▶ Ss work in pairs. They ask and answer about where to find the items listed in the box.

Answers
aspirin – Pharmacy on top floor
CD player – Electronic goods in basement
computer – Computer department in basement
dictionary – Bookshop in basement
football – Sports hall in basement
pencil – Stationery on ground floor
sofa – Furniture department on top floor
women's jeans – Women's clothes on ground floor

3 ▶ Ss work in pairs. A pairs work in a gift shop and B pairs are potential customers. A pairs read the information on page 130, B pairs on page 66. Give Ss time to prepare. As decide what they sell and the price of the goods on offer. Bs decide on what gifts they want to buy and how much they want to spend.

▶ A pairs set up shops around the room. B pairs circulate, asking about the goods and prices. They must decide where they will buy the presents. An example dialogue is provided for them.

▶ Do not worry about mistakes during this activity. Monitor and note down any obvious errors to deal with later. In feedback, compare presents and prices.

OPTIONAL EXTENSION

Ss think of gifts they have received or given. They tell their partner about (1) a particularly nice gift they received/gave and (2) a gift they weren't so happy with.

6 Review and practice

1 ▶

> **Answers**
> + *ed*: finished, looked, owned, started, wanted
> + *d*: changed, closed, decided, lived, moved
> -*y* + *ied*: married
> + consonant + *ed*: planned, stopped

2 ▶

> **Answers**
> They <u>were</u> lovely people
> <u>worked</u> in a car factory
> he <u>owned</u> a car
> she <u>was</u> a girl
> She <u>married</u>
> she <u>stayed</u> at home
> My great-grandfather <u>stopped</u> work
> always <u>carried</u> a little bag
> <u>died</u> too

3 ▶

> **Answers**
> 1 had
> 2 spent
> 3 made
> 4 met
> 5 left
> 6 went

4 ▶

> **Answers**
> 1 Was Pablo Picasso Spanish? Yes, he was.
> 2 Did Mozart play the guitar? No, he played the piano.
> 3 Was President Kennedy Russian? No, he was American.
> 4 Was the Hoover Building a factory 70 years ago? Yes, it was.
> 6 Did Alexander Graham Bell invent the computer? No, he invented the telephone.

5 ▶

> **Answers**
> Across
> 1 bookshop
> 5 supermarket
> 8 stationery
> 9 shoe
> Down
> 2 park
> 3 gallery
> 4 store
> 5 stations
> 6 post
> 7 hotel

6 Writing bank

1 ▶

> **Answers**
> No. We don't know exactly when they went (i.e. which month). We know they stayed in the city centre but not where. We know the trip was expensive but we don't know how much it cost. All the other questions were answered.

2 ▶

> **Answers**
> Positive things: a pretty lake in the city centre, small so easy to walk around, countryside very different from Scotland
> Negative things: expensive, very cold, dark most of the time

3 ▶

> **Answers**
> 1 because
> 2 so

4a ▶

> **Answers**
> 1 so
> 2 because

b ▶ Ss' own answers

5a ▶ Ss' own answers

b ▶ Ss cross-check their notes with the TravelBuddy guidelines.

c ▶ Ss write a short text for TravelBuddy.

7 People

Overview

CEFR Can do objectives
7.1 Understand and tell a simple story
7.2 Describe people and understand descriptions
7.3 Understand and use dates and months
Communication Identify a person from a simple description
Writing bank Respond to an event in writing

CEFR Portfolio ideas
a) Write a short story about a recent experience. The story can be exciting, funny or unusual.
b) Make a picture crossword puzzle for your friends. All the answers in the crossword are words to describe people.
c) You are flying to Tokyo next month. Write an email to Sandra Shimoyu (she works in the same business but she does not know you). Tell her the date and time when you will arrive. Sandra will meet you at the airport. Describe your appearance so that Sandra can find you.
d) One of your friends/relatives is going to be 50 years old next week. Write a short message to him/her. Your message can be serious or funny!

Lead-in

OPTIONAL WARMER

Ss work in pairs. They tell each other about their impressions when they meet people for the first time. Ask: *What do you notice first about (1) men and (2) women: face, eyes, body, clothes, etc.?*

1a ▶ Ss focus on the pictures. Ask: *Where do you think these people are?*

▶ Ss match the people in the photos to the descriptions 1–12.

Answers	
1	G
2	B
3	F
4	G
5	F
6	B
7	C
8	F
9	A
10	C
11	E
12	F

b ▶ ◉ 2.01 Play recording 2.01. Ss listen to check their answers.

▶ Focus on the contracted form of *has got* in spoken English, e.g. *G's got blue eyes*; *B's got fair hair*. Note: *Hair* is singular in English. Point out to Ss *She's got fair hair* but *He's bald. She wears glasses.*

2a ▶ Ss match adjectives to people in the photos. The answers will be subjective and more than one answer is possible.

b ▶ Ss compare answers. Teach *He/She looks* + adjective: *He looks friendly. She looks pretty.*

3 ▶ Direct Ss to the example given. In pairs, Ss describe and identify one of the people from the photos. Monitor closely, helping with vocabulary and correcting any obvious errors.

EXTEND THE LEAD-IN

Ss work in small groups. They describe what their ideal partner would look like. (E.g. *My ideal partner has blue eyes and dark hair. I don't like beards but I like moustaches.*) Do not worry about Ss making mistakes during this activity. In feedback focus on any differences of opinion.

7.1 Finders keepers!

'Finders keepers' is an adage meaning that when
something is lost, whoever finds it becomes the new
owner. Children commonly say this to each other when
they find something they like. Generally, if you find
something in a public place, you have to bring it to the
local police station or local Lost Property office. Most
public buildings also have a Lost Property desk. ('Lost
and Found' is the term more commonly used in North
America.) Usually, an attempt will be made to contact
the owner if they can be easily identified. The finder of
the object or money can reclaim the property after a set
period of time has elapsed, usually six months to a year.
Otherwise, unclaimed property is given to charity or
thrown away.

In this lesson, Ss read about how two schoolgirls found
thousands of pieces of banknotes on their way to school
and what they did with the money. They practise telling
each other interesting stories.

OPTIONAL WARMER

Ss work in small groups. They discuss what they would
do in the following situations: (1) they find a large sum
of money in a rubbish bin, (2) the shop assistant gives
them change for 100 pounds instead of 10 pounds,
(3) they realise outside the shop that they have forgotten
to pay for books. Do not worry about Ss making mistakes.
They will be able to use only very basic language for this
discussion.

Reading

1 ▶ Ss look at the headline. Elicit the meaning of *jigsaw
puzzle*. Explain the difference between games and puzzles
and give some examples (e.g. Monopoly and Trivial Pursuit
are games; crossword puzzles, Sudoku puzzles and the
Rubik cube are puzzles).

Answers
A jigsaw puzzle is a picture that has been cut up into
irregularly shaped pieces, which you put together again
to re-form the picture.

2 ▶ Skimming: Explain to Ss that before they read the
text properly, they will read it very quickly to get an idea
of what it is about. Direct them to the question and tell
them they have two minutes to find what the jigsaw puzzle
referred to in the headline is. Explain that they do not need
to understand the text fully at this point. Stop the activity
after two minutes.

Answer
Putting all the banknote pieces back together.

3 ▶ Ss look at the eight statements. They read the text
again, this time more slowly to find the correct order of
events. Ss check answers in pairs, then as a whole class.

Answers
1 g
2 e
3 d
4 b
5 c
6 a
7 h
8 f

4 ▶ Explain to Ss that they are going to learn about
effective ways to read English texts. Ss look at the types
of questions asked in ex. 2 and 3. Tell Ss that the two
exercises help develop different reading skills. Explain
that ex. 2 helped Ss to get an overview of the text and
to identify the main events – this is step 1; ex. 3 helped
Ss read in a more detailed way – this is step 3. The other
important step in reading is to find the meaning of new
words. Ss can use a dictionary for this of course, but
explain that a very important reading skill is to guess the
meaning of unfamiliar words, using the context.

▶ Ss find *set off* in the text and read the sentence which
contains this expression. They then read the tips for
guessing the meanings of new words which are given in
the Lifelong learning box.

▶ Ss then look at the new words. First, they find these
words in the text and read the whole sentence. Then, they
use the tips to try to guess the meanings.

5 ▶ Ss look at the list of adjectives and select the ones
that represent their reactions to the story. Help with the
meaning, word stress and pronunciation of the words.
Then, in pairs, Ss tell each other what they thought of the
story and why.

OPTIONAL PAST TENSE REVIEW

In pairs, Ss look at the text again and find (1) six
examples of past forms of regular verbs, (2) two
examples of past question forms for irregular verbs and
(3) nine other examples of past forms for irregular verbs.

Vocabulary | phrasal verbs

6a ▶ Ss scan through the text quickly to find the second
part of the verbs.

Answers
1 pick up   3 pull out   5 give back
2 look at   4 hand in   6 put together

b ▶ Ss look at the pictures and match them with the
correct two-part verbs. Ss check answers in pairs then as a
whole class.

Answers		D	pull out
A	set off	E	look at
B	hand in	F	put together
C	pick up	G	give back

c ▶ Ss use the verbs to complete the sentences about the pictures.

Answers		2	hand in	4	put together
1	Look at	3	pick up	5	set off

▶ Direct Ss to the Reference section on page 77 for other examples of phrasal verbs found in previous units.

Grammar | articles

7a ▶ Ss read the two extracts from the text, focusing on the use of *a/an* and *the*. Ask Ss: *Why do you think* a *is used in the first sentence and* the *in the second sentence?* Give Ss a minute or two to think about this but don't give feedback until after Ss have completed the Active grammar box.

▶ Ss complete the Active grammar box. They check answers in pairs, then as a whole class.

> **Active grammar**
>
> a/an, the

▶ Remind Ss of the use of *a* and *an* (a *teacher*, a *trip*, etc. but an *apple*, an *architect*, etc.). We use *an* for nouns starting with a vowel sound and *a* for all other sounds.

▶ Write *We picked up __ paper* on the board. Remind Ss that we don't use *a/an* with uncountable nouns. (This was dealt with in Lesson 4.2). Elicit some uncountable nouns to illustrate the point (e.g. *tea*, *snow*, *paper*). We can't count these things one, two, three – so we can't say *We picked up a paper* here. Instead we say *a piece of paper* or *some paper*.

▶ This grammar point is easier for some language speakers than others. If you feel Ss are not finding this grammar point too difficult, draw their attention to the fact that we say *The sun is shining* and *We need to protect the earth* not *A sun is shining* or *We need to protect an earth*. Ask: *Why is this?* (There is only one sun and one earth so we do not need to use *a/an* when talking about these for the first time in a conversation. It is clear already which one we are referring to.)

▶ Direct Ss to the Reference section on page 77.

b ▶ Ss choose between *a/an* and *the* to complete the sentences. They check answers in pairs, then as a whole class.

Answers		2	a, a, The, the, the
1	a, The	3	a, the

8a ▶ Ss complete the story with the correct use of articles.

Answers	
1	a
2	the
3	a
4	a
5	the
6	a
7	the
8	the
9	the
10	a

b ▶ Ss close their books. Ss work in pairs and take turns to practise telling each other the story without looking at the text.

Speaking

9a ▶ Ss work in pairs, A and B. As turn to page 130 and Bs turn to page 133. Explain that As will see pictures for the first half of the story and Bs will see pictures for the second half of the story. Give Ss a few minutes to look at the pictures and prepare what they will say. Ask them to think of the past forms of the verbs they will need to tell the story.

▶ Ss tell each other about their half of the story. As must go first and then Bs.

▶ As an alternative to asking Ss to re-tell the story during feedback, Ss can look at each other's pictures on pages 130 and 133. Elicit the verbs Ss used for each picture in the story.

b ▶ Put the following headings on the board: *something I lost/something I found; winning money/losing money*. Give Ss a few minutes to think of a true story which relates to one of the headings. The story can be about themselves or someone they know. (If Ss can't think of a story, they can invent one or think of another interesting story about themselves.)

▶ Ss work in small groups of three or four and tell their story to the others in the group. Help Ss with new vocabulary as you monitor but do not worry about Ss making mistakes during this activity. Make a note of any mistakes relating to the use of past forms and articles as you monitor and deal with them later.

> **OPTIONAL EXTENSION**
>
> Ss conduct a roleplay in pairs. A is one of the girls who found the money and B is the reporter who wrote the newspaper article. Bs interview As about the incident. Encourage Ss to ask and imagine answers where the information is not given in the text. (E.g. *Did you always go that way to school? Was there anything else in the bag? How long did it take you to put together one note?* etc.) Do not worry about Ss making mistakes during this activity. Note down any obvious errors to deal with later.

7.2 The girl from …

Ipanema Beach, located in a fashionable part of Rio de Janeiro, is one of the most famous beaches in Brazil, along with neighbouring Copacabana Beach. The well-known song *The Girl from Ipanema*, sung by Astrud Gilberto, was a huge hit in the US in 1964 and many other artists have subsequently recorded it. The song describes the love felt by a young man as he watches a beautiful woman walk by each day – but he is too shy to speak to her.

In this lesson, Ss read an email from Marianne who is staying with a host family while studying near Ipanema Beach in Brazil and listen to Marianne describing a man she has met to her friend. Ss take turns to describe people.

OPTIONAL WARMER

Ss imagine they are going to an English-speaking country they have not been to before to do a course in English. Elicit the types of accommodation available (e.g. host family, youth hostel, etc.). In pairs, Ss think of two advantages and two disadvantages for the different types of accommodation: *A host family is good because you can practise English with the family. But it is bad because I like to cook for myself*, etc.

Reading

1 ▶ Ss look at the photos. Explain who Marianne is and why she is in Brazil. Ss discuss the two questions.

Answers
1   It is Ipanema Beach in Rio de Janeiro.
2   Ss' own answers

2a ▶ Teach *host family* (a local family who you stay with if you are visiting a different city or country). Ss look at the three questions and read the text to find the answers. Explain that they do not need to understand the text fully at this point. Write *my age* and *tanned* on the board and ask Ss to try to guess what these words mean as they read (*the same age as me*, *brown from the sun*). Ss check answers in pairs, then as a whole class.

Answers
1   She arrived in Rio de Janeiro to do a course.
2   She lives with the Silva family.
3   She usually goes to the beach.

b ▶ Ss read the text again and match the statements to the paragraphs.

Answers
2   E
3   A
4   D
5   B

c ▶ Ss read the email again and match the people to the adjectives. Ss check answers in pairs, then as a whole class.

Answers
1   c
2   d
3   a
4   f
5   b
6   e

3 ▶ Direct Ss to the vocabulary learning tip in the Lifelong learning box. Point out that it is useful to write the noun too when noting down opposites. For example, *old* can be the opposite of *young* or *new* (depending on who/what we are describing).

Ss look at the adjectives in ex. 2c again and match them to their opposites. Ss check answers in pairs, then as a whole class.

Answers
1   dark
2   shy
3   nice
4   handsome/pretty
5   short

We usually use *pretty* to talk about a woman and *handsome* to talk about a man. We use *short* and *tall* (not *long*) for people. We use *young* (not *new*) to talk about people, except for a new baby.

Vocabulary | adjectives (4): people

4a ▶ In pairs, Ss put the adjectives into the different columns.

Answers
Body: (not very) slim
Face: handsome, nice, pretty, unattractive
Skin: dark, pale, fair
Hair: dark, fair
Height: short, tall
Age: middle-aged, old, young
Personality: nice, shy, confident, horrible

▶ Ask Ss: *Which adjectives can go in more than one of the columns?* *Fair* and *dark* can be used to describe both hair and skin colour. *Nice* can describe appearance or personality.

b ▶ Ss add to the columns in pairs. You might like to do this activity as a team game. Each pair/team must try to extend the list in each category without using a dictionary. Give Ss two minutes per category. Each team gets one point for each new vocabulary item. The team with the most points at the end wins.

c ▶ Draw Ss' attention to the three main categories in ex. 4a and b, appearance, age and personality. Direct Ss to the *How to... describe people* box. Ss match the categories to the expressions. They check answers in pairs, then as a whole class.

Answers
1 age
2 appearance
3 personality

▶ Review modifiers (*really*, *quite*, *very*, *not very*). Ask Ss to look at the email again and to underline the modifiers (*very nice*, *very friendly*, *quite short*, *very tanned*, *not very slim*, *really interesting*, *really handsome*, *quite shy*).

d ▶ Explain that this is a tip to make descriptions more interesting and personal. Ss read the tip in their books, then think of examples to illustrate the adjectives in the box in pairs. Elicit one or two examples for each adjective during feedback.

OPTIONAL EXTENSION

Ss think of someone in the class, or a famous person. They describe him/her to their partner, but don't say his/her name. The partner tries to guess who it is, e.g *She's 22. She's got dark hair. She's confident, she asks a lot of questions. – That's Ana Maria!*

Grammar | pronoun *one/ones*

5a ▶ Ss focus on the excerpts from the email in ex. 2a. Ask Ss to find the sentences in the email. Ss match the underlined words to the correct meaning. They check answers in pairs, then as a whole class.

Active grammar
1 d
2 a
singular
plural

▶ *One* replaces singular nouns, *ones* replaces plural nouns. We often use *one* and *ones* to replace the noun after an adjective or after *this/these* and *that/those*. We also use *one* after *each* and in expressions like *the one/ones on the left/right*, etc.

▶ Direct Ss to the Reference section on page 77.

b ▶ Ss complete the exercise, then check answers with a partner.

Answers
1 ones
2 one
3 one
4 ones

c ▶ Ss read the paragraph and find four words which could be replaced by *one* or *ones*. Ss check answers in pairs, then as a whole class.

Answers
The second one
The third one
the one on the second floor
The other ones

Listening

6a ▶ 2.02 Ss look at the four photos. Play recording 2.02. Ss identify Luis from the photos.

Answer
photo 3

b ▶ Elicit ways of describing the men in the photos, e.g. *He's got glasses*, *He's got grey hair*, etc.

▶ Ss listen again and make notes about Marianne's description. Ss compare answers in pairs, then as a whole class.

Answers
He's Brazilian. He works in a hotel. He speaks English. He's very handsome. He's tanned. He's about 22 or 23. He's slim. He's got short, dark hair. He's got a little beard. His name's Luis. He's single.

Speaking

7a ▶ Ss take turns to describe another man in the photos and guess who it is.

b ▶ Ss work in pairs. Each pair prepares a description of someone who everyone in the class knows, either a famous person or someone in the class/school. Give Ss a few minutes to do this. Then, Ss form new pairs. Ss take turns to describe their person to their partner, who tries to guess who it is.

OPTIONAL EXTENSION

Ask: *How did Marianne meet Luis?* (He spoke to her.) *Have you ever liked someone from a distance but were too shy to speak to the person?* In pairs, Ss think of advice to give to someone in this situation. (E.g. Say hello to him/her; Bump into him/her 'accidentally', etc.) Elicit all the suggestions in feedback and decide as a class on the best piece of advice.

7.3 Special days

> Canada Day, often referred to as 'Canada's birthday', takes place on 1st July and celebrates the enactment of the British North American Act in 1867.
> Halloween, celebrated in many parts of the English-speaking world, takes place on 31st October and is thought to have its origins in the Irish pagan Samhain festival. The following day, 1st November, is the Christian feast of All Hallows or All Saints, when people traditionally visit graves of dead relatives. Fancy dress parties are particularly common at Halloween, as is 'trick or treating', children in masks and costumes knocking on neighbours' doors and receiving sweets.

In this lesson, Ss read about special days when gifts are given. They listen to a woman describing two important days in Canada and also to a phone conversation where two people talk about presents. Ss practise asking each other about birthdays and other special occasions.

Reading and listening

OPTIONAL WARMER

Ss work in pairs and make a list of all the occasions when they might buy/receive a present (e.g. moving house, holidays like Christmas or Eid, thank you gifts, etc.).

1a ▶ Elicit national holidays/special events and whether people give presents on these occasions.

b ▶ Remind Ss of the reading steps they learned about earlier in the unit (in the Lifelong learning box in Lesson 7.1). Explain that they will read the text twice, the first time quickly and the second time more slowly. Tell them they won't have more than two minutes for their first reading.

▶ Ss read the text quickly to find three special days mentioned (note: more than three are given). After two minutes, stop the activity.

Answers
New Year's Day, International Women's Day, Mother's Day, Ochugen

c ▶ Ss read the questions, then the text again to find the answers. Ss check answers in pairs, then as a whole class.

Answers
1 the first Sunday in May
2 food or sweets
3 yellow
4 red is the colour of good luck

▶ Explain that dates can be written either *8th March* (pronounced *the eighth of March*) or *March 8th* (pronounced *March the eighth*).

2a ▶ 🔵 2.03 Ss look at the two photos at the top of the page. Don't explain which photo refers to Canada Day and

which to Halloween but use the photos to teach *parade* and *costumes* which come up in the questions.

▶ Ss read through the question. Play recording 2.03. Ss listen and tick the appropriate occasion for each activity. Ss check answers in pairs, then as a whole class.

Answers
costumes: Halloween
parade: Canada Day
candy: Halloween
day off work: Canada Day
'trick or treat': Halloween

b ▶ Ss match some of the activities with the photos.

Answers
top photo: people dress up in costumes
bottom photo: there is a parade

c ▶ Put the following headings on the board: *food, clothes, activities*. Ss discuss national holidays and special occasions in their countries using the headings.

Vocabulary | ordinal numbers and months

3a ▶ Ask: *When is International Women's Day?* Write *8th March* on the board. Point at the number. Ask: *What number is this?* The number is *8* but explain that we say *8th* for dates – *the 8th of March* or *March the 8th*.

▶ Ss read the text in ex. 1 and the audioscript for ex. 2a on page 154. Ss find all the dates mentioned in the two texts and then complete the table in their books.

b ▶ 🔵 2.04 Play recording 2.04. Ss listen to check if they were right.

Answers
first	sixth	eleventh	thirtieth
second	seventh	12th	thirty-first
	8th	thirteenth	
	9th	15th	
	tenth		

▶ Help Ss with the pronunciation of the words, especially *first* and the *-th* sound at the end of most ordinal numbers. Draw Ss' attention to the hyphen in *twenty-second* and *thirty-first*.

▶ Play recording 2.04 again. Ss repeat each number.

4 ▶ Ss complete the exercise by choosing the correct word. Ss check answers in pairs, then as a whole class.

Answers
1 first
2 three
3 second
4 third
5 ninth

5a ▶ Ss find three different months in the text.

Answers March, May, July

b ▶ Ss look at the jumbled months and put them in order. Ss practise saying the months.

Answers	May 5	September 9
February 2	June 6	October 10
March 3	July 7	November 11
April 4	August 8	December 12

c ▶ Put today's full date, including the year, on the board. Review how to say the year in dates from Unit 6. Ss practise saying the dates.

The conventions for writing dates in figures are different in British and American English. In British English, the day of the month goes first and the month second; in American English, it is the reverse. This means that Christmas Day in 2011 would be written in figures as 12/25/2011 in North America and as 25/12/2011 in other parts of the English-speaking world.

d ▶ Ss take turns to tell their partner their birthdays and give the dates of national holidays in their country. In monocultural classes, Ss can exchange other important dates in their lives, e.g. various anniversaries and birthdays of other family members.

Grammar | possessive pronouns

OPTIONAL LEAD-IN

Ss work in pairs. They discuss present-giving in their families. (1) *Who usually buys the presents in your family?* (2) *Do you usually buy individual or shared presents?* (E.g. My mother and I buy a present together for my father's birthday.) (3) *Who is the hardest to buy for?* (4) *Do you like wrapping presents?* (Note: *to wrap* comes up in the listening.)

6a ▶ Ss look at the pictures, some of which are presents Jane has bought for her friends. They match the words to the pictures.

Answers	C diary	E umbrella
B DVDs	D trainers	F handbag

b ▶ 🔊 2.05 Play recording 2.05. Ss listen and match the items to the people. Ss check answers in pairs, then as a whole class.

Answers	Jane's parents – clock
Davy – trainers	Gordon – DVDs
Tara – diary	

7a ▶ Ss look at the excerpts from recording 2.05. They match the underlined words to the correct meaning. Ss check answers in pairs.

Answers	1 b	2 a

b ▶ Ss look at the audioscript on page 155 and complete the Active grammar box.

Active grammar

mine	ours
his	yours
hers	theirs

▶ Write *It is mine* and *It belongs to me* on the board. Underline the verbs to emphasise the different structures. *It is mine* can mean both *It belongs to me* and *It is for me.*

▶ Direct Ss to the Reference section on page 77.

8 ▶ Ss rewrite the sentences using possessive pronouns. Ss check answers in pairs, then as a whole class.

Answers		3 hers	6 his
1 yours		4 was theirs	7 theirs
2 is mine		5 ours	8 Is (this) his?

OPTIONAL EXTENSION

Ask Ss to select something from their bag, wallet or pencil case. Collect the items in a bag so Ss cannot see who is giving what. Put all the items on the desk. Ask: *Who does this belong to?* Ss guess whose it is, e.g. *it's Paul's* or *it's Maria's*. Check who the items really belong to, e.g. *Is it yours, Paul? Yes, it's mine. No, it's not his*, etc.

Pronunciation | /θ/

9a ▶ 🔊 2.06 Write *brother* and *bathroom* on the board. Underline the *th* in both words. Say the two words. Ask: *Is the th sound the same?* (No, in *brother*, it is /ð/ and in *bathroom*, it is /θ/). Write the two phonetic symbols on the board.

▶ Write *birthday* on the board. Do not pronounce it yet. Ask: *Which sound is* th *in this word?* Play recording 2.06. Ss listen and identify the /θ/ sound. Ss practise saying the words *birthday* and *bathroom*.

b ▶ 🔊 2.07 Ss look at the words. Play recording 2.07. Ss listen and identify which word they hear. They check answers in pairs, then as a whole class.

Answers		2 think	4 thirst
1 free		3 thick	5 three

c ▶ 🔊 2.08 Play recording 2.08. Ss listen and tick or cross the numbers.

Answers		3 ✗	6 ✓
1 ✓		4 ✗	7 ✗
2 ✓		5 ✓	8 ✓

▶ Direct Ss to the Pronunciation bank on page 147.

Speaking

10 ▶ Ask Ss to stand up and come to wherever there is most space in the room. Ss mingle and ask each other about their birthdays (*When is your birthday? It's on the first of February*, etc.). Ss note down the different dates. When they have found the five students they're looking for, they sit down. Ss call out the answers during feedback.

7 Communication

In this lesson, Ss listen to people asking about and describing what someone looks like. They practise describing and identifying people.

> **OPTIONAL WARMER**
>
> Ss discuss the following questions with a partner: *Do you forget faces easily? Do you normally remember people's names or their faces? What do you notice about people – hair colour? eye colour? clothes? body shape?* etc.

1 ▶ Ss focus on the picture. Discuss as a whole class where the picture is and where the people are.

> **Answer**
> arrivals hall at the airport

2a ▶ 🔵 2.09 Explain to Ss that they will hear the recording twice. The first time they should listen to get the general idea and the second time for more details.

▶ Play recording 2.09. Ss listen to get the general idea of what the problem is. Ss check answers in pairs, then as a whole class.

> **Answers**
> She is too busy to go to the airport to meet Mr Schäfer.

b ▶ Play the recording a second time. Ss listen and note down the details to complete Geoff's notes. They check answers in pairs, then as a whole class.

> **Answers**
> late 40s
> 2 metres
> dark
> grey
> short
> slim
> pale
> short beard
> glasses

c ▶ Ss decide in pairs which man in the picture is Mr Schäfer.

> **Answer**
> man on the right, wearing a red tie and holding a piece of paper

3 ▶ Play the recording again. Ss listen and complete the *How to...* box.

> **Answers**
> 1 look
> 2 old
> 3 colour
> 4 Does
> 5 hair
> 6 Is
> 7 colour
> 8 like

4 ▶ Ss work in pairs. Student A reads the information on page 130 about meeting Ms Andrews at the airport. Student B looks at the pictures on page 134 and chooses one of the people to describe as Ms Andrews. Student A asks questions and takes notes, then identifies Ms Andrews on page 134 from B's description.

▶ Ss then swap roles. Student B looks at the information about meeting Mr Gardner at the airport on page 134. Student A looks at the pictures on page 130 and chooses one of the people to describe as Mr Gardner. This time, Student B identifies Mr Gardner on page 130 from A's description.

> **OPTIONAL EXTENSION**
>
> Cut out photos of people from magazines. Ss work in pairs. Student A has just witnessed a robbery. Student B is a police artist who draws people based on descriptions of eyewitnesses. Give As one of the photos and tell them to imagine this is the person they saw. They describe the person and Student B draws an 'identikit' picture. Ss compare the photo and the picture during feedback. Note: Ss do not have to be good at drawing for this activity.

7 Review and practice

1 ▶

Answers
1 a
2 the
3 a
4 the
5 a
6 a
7 The
8 a

2 ▶

Answers
1 put together
2 pick up
3 give back
4 look at
5 set off

3 ▶

Answers
the red one?
modern ones?
those big ones in the corner
The metal ones?
how about this one?
I don't like that one
a different one

4 ▶

Answers
2 h
3 b
4 a
5 d
6 c
7 g
8 f

5 ▶

Answers
1 eighth
2 twenty-fifth
3 first
4 eighteenth
5 ninth

6 ▶

Answers
1 C
2 B
3 D
6 A

7 Writing bank

1a ▶ Ss' own answers

b ▶

Answers
1 D   3 D   6 A
2 B   4 C   7 B
      5 E or B   8 C

2 ▶

Answers
a 7   c 4   f 2
b 5   d 6   g 8
      e 1   h 3

3a ▶

Answers
1 exclamation mark
2 dash

b ▶

Answers
1 – (dash), ! (exclamation mark)
2 – (dash)
3 ! (exclamation mark)
4 ! (exclamation mark)

c ▶

Answers
1 Thanks for the present – it's just what I wanted.
2 I'm really pleased you got the job – good luck!
3 Enjoy your trip – send me a postcard!
4 I'm sorry I missed your birthday – I was on holiday.

4 ▶

Answers
1 I hope
2 I'm sorry
3 I'm really pleased
4 I hope
5 I'm sorry

5a ▶

Answers
1 cousin: D
  aunt: E or B
  teacher: A
  best friend: B or D
2 Ss' own answers

b ▶ Ss write messages for their cards.

Overview

Lead-in	Revision: Clothes; seasons
8.1	**Can do:** Describe what people are doing now **Grammar:** Present Continuous **Speaking and Pronunciation:** Sentence stress **How to...** describe a picture **Listening:** Festivals around the world Describing a picture
8.2	**Can do:** Talk about what you wear **Grammar:** Position of adjectives **Vocabulary:** Clothes **Speaking and Pronunciation:** Quiz: What kind of dresser are you? **Reading:** Street fashion
8.3	**Can do:** Talk about the weather **Grammar:** Present Simple and Present Continuous **Vocabulary:** The weather **Speaking and Pronunciation:** /ɒ/ and /əʊ/ **Reading:** Extreme weather
Communication	Describe problems and ask for solutions **How to...** describe problems and ask for solutions
Reference	
Review and Practice	
Writing bank	Write a postcard **How to...** make your writing more interesting

CEFR Can do objectives
8.1 Describe what people are doing now
8.2 Talk about what you wear
8.3 Talk about the weather
Communication Describe problems and ask for solutions
Writing bank Write a postcard

CEFR Portfolio ideas
a) Imagine you are at a local festival. Write a short message to your pen friend about the weather and what people are doing.
b) Choose a photograph from a recent holiday. Describe the people in the photograph and say what they are doing.
c) Write a short postcard to your teacher from a recent a recent holiday.

Lead-in

The dress code for office work in the English-speaking world is generally a suit (or just trousers), shirt and tie for men and suit (or skirt/trousers) and blouse for women. However, some companies now have a more relaxed dress code on Fridays when jeans are sometimes permitted and men need not wear a tie. This is often referred to as a 'dress-down Friday' or 'casual Friday' policy.

OPTIONAL WARMER
Ss discuss the following questions in small groups of three or four: *Do you like shopping for clothes? How often do you do it? Which clothes item do you have the most of?* (E.g. *shoes, coats, jeans*, etc.)

1a ▶ Ss look at photos A–D. Elicit what the seasons are in each photo. Ss look at the clothes vocabulary and check unfamiliar words in the dictionary.

▶ Ss then match the clothes in the photos to the words.

Answers	hat A	shorts C	tie D
coat B	jeans A, B	skirt C	
dress C	pullover A	suit D	
gloves A	scarf A	T-shirt C	

b ▶ Ss work in pairs and name other clothes in the pictures. They can use their dictionaries. These include *mac* (B), *belt* (C), *braces, shirt, jacket* (D).

2 ▶ Ss work in pairs and decide which clothes can be worn in which seasons. Ask: *What do we wear in spring/ summer?* etc. during feedback.

3 ▶ Ss match the adjectives to their meanings. Ss check answers in pairs, then as a whole class.

Answers	3 f	5 a
2 e	4 b	6 c

OPTIONAL LEAD-IN TO THE LISTENING
Write: *jeans or formal clothes; loose/tight shirts and pullovers; jackets or winter coats* on the board. Ss discuss their preferences about clothes with a partner.

4a ▶ 🔘 2.10 Ss look through the four sentences. Play recording 2.10. Ss listen and complete the gaps. Ss check answers in pairs, then as a whole class.

Answers	3 Tight
1 jeans	4 coats
2 formal	

b ▶ Ss give their opinions on the four statements.

8.1 Festivals around the world

The world's largest open air music festival takes place on the last weekend in June in Glastonbury, England. One ticket buys you entry to over 80 stages and numerous musical acts, featuring some of the biggest names in the music industry every year. The festival is mainly run by volunteers and most of the proceeds go to charity. The festival-goers mainly camp out for the weekend and the conditions can be notoriously wet and muddy.

In this lesson, Ss listen to reporters describing what is happening at three different festivals. They also listen to a description of a festival scene in a photo. Ss practise describing what people are doing in the pictures.

Listening

OPTIONAL WARMER

Elicit different types of festivals, e.g. street theatre and entertainment, indoor arts festival with cultural events, parade-type festival like the Rio Carnival, jazz or music festival, etc. Give Ss a few minutes to make a list of famous festivals around the world in pairs. Put all the suggestions on the board. Ask Ss if they have ever been to any of these festivals.

1 ▶ Ss look at the six photos and discuss the questions with a partner. Do not give feedback yet.

Answers
1   Boston Carnival: photos A and D
    Mariachi Festival in Mexico: photos B and E
    Helsinki Arts Festival: photos C and F
2   Boston in the US, Guadalajara in Mexico, Helsinki in Finland

2a ▶ 🔘 2.11 Play recording 2.11. Ss listen and check their answers from ex. 1. Ss also match the reporter to the festival photos.

Answers
photos A and D – reporter Anna
photos B and E – reporter Justin
photos C and F – reporter Pam

b ▶ Ss match the people to the photos.

Answers
a Mariachi group – B
dancers in colourful costumes – A
Whitney – D

c ▶ Ss match the sentence halves in pairs, then listen to the recording again to check their answers.

Answers
1   e
2   f
3   a
4   b
5   d
6   h
7   g
8   c

3 ▶ Ss discuss the questions in pairs.

▶ Ask: *Which kind of festival do you/would you prefer?* and compare preferences during feedback.

Grammar | Present Continuous

4a ▶ Ss look at the sentences in ex. 2c and use them to complete the Active grammar box. Ss check answers in pairs, then as a whole class.

Active grammar
Affirmative: is, are
Negative: isn't, aren't

▶ Demonstrate the contracted forms: *I am (I'm) dancing; He is (He's) dancing; They are (They're) dancing; He is not (isn't) talking; They are not (aren't) talking*, etc. Explain we use these when speaking. Ss will have an opportunity to practise saying the contracted forms in ex. 6 so it is enough to draw their attention to them at this stage. They should be familiar with the contracted forms for the verb *to be* already.

b ▶ Ss complete the sentence in pairs.

Answer
2

▶ Emphasise the difference between *Whitney cooks Caribbean food every day* and *Whitney is cooking Caribbean food now* (at the moment of speaking).

c ▶ Ss complete the rule for the Present Continuous.

Answer
to be

d ▶ Focus on the spelling of the *-ing* form of the verb. Ss look at the box and write the *-ing* forms. They check answers in pairs. Ss can then check their answers in the audioscript on page 155.

Answers
1   watching, playing
2   having, moving, dancing
3   sitting, clapping

▶ Direct Ss to the Reference section on page 87.

5a ▶ Ss write sentences using the Present Continuous. Ss check answers in pairs, then as a whole class.

Answers
1 All the people are having a good time.
2 She isn't dancing now.
3 They're wearing traditional costumes.
4 We're reading an interesting book.
5 I'm wearing a coat.
6 I'm not studying any languages at the moment.
7 We're not writing an exercise.
8 What are you doing at the moment?

b ▶ Ss re-write sentences 4–7 so that they are true sentences about themselves. Ss compare sentences with a partner, then answer question 8.

Pronunciation | sentence stress

6 ▶ ⬤ 2.12 Play recording 2.12. Ss listen and underline the stressed syllables they hear. Ss check answers in pairs, then listen again and repeat.

Answers
1 She's <u>dan</u>cing.
2 They're <u>talk</u>ing.
3 Are you <u>lis</u>tening?
4 We aren't <u>leav</u>ing.

▶ Ask: *Is the -ing part of the word stressed?* (No.) *Is the verb* to be *stressed?* (Usually not, except in negative sentences.) Explain that the words that tend to be stressed are the words which carry the most meaning, not the grammar words.

▶ Direct Ss to the Pronunciation bank on page 148.

Speaking

7 ▶ Ss take turns to mime one of the verbs in the box and the others try to guess which action it is. Model an example first.

8 ▶ Ss look at the picture. Elicit where it is and what is happening in the photo.

OPTIONAL VARIATION

Team game. Divide the class into two large groups. Each group takes turns to make a sentence about the picture. (*People are dancing; There are tall houses in the picture*, etc.) Ss cannot repeat sentences. Keep the pace snappy and don't give Ss too long to think of sentences. Keep going back and forth until one team cannot think of a new sentence. The team which keeps going for the longest wins.

9a ▶ ⬤ 2.13 Ss match the descriptions to the part of the picture. Ss check answers in pairs, then listen to recording 2.13 to check their answers.

Answers
1 c
2 b
3 a
4 d

b ▶ Ss complete the *How to...* box in pairs.

Answers
1 back/front
2 On, right
3 are
4 There
5 There

10 ▶ Ss work in pairs. Student A looks at the picture on page 131. Student B looks at the picture on page 134. The scenes are similar but there are six differences which Ss must find by asking and answering questions about each other's picture. (e.g. *How many people are dancing? What is happening at the front of your picture?*, etc.). Ss compare pictures in feedback.

Answers
Student A's picture:
A man and a woman are serving burgers.
The woman at the front of the queue is ordering a burger.
Two girls are sitting on a bench.
The musician on the left is playing the guitar.
The musician on the right is singing.
Two men on the right are clapping.
Student B's picture:
A man is serving burgers.
The woman at the front of the queue is eating a burger.
Two girls are standing, watching the musicians.
The musician on the left is singing.
The musician on the right is playing the guitar.
One man on the right is clapping.

OPTIONAL EXTENSION

Cut out about six or seven interesting photos/images which contain people from magazines or newspapers. Adverts are often good for this. Number the pictures and put them around the room. Give Ss a few minutes to walk around the room to look at the pictures. Ss then work in pairs. They select one of the pictures and decide (1) where the person/people in the photo are, (2) what they are doing and (3) how they are feeling and why. E.g. *The woman in this picture is sitting on a bed in her bedroom. She is dressed in formal work clothes. She is thinking about something. She looks sad. Maybe she is having problems at work at the moment.* They write a short caption on cards to go with their chosen picture/image without identifying the picture. Collect all the cards and stick them on the board. All the pairs come to the board, read the cards and match the various captions to the photos.

8.2 You are what you wear

In this lesson, Ss read about how five different people like to dress and talk about their own and other people's clothes preferences.

Reading

OPTIONAL WARMER

Ss work in pairs. They tell each other the kind of clothes they would choose to wear on the following occasions: (1) a wedding; (2) going to the cinema on a first date; (3) special family celebrations (e.g. birthdays, Christmas, etc.); (4) a long plane journey. Write the occasions on the board. Explain *wedding* (marriage party) and *date* (romantic appointment, when the two people don't know each other very well).

1 ▶ Skimming: Explain to Ss that they will read the text twice, the first time very quickly and the second time much more slowly. Direct them to the exercise and tell them they have two minutes to name the people in the pictures A–E. Explain that they do not need to understand the text fully at this point. Stop the activity after two minutes. Ss compare answers in pairs and then as a whole class.

Answers
A Danny
B Sunny
C Simon
D Karen
E Tara

2a ▶ Ss match the clothes with the people in pairs.

Answers
boots – Karen
jacket – Danny, Karen, Tara
jeans – Simon
pullover – Danny
sandals – Tara
sari – Sunny
shoes – Danny
a skirt – Karen, Tara
a suit – Tara
sunglasses – Simon
trainers – Simon
trousers – Danny

▶ Focus on the pronunciation of these words, especially the initial /dʒ/ in *jacket* and *jeans* and the /uː/ sound in *suit*.

OPTIONAL EXTENSION

In pairs, Ss categorise the vocabulary into (1) clothes worn on the top half of the body and (2) clothes worn on the lower part of the body. Ss add clothes to each category.

b ▶ Ss discuss the questions with a partner. Ask questions like: *Who do you think is the most fashionable/ least fashionable? Who has the nicest clothes?* etc. in feedback.

c ▶ Ss read the texts more slowly, this time focusing on the five sentences. Teach *cool* (a little bit cold). Ss read through the texts and complete the sentences. Ss read at their own pace. Ss check answers in pairs, then as a whole class.

Answers
1 Karen
2 Danny
3 Sunny
4 Tara
5 Simon

3 ▶ Ss discuss fashion in pairs.

OPTIONAL VARIATION

Elicit what Ss think is important when shopping for clothes. Write all suggestions on the board (e.g. price; fashion; designer label; comfortable to wear; the colour/ style suits you; the material will wash/keep clean easily; natural materials, etc.). Make sure there are at least seven items on the board. Add one or two if necessary if Ss' list is short. Ss rank the list in order of personal importance when buying clothes, 1 being the most important thing. Ss do this individually first and then they discuss their choices in small groups of three or four.

Vocabulary | clothes

4a ▶ Ss focus on the vocabulary in the text. They find words with opposite meanings to those listed. Ss check answers in pairs, then as a whole class.

Answers
1 thick
2 warm
3 tight
4 bright
5 fashionable
6 natural

▶ Draw Ss' attention to the prefix *un-* but do not spend too long on this.

b ▶ Ss match the four words from the text to their meanings. Ss check answers in pairs, then as a whole class.

Answers
1 b
2 c
3 d
4 a

▶ Focus on the pronunciation of these words, especially *wool* and *leather*.

Grammar | position of adjectives

5a ▶ Focus on the pictures in the text. First, ask factual questions, e.g. *What colour are Simon's jeans? Do you all agree?* (Yes.) *Is his T-shirt tight or loose?* (tight) *Do you all agree?* (Yes.) etc. Then, ask some opinion questions, e.g. *Is Tara's suit nice? What adjective would you use to describe Simon's jeans?* etc. (Elicit various answers.) *Do you all agree?* (Some may do and some may not.) Explain the difference between adjectives which describe facts and adjectives which describe an opinion.

▶ Ss focus on the sentences from the text. They discuss the questions in pairs.

> **Answers**
> 1   young, silk, brown
> 2   lovely, beautiful, smart

b ▶ Ss choose the correct word to complete the rule. They check answers in pairs, then as a whole class.

> **Active grammar**
> before
> before
> after

▶ Help Ss with the falling intonation pattern at the end of these sentences.

It is not necessary to explain more complicated rules for the position of adjectives at this stage. The opinion/fact distinction is enough for this level.

▶ Direct Ss to the Reference section on page 87.

6 ▶ Ss look at the pictures. Elicit one or two adjectives to describe each one.

▶ Ss choose words from the box to label the pictures. Ss compare answers in pairs, then as a whole class.

> **Suggested answers**
> beautiful cotton dress
> expensive Swiss watch
> scruffy brown shoes

7 ▶ Ss order the words to make sentences. Ss check answers in pairs, then as a whole class. Ss practise saying the sentences, using falling intonation at the end.

> **Answers**
> 1   She's wearing a beautiful silk dress.
> 2   That suit looks smart.
> 3   Second-hand clothes aren't expensive.
> 4   I love my comfortable wool pullover.
> 5   Your jeans look fantastic.
> 6   Mario always wears nice cotton T-shirts.

8 ▶ Ss take turns to describe another student in the class to their partner. Their partner must guess who is being described.

Speaking

9a ▶ Make sure Ss are working with a new partner for this activity. Ss work in pairs and use the questionnaire to interview each other about their clothes preferences. Each student should make notes about their partner's answers.

b ▶ Ask individual Ss to tell the class about their partner's clothes preferences. With large classes, it can be easier and more time efficient to have Ss describe their partner in groups rather than to the whole class.

▶ You might like to direct Ss to the model texts in ex. 1 and ask them to prepare a similar text to describe what kind of dresser their partner is.

> **OPTIONAL EXTENSION**
> Ss discuss the following questions in pairs or small groups: *How do you organise your wardrobe and clothes drawers? How often do you throw clothes out? Do you have clothes in your wardrobe that you never/rarely wear? Do you take good care of your clothes?*

8.3 Changing weather

In this lesson, Ss read about how global warming is affecting the weather. They talk about weather conditions and practise comparing what people usually do and what they are doing now.

OPTIONAL WARMER

Ss think of three reasons to like each of the four seasons, e.g. *Spring: flowers grow in the gardens; the weather begins to get warmer; people put their winter coats away*, etc. In feedback, establish which season Ss like best.

Vocabulary | the weather

1 ▶ Ss match the weather symbols to the weather words. Ss check answers in pairs.

Answers		4	C		7	H
2	A	5	F		8	D
3	G	6	B			

▶ Highlight that *It's snowing* and *It's raining* are Present Continuous verbs here and the other weather words are adjectives.

2a ▶ 🔊 2.14 Play recording 2.14. Ss listen to see how many of the weather words from ex. 1a they hear.

Answers
warm (x3)
sunny (x3)
snow(ing)
foggy
raining

b ▶ Play the recording again. Ss listen and complete the gaps in the text. Check answers as a whole class.

Answers		3	degrees	6	sunny
1	warm	4	foggy	7	hot
2	snow	5	summer	8	raining

c ▶ Elicit what the weather is like in Ss' countries.

Pronunciation | /ɒ/ and /əʊ/

3a ▶ 🔊 2.15 Direct Ss to the four words. Play recording 2.15. Ss listen to identify the two sounds /əʊ/ and /ɒ/. Ss check answers in pairs, then as a whole class. Write the phonetic symbols on the board.

Answers
Cold and *snowing* are /əʊ/ sounds.
Hot and *foggy* are /ɒ/ sounds.

b ▶ 🔊 2.16 Play recording 2.16. Ss listen and decide whether the sounds are the same or different in each pair of words. They do not need to practise saying the sounds yet.

Answers
1 same
2 different
3 different
4 same

c ▶ 🔊 2.17 Play recording 2.17. Ss listen and list the words they hear under the two columns. They check answers in pairs, then as a whole class. Ss practise saying the words.

Answers
/ɒ/: clock, cost, not, on, bottle
/əʊ/: old, note, hotel, wrote, own

OPTIONAL EXTENSION

Ss take turns to practise saying these sentences: (1) *It snows a lot in Poland.* (2) *The doctor told me not to get cold.*

Reading

4 ▶ Ss look at the photos and discuss the questions with a partner. Do not give feedback yet.

5a ▶ Explain to Ss that they will read the text twice, the first time very quickly and the second time much more slowly. Explain that they do not need to understand the text fully at this point. Ss read quickly to match the text to one of the photos. Stop the activity after a minute. Ss check answers in pairs, then as a whole class.

Answer
The text matches with the top picture of London. The bottom photo shows New York.

b ▶ Ss read the text again, this time at their own pace, and answer the questions. Ss check answers with a partner, then as a whole class.

Answers
1   46 degrees Celsius
2   Everybody turned on their air conditioning and so there were power cuts and people didn't have lights in the evening.
3   for several weeks
4   Buses and trains didn't run because of the bad weather.

6 ▶ Ss focus on the new vocabulary in the text. They match the words to the correct meaning. Ss check answers in pairs, then as a whole class.

Answers		4	b
1	f	5	c
2	d	6	a
3	e		

7 ▶ Write *act – action* and *communicate – communication* on the board. Ss should be familiar with these words. Ask *Which are the verbs?* (act, communicate) *Which are the nouns?* (action, communication) Explain that the suffix *-ion* is added to *act* and *communicat(e)* to make a noun.

▶ Write *dark – darkness* on the board. Ask: *Which word is the noun?* (darkness) *What type of word is dark?* (an adjective) Explain that *-ness* is similar to *-ion*. The suffix *-ness* is added to adjectives to make them nouns.

▶ Ss look at the nouns with the suffix *-ness* and say which adjectives they come from. Ss check answers in pairs, then as a whole class.

Answers		4	sick
1	tired	5	bald
2	happy	6	crazy
3	fit		

▶ Ask Ss: *What do you notice about* happiness *and* craziness? (No *-y* at the end and *-iness* instead.)

Encourage Ss to look out for different word endings and note the different forms in their vocabulary journals.

Grammar | Present Simple/Present Continuous

8a ▶ ⦿ 2.18 Play recording 2.18. Ss listen and decide why Luke isn't at work.

Answer
He can't get to work because of the snow.

b ▶ Ss look at the statements. Play the recording again. Ss listen and decide whether the statements are true or false. Ss check answers in pairs, then as a whole class.

Answers
1   F
2   T
3   F
4   F
5   T

c ▶ Ss discuss the questions in pairs.

Answers
1   because everything looks beautiful
2/3 Ss' own answers

OPTIONAL VARIATION

Ss work in small groups. They discuss (1) which type of weather they like best/least and why and (2) how the weather affects their health/mood.

9a ▶ Direct Ss to the extracts from the listening text. Explain that some of the verbs are Present Continuous and some are Present Simple.

▶ Ss look at the sentences. They circle the Present Simple verbs and underline the Present Continuous verbs. Ss check answers in pairs, then as a whole class.

Answers
Present Continuous: isn't working, aren't running
Present Simple: snows, phone

▶ Quickly review how the Present Simple and Present Continuous are formed.

b ▶ Ss complete the rules by filling in the correct tense.

Active grammar
1   Present Continuous
2   Present Simple

▶ Check Ss understand that we use the Present Simple to talk about routines and facts and the Present Continuous to talk about actions happening now.

▶ Direct Ss to the Reference section on page 87.

10 ▶ Ss choose the correct form of the verb in each sentence.

Answers		4	isn't wearing
1	is raining	5	are studying
2	take	6	don't drink
3	carry		

11a ▶ Ss write sentences about the people in the pictures, using the prompts. Ss check answers in pairs, then as a whole class.

Answers
2   Laura usually walks to work but today she is driving her new car.
3   Sally usually cleans the house every day but today she is playing football.
4   Anna usually wears jeans but today she is wearing a dress.

b ▶ Ss practise the two tenses by asking each other questions about the people in the pictures.

OPTIONAL EXTENSION

Elicit the different things people do/don't do on their summer holidays (e.g. beach in the afternoon, breakfast in bed, no work, no traffic jams, etc.). Explain that 'James' is on a beach holiday with his family. You can draw a matchstick picture of James or bring in a photo from a magazine. Ss make sentences describing what James usually does when he is at work and what he is doing now. Put different times of day on the board: *in the morning, at lunchtime, in the afternoon, in the evening, at night*. E.g. *In the morning: James usually gets up early. He moves quickly and has breakfast in the kitchen but today he is having breakfast in bed with his wife. He is eating slowly*, etc.

8 Communication

People in the UK and in Ireland are generally slow to complain about bad service in bars and restaurants. If food is cold or service is poor, they will not complain verbally, but will instead leave and not use the restaurant or service provider again. It is considered impolite to complain loudly or with aggressive gestures. If people complain, they often do so indirectly (e.g. *I'm sorry to bother you, but …*; *You may not have noticed, but …*, etc.). Complaining tends to be much more direct in North American and Australian cultures.

In this lesson, Ss practise describing a problem to a service or goods provider and asking for a solution to the problem, such as a refund, exchange or repair.

OPTIONAL WARMER

Ss work in pairs. Write the following situations on the board: people talking in the cinema, cold food in a restaurant, a mark on a shirt you have bought, noisy neighbours, the bus is late. Ss discuss whether they would complain in these situations or not. Ss will only be able to express their views in very basic English.

1a ▶ Ss look at the pictures in pairs and decide where each one is.

Answers
1 F
2 B, C, E
3 A, D

b ▶ Ss look at the pictures again. Elicit what is happening in each picture without focusing on the phrases. Ss then match the phrases to the pictures. Help Ss with the pronunciation of *receipt*. Explain the difference between *a refund* and *an exchange*.

Answers
It isn't working. – D
a receipt – B
a refund – C
to repair something – F
an exchange – E

2 ▶ 🔘 2.19 Play recording 2.19. Ss listen and identify which pictures correspond to which dialogue.

Answers
Dialogue 1: F
Dialogue 2: B, D, E
Dialogue 3: A, C

3a ▶ Elicit the stages in making a complaint. *What do you do first/second?*, etc. (Explain the problem, ask for money/exchange, etc.). Ss look at the stages in the *How to…* box.

▶ Play the recording again. Ss listen and complete the *How to…* box.

b ▶ Ss check their answers in the audioscript on page 156.

Answers
1 Can
2 bought
3 hot
4 problem
5 doesn't
6 isn't
7 exchange
8 like
9 repair

c ▶ Ss practise the dialogues with each other. Monitor closely, correcting any pronunciation errors.

4 ▶ Ss work in pairs. They take turns to describe problems with something they have paid for. Ss read Roleplay 1. One student is a customer and the other is a shop assistant. Student A's information is on page 131 and Student B's is on page 86. Give Ss a minute or two to read through the information. They can use their dictionaries for words they don't understand. When they are ready, they work in pairs to complete the roleplay.

▶ When they have finished, they exchange roles and read the information for Roleplay 2. They conduct the second roleplay in pairs and so on with Roleplays 3 and 4. Do not worry if Ss make mistakes during this activity. Any obvious errors you hear can be dealt with later.

▶ When Ss have completed the roleplays in pairs, ask: *Did you find a solution for the problem with the computer? What about for the problem with the jacket?*, etc. and elicit the different solutions which Ss found. It is not necessary to have Ss act out the roleplays again in front of the class.

OPTIONAL EXTENSION

Ss write an email to the company explaining the problem and asking for a solution for one of the roleplay situations in ex. 4. Teach *Dear Sir/Madam* to begin and *Yours faithfully* to end a formal email or letter.

8 Review and practice

1a ▶

Answers			
1	clapping	7	studying
2	making	8	swimming
3	planning	9	using
4	reading	10	waiting
5	riding	11	writing
6	sitting	12	carrying

b ▶

Answers			
1	'm writing	4	's using
2	'm waiting	5	's making
3	's studying	6	'm reading
		7	are planning

2 ▶

Answers
1 Are you reading a good book? Yes, I am.
2 Are you studying German? No, I'm not studying German. I'm studying English.
3 Is she cooking dinner? No, she isn't cooking dinner. She's preparing tomorrow's lunch.
4 Is he working at home today? Yes, he is.
5 Are they playing tennis? No, they aren't playing tennis. They're playing basketball.

3 ▶

Answers
1 The new James Bond film looks exciting.
2 I bought a fashionable leather jacket yesterday.
3 The weather is very hot today.
4 You look awful in those old jeans.
5 Our teacher is a friendly middle-aged woman.
6 I gave my girlfriend a beautiful red scarf.

4 ▶

Answers
1 She usually wears a formal business suit.
2 Today she's wearing jeans and a T-shirt.
3 She usually talks to people in the office.
4 Today she's talking to clients at the match.
5 She usually has a sandwich for lunch in the office.
6 Today she's having a big meal in a restaurant.

5 ▶

Possible answers			
1	a coat	4	a dress
2	a hat	5	a suit
3	boots	6	a jacket

6 ▶

Possible answers
Picture 1: It's spring. It's sunny. The sun is shining. It's hot.
Picture 2: It's windy. It's cold. It's raining.

8 Writing bank

1 ▶

Suggested answers
swim, surf, go for a walk, sail, eat fish

2 ▶

Answers
1 Polly
2 a lovely apartment near the beach
3 fantastic
4 two children: Patrick and Melanie

3a ▶

Answers
lovely, fantastic, wonderful, amazing, great

b ▶

Suggested answers
attractive, bright, colourful, comfortable, delicious, exciting, fashionable, friendly, luxurious, perfect, popular, pretty, relaxing

4 ▶ Ss' own answers

5 ▶

Answers
1 Dear Polly, Love Lara
2 a paragraph 2
  b paragraph 3
  c paragraph 4
  d paragraph 1

6a ▶ Ss' own answers

b ▶ Ss write the postcard.

9 Culture

Overview

CEFR Can do objectives
9.1 Make comparisons between things and people
9.2 Compare one thing with several others
9.3 Talk about personal preferences
Communication Make and respond to suggestions
Writing bank Write a short biography

CEFR Portfolio ideas
a) Choose your favourite film star and write his/her biography.
b) Imagine yourself in your dream job. Write your imaginary biography.
c) *Who's Who?* is a directory of famous people. The people in *Who's Who?* write their own short biographies. Write your biography in 200 words or less.
d) Audio or Video recording. With a partner, plan the questions he/she will ask you in an interview about your life for local radio or TV. Record the interview.

Lead-in

1a ▶ Ss look at the jumbled letters and reorder them to match the four pictures.

Answers
1. music B
2. film A
3. theatre C
4. painting D

b ▶ Ss work in pairs. They name one example of each of the art forms in the box, e.g. *ballet* – Swan Lake; *cartoon* – The Simpsons, etc.

2a ▶ Ss look at the picture of the incomplete word map. The head word is *THE ARTS*. Explain there are five subheadings. Ss use the words from ex. 1 to complete the word map. Tell Ss they can put words in more than one category if they wish. Ss compare answers with a partner. Do not give feedback until after ex. 2b.

b ▶ 🔊 2.20 Play recording 2.20. Ss listen and compare their word map to that of the two people on the recording.

Answers
(This is the word map from the recording but there are several possible variations.)
Painting: cartoon, modern art
Literature: horror, novels, poetry, comedy
Music: classical music, opera, rock music
Theatre: opera, dance, ballet, comedy, plays
Film: horror, comedy

c ▶ Ss think of more words to add to the word map, e.g. *sculpture*, *modern dance*, *choir*, etc.

3 ▶ Ss work in groups and answer the questions. Encourage Ss to explain why they like a particular novel or film. (E.g. *My favourite book is* War and Peace *by Leo Tolstoy. I love long historical novels. It is about life*, etc.) Ss will only be able to express very basic opinions about the various works of art.

EXTEND THE LEAD-IN
Ss imagine they are going to visit a famous capital city for the weekend, e.g. New York, Paris, Beijing, etc. Write the following things to do on the board: *go shopping, visit an art gallery, visit a museum, go to an expensive restaurant, go to local bars and clubs, go to the theatre, travel around the city on foot/by bus, etc., visit famous historical buildings, go to the zoo*. Ss rank the activities in order of preference. They do this individually first and then they discuss the various activities and compare preferences in small groups.

9.1 Making news

In this lesson, Ss read and listen to different opinions about trends and preferences in relation to news sources today. Ss express their own opinions about this and a range of other topics.

OPTIONAL WARMER

Bring a newspaper to class if you can. Elicit from Ss the different sections of the newspaper and write them on the board, e.g. *TV pages*, *international news*, *national news*, *sports section*, *classifieds*, etc. Ss work in pairs. They tell each other (1) which parts of the newspaper they would read first and (2) which parts they would not read.

Reading

1 ▶ Ss discuss the two questions with a partner. In feedback, elicit the big news stories at the moment. Discuss the different ways of finding out about the news with Ss. Elicit different news sources (radio, TV, newspaper, the Internet, etc.).

2a ▶ Ss look at the list of news sources in the first column of the table. They match the words to the photos in the text. They check answers in pairs, then as a whole class.

Answers
1 the radio
2 the Internet
3 mobile phone
4 newspapers
5 the TV

b ▶ Ss read the text quickly to find out which news sources the three people like. Point out that sometimes two preferences are mentioned. Ss check answers in pairs, then as a whole class. Ask: *Do you agree with Fuad/Katie/ Magnus?*

Answers
Fuad: newspapers and the radio
Katie: the Internet and TV
Magnus: mobile phone

c ▶ Direct Ss to the table. Teach *detailed* (a lot of information) and *convenient* (it is easy to find information in this way).

▶ Write *realistic*, *visual* and *old-fashioned* on the board and ask Ss to try to guess what these words mean as they read. Ss read the text again and complete the table. Ss call out the answers during feedback.

Answers
Newspapers: (detailed), easy, cheap
The radio: convenient, easy, cheap
The TV: exciting
The Internet: fast, detailed
Mobile phone: fast, convenient

Vocabulary | news sources

3a ▶ Ss complete the phrases with verbs from the box. Check answers.

Answers
1 read
2 watch
3 read
4 go
5 listen to
6 use

b ▶ Ss discuss the questions with a partner. Elicit Ss' opinions during feedback.

Grammar | comparison of adjectives

4 ▶ Direct Ss to the table in ex. 2a. Ask: *Which news sources are fast?* (the Internet, mobile phones) Ask: *Are newspapers fast?* (No.) Say and write on the board *The Internet is faster than newspapers*.

▶ Ss use the underlined words in the text to complete the first part of the Active grammar box. Ss check answers in pairs.

Active grammar

easier
more realistic
more exciting
better

▶ Ss read through the four rules in the second part of the Active grammar box. They find examples of each rule from the list. Ss check answers in pairs.

Answers
2 easier
3 more realistic, more exciting
4 better, worse

▶ Explain that only two-syllable adjectives which end in *-y* take *-er*. (*easier/funnier than*). Other two-syllable adjectives take *more ... than* (e.g. *more modern than*, *more polite than*).

▶ Direct Ss to the Reference section on page 97.

Pronunciation | /ə/ in comparatives

5a ▶ 🔘 2.21 Focus on the sentence stress of comparative sentences, especially the weak vowel sound. Write *The Internet is faster than newspapers* on the board. Underline the /ə/ sounds. Say the sentence for Ss.

▶ Play recording 2.21. Ss listen to the phrases and underline the /ə/ sounds. Ss check answers in pairs, then as a whole class. Ss practise saying the phrases.

Answers
2 faster than
3 colder than
4 healthier than

b ► Ss write the sentences and practise saying them with a partner. Monitor closely, correcting any pronunciation errors you hear.

Answers
1 Iceland is colder than Egypt.
2 Maths is easier than English.
3 Fruit is healthier than chocolate.
4 A Ferrari is faster than a Fiat.

► Direct Ss to the Pronunciation bank on page 148.

6 ► Ss complete the sentences by using the correct comparative form of an adjective and another news source. The sentences they make should express their own opinions. Ss compare sentences in pairs. Elicit one or two sentences for each news source during feedback.

OPTIONAL VARIATION

Elicit the names of ten people and things from Ss. Ss call out the first ones that come into their heads, e.g. Colin Farrell, eggs, football, apples, etc. The less obvious connection between the nouns the better. Ss work in small teams of three or four. They make as many sentences as they can comparing two of the nouns on the board. They cannot compare the same two things with each other twice and they cannot use the same adjective twice. Monitor closely, correcting any errors you hear. At the end, the team with the most sentences wins.

Listening and speaking

7a ► 🔵 2.22 Direct Ss to the three bullet points at the top of the reading text on page 90. Teach *percent* and (*presidential*) *election* which come up in the listening text. Ss read the bullet points again. Ask: *Do these figures surprise you? Why/Why not?*

► Tell Ss that they are going to listen to Petra and Nick discussing these facts and figures. Explain that Petra is female and Nick is male. Give Ss a few minutes to read the opinions before playing the recording.

► Play recording 2.22. Ss listen and match the opinion to the person.

Answers
1 P
2 N
3 N
4 P

b ► Ask: *Do Petra and Nick have exactly the same opinion?* (No.) Direct Ss to the audioscript on page 156. Play recording 2.22 again. Ss read and listen and then complete the expressions in the *How to...* box. Ss check answers in pairs, then as a whole class. Help with the intonation patterns for these sentences. Ss practise saying the expressions.

Answers
1 think
2 think
3 believe
4 don't
5 find
6 my

8 ► Ss look at the four topics: entertainment, music, sports and books. Direct them to the adjectives in the box but explain that they can use any adjectives they like to talk about the topics. Draw their attention to the suggested language in the sample dialogue.

► Ss work in pairs. They discuss the topics using the headings given for each one. Elicit Ss' preferences in relation to the topics during feedback.

OPTIONAL EXTENSION

Write on the board: *The* Washington Post *is more serious than* Hello! magazine. Ask: *Do you agree/disagree?* Elicit other serious type newspapers or magazines (e.g. *The Guardian*, *The New York Times*, *Time Magazine*, etc.). Elicit other tabloid-type magazines and newspapers (e.g. *The Daily Mirror*, *USA Today*, etc.). Include examples from Ss' own countries. Ss work in small groups and compare the two types of print media. Put the headings *types of stories, the truth, photos, style of writing, personal details* on the board to guide the discussion. Explain that there are no right or wrong sentences or opinions for this activity. Do not worry about Ss making mistakes as they try to express their opinions during this activity.

9.2 Movie magic

The Sundance Film Festival is the largest film festival in the United States and is held in Utah in January each year. The Festival chairman is the actor Robert Redford, who took the name from one of his most famous films, the 1969 western *Butch Cassidy and the Sundance Kid*, regularly rated as one of the most popular American films of all time. The Sundance Film Festival showcases independently made films.

In this lesson, Ss listen to a film critic giving her opinion about various films from the last ten years and read some interesting facts about films. Ss discuss different films and film genres.

OPTIONAL WARMER

Teach *ingredients* (the different things you need to make a particular recipe or dish). Elicit the ingredients of pizza or some other well-known dish. Write *horror film, a love story, a science fiction film* on the board. Ss work in pairs and list the typical ingredients of these types of films (e.g. horror film: blood, an evil person or monster, a beautiful girl alone, etc.). Write the suggestions on the board during feedback.

Vocabulary | films

1a ▶ Ss look at the four photos of different films. Elicit the names of the four films. Ss match the film genre to the film. They check answers in pairs, then as a whole class.

Answers
A (*War of the Worlds*, 1953 version) a science fiction film
B (*Pink Panther 2*) a comedy
C (*The Fugitive*) a thriller
D (*Dracula*) a horror film

b ▶ In pairs, Ss think of one film for each of the genres in the box.

c ▶ Ss use the adjectives to describe the different film genres. Teach *scary* (makes you afraid), *romantic* (about love) and *violent* (a lot of fighting and killing in the film). A great deal of overlap is possible here. Focus on the pronunciation of these words.

Possible answers
sad: a love story, a documentary
exciting: an action/adventure film, a horror film, a thriller, a science fiction film
violent: horror, thriller, action/adventure, documentary
clever: science fiction, comedy and thriller
funny: comedy, a cartoon, but other genres also
scary: horror, thriller, science fiction
romantic: love story, a musical
happy: comedy, love story, musical, cartoon
interesting: documentary, any of the films

2 ▶ Ss discuss the types of film they like and dislike and explain why.

Listening

3a ▶ 🔵 2.23 Ss look at film titles in the box. Elicit which genre these films might fall into. Ss may not have seen the films but may know about them. Go through the list of opinions first to ensure Ss understand the vocabulary. Teach *foreign film* (in Hollywood, this means not in English), a *fresh* musical (new, modern, different). Avoid any overt focus on the superlatives yet.

▶ Play recording 2.23. Ss listen and match the film to the opinion of Mariela. Ss check answers in pairs, then as a whole class.

Answers
An Inconvenient Truth 3
Casino Royale 2
Chicago 7
Little Miss Sunshine 6
No Country for Old Men 5
Slumdog Millionaire 1
The Lives of Others 4

b ▶ Play the recording again. Ss listen and correct the mistakes. Ss check answers with a partner, then as a whole class.

Answers
1 the *Lord of the Rings* series (not the *Harry Potter* series)
2 *Slumdog Millionaire* (not *Casino Royale*)
3 a documentary (not a thriller)
4 a bad guy (not a good man)
5 doesn't usually like musicals (not loves musicals)

c ▶ Ss match the words from the listening text to the meanings.

Answers
1 e
2 a
3 d
4 b
5 c

4 ▶ Elicit Ss' opinions about the films which Mariela talked about. Ask: *Do you agree with Mariela?*

Grammar | superlative adjectives

5a ▶ Ss look at the example sentence and then match it to the correct meaning. Ss check answers in pairs, then as a whole class.

Answer
2

b ▶ Ss use the superlative adjectives from ex. 3a to complete the Active grammar box.

> **Active grammar**
>
> most exciting
> freshest
> funniest
> best
> most violent

▶ Direct Ss to the rules at the bottom of the Active grammar box. Ask Ss: *What about two-syllable adjectives?* When they end in *-y*, we drop the *-y* and add *-iest*, e.g. *funny – funniest*. For other two-syllable adjectives, we use *the most*, e.g. *famous – the most famous, polite – the most polite*. Emphasise the use of the definite article in superlatives ('Slumdog Millionaire *is best film*' is incorrect). Focus on the typical sentence stress used in superlative sentences: *It's the most exciting film, It's the freshest musical.*

▶ Direct Ss to the Reference section on page 97.

6a ▶ Ss write superlative sentences using the prompts. They check answers in pairs, then as a whole class.

> **Answers**
> 1 the funniest
> 2 the scariest
> 3 the best
> 4 the most handsome
> 5 the most beautiful
> 6 the most romantic

b ▶ Ss make changes to the sentences so that they express their true opinions. Ss compare sentences with a partner. Elicit one or two sentences for each superlative during feedback.

> **OPTIONAL EXTENSION**
>
> Ss discuss the following questions with a partner: *What makes you decide to go to a particular film? What is your favourite time of day/day of the week to go to the cinema? Who do you like to go with? Do you usually buy popcorn, ice cream, etc., when you go to the cinema?*

Reading and speaking

7 ▶ Ss look at the list of superlatives in the table. Elicit suggestions for the answers but do not give any feedback yet.

▶ Ss work in groups of three, A, B and C. Each student is given a text to read which contains three of the answers to the table. Student A reads the text on page 131, Student B reads the text on page 132 and Student C reads the text on page 93.

▶ Direct Ss to the suggested language in the sample dialogue. They ask and answer questions in order to complete the table. Ss should give any extra information they have found about each film.

> **Answers**
> longest film: *The Cure for Insomnia*
> most expensive film: *Pirates of the Caribbean: At World's End*
> earliest film with sound: *The Jazz Singer*
> most successful cartoon: *Shrek 2*
> richest film star: Julia Roberts (female) and Tom Cruise (male)
> youngest Oscar winner: Tatum O'Neal
> most romantic love story: *Casablanca*
> scariest horror film: *Psycho*
> worst villain in a film: Hannibal Lecter

8 ▶ Ss discuss the questions in pairs. Compare Ss' suggestions for part 2 in feedback.

> **OPTIONAL EXTENSION**
>
> Conduct an *Academy Awards of all time* in class. Elicit nominations for different categories. Limit the nominations to about four or five names. Suggested categories are: *Best Film ever, Best Actor, Best Actress.* (You can elicit suggestions from Ss for other categories.) Write the nominations for each category on the board and ask Ss to vote. Collect the votes and ask two Ss to count the votes for each category and to announce the winner (e.g. *The nominations for Best Film ever were … And the winner is …*).

9.3 Popular culture

Banksy is the pseudonym of an English graffiti artist, thought to be from Bristol. He works hard to preserve his anonymity and his real identity remains unknown even though he has been exhibiting street art and graffiti since the late 1980s. His art is characterised by a distinctive style of stencilling and often focuses on political and ethical themes. People travelled from all over the world to see the first gallery exhibition of his works, at Bristol Art Gallery in 2009. His first film, *Exit Through the Gift Shop*, premiered at the Sundance Film Festival in 2010. Even though Banksy himself features in the film, his face is never seen and his voice is distorted so that his identity remains unknown.

In this lesson, Ss read about the artist known as Banksy and listen to a short conversation about art. Ss discuss their preferences in relation to art and cultural activities.

OPTIONAL WARMER

Elicit the name of some famous artists and sculptors and some of their works. Write the suggestions on the board. Ss work in pairs. Ask: *What is your favourite work of art?* Ss discuss in pairs.

Reading

1 ▶ Ss look at the pictures and discuss the questions. Elicit their opinions on the pictures as 'art'.

2a ▶ Scanning: Explain to Ss that they will read the text twice, the first time very quickly and the second time much more slowly. Direct them to the heading and tell them they have one minute to match the art described in the text to one of the pictures. Explain that they do not need to understand the text fully at this point. Stop the activity after one minute.

Answer
Picture A

b ▶ Ss read the text more slowly, focusing on evidence for the five statements. Teach *scary* (makes you afraid). Ss read the text and decide whether the statements are true or false. Ss check answers in pairs, then as a whole class.

Answers
1 F
2 T
3 F
4 T
5 F

c ▶ Ss find the words in the text and read them in context. They match the words to the definitions given. Ss check answers in pairs, then as a whole class.

Answers
1 b
2 d
3 f
4 e
5 a
6 c

3 ▶ Direct Ss to the title of the text and the photos on page 94. Conduct a whole-class discussion based on the three questions. Elicit Ss' views and opinions in relation to what constitutes 'art' and 'popular culture'.

OPTIONAL VARIATION

Elicit the kind of places you would usually find graffiti (walls, the underground, etc.) and the kind of people who do it. Ss work in groups of three or four. They discuss the following: *Is graffiti art? Why/Why not?* (E.g. *No, it makes the streets look dirty/Yes, it is street art. Graffiti artists are very skilful*, etc.) Do not worry about Ss making mistakes during this discussion but encourage them to express their views as best they can.

Listening

4a ▶ 2.24 Ask Ss: *Would you like to go to see the Banksy exhibition?* Play recording 2.24. Ss listen and identify the two photos matching what they mention in the conversation.

Answers
A, E

b ▶ Play the recording a second time. Ss listen and write the name of the speaker beside the activity they like. Ss check answers in pairs, then as a whole class.

Answers
1 S
2 S
3 J
4 S
5 J

Pronunciation | *yes/no* questions

5a ▶ 2.25 Ss focus on the two questions from the recording in ex. 4. Play recording 2.25. Ss listen and note whether the voice goes up or down at the end in each sentence. Ss check answers in pairs, then as a whole class.

Answer
The voice goes up at the end in both questions.

b ▶ 2.26 Ss look at the six sentences. Establish that some are questions and some are answers. Play recording 2.26. Ss listen and note whether the voice goes up or down at the end. Ss check answers in pairs, then as a whole class.

Answers
The voice goes up in the questions (1, 3, 5, 6) and down in the answers (2, 4).

▶ Play the recording again and Ss repeat the sentences. Ask: *What kind of questions are these?* (*yes/no* questions, not question-word questions)

c ▶ Ss make sentences using the prompts and practise saying them in pairs.

Answers
1 Is it cheap?
2 Is it new?
3 Does she smoke?
4 Do they work?

▶ Direct Ss to the Pronunciation bank on page 148.

Grammar | *like/love/hate/prefer*

6 ▶ Write the word *prefer* on the board. Say the word but do not explain what it means or how to use it yet. Ss look at ex. 4b and focus on (1) how *prefer* is used and (2) what it means. They choose the correct option to complete the Active grammar box. Explain that they can tick more than one answer in no. 1. Ss check answers in pairs, then as a whole class.

Active grammar
1 a, c
   going to, listening
2 a
   to

▶ Write I prefer traditional paintings to modern ones; I like going to exhibitions and I hate watching talent programmes on TV on the board. Focus on the underlined words.

▶ Direct Ss to the Reference section on page 97.

7a ▶ Ss work in pairs. They take turns to ask each other about what they like doing, using the prompts given. Elicit one or two questions and answers in feedback.

b ▶ Ss work in pairs. They take turns to ask each other about their preferences using the prompts. Elicit one or two questions and answers during feedback.

c ▶ Ss look at the audioscript on page 156 and complete the *How to...* box. Ss check answers in pairs, then as a whole class.

Answers
1 like/love
2 hate
3 prefer
4 prefer
5 more

Speaking

8a ▶ Ss work in pairs. Try to ensure they are working in different pairs from ex. 7. They discuss the three questions. Encourage them to use both *prefer ... to ...* and *like ... more than ...* in their answers.

b ▶ Ss stand up and move around the room. They talk to other Ss in the class and ask and answer about their preferences based on the four questions in their books. Ss must give a reason for their preferences.

▶ Conduct a class survey for feedback. Put the four headings on the board, leaving a space to add the number beside each activity. Ask: *How many of you prefer museums? How many of you prefer concerts?* and so on. Write the number beside the activity.

OPTIONAL EXTENSION
Ss write a short report based on the results of the survey in ex. 8b, e.g. *In our class, X students prefer going to concerts to going to museums*, etc.

9 Communication

In this lesson, Ss arrange a group outing for the next evening.

OPTIONAL WARMER

Write up a list of things to do in your free time: *shopping, the cinema, a restaurant, the pub, a nightclub, the swimming pool, a sports event, a concert.* Ss categorise the activities into things you usually do during the day and things you usually do in the evening. Some things, e.g. the cinema, can be both. Ask Ss about their preferred times for these activities.

1a ▶ Ss make a list of things they usually do on Saturdays with a partner.

b ▶ ⚫ 2.27 Ss look at the list of activities. Explain that column 1 relates to ex. 1b and column 2 relates to ex. 1c. Play recording 2.27. Ss listen and tick the things the friends talk about under column 1. Ss check answers in pairs. Do not give class feedback until after ex. 1c.

Answers
go to a football match
go to the cinema
see a band
have dinner
They decide to see a band.

c ▶ Ss order the activities under column 2. Check answers as a whole class.

Answers
go to the cinema 1
have dinner 2
go to a football match 3
see a band 4

2 ▶ Play the recording again. Ss read the audioscript on page 157 as they listen and complete the *How to...* box. Ss check answers in pairs, then as a whole class.

Answers
1 to the cinema
2 going out
3 don't (we) go
4 great idea
5 good
6 think
7 don't
8 meet

▶ Ask: *What happens to the verb after* How about... *and* What about... ? (-ing form) *What happens to the verb after* Why don't we... *and* Let's... ? (infinitive without *to*)

▶ Explain that the question forms used to make suggestions are not really questions. We do not respond to *Why don't we go to the cinema?* with *Because...*, but instead we use one of the responses in the *How to...* box.

3a ▶ Ss focus on the list of places. Ss match four places to the pictures.

Answers
a 1 Cinderella
b 4 The Waterfront Restaurant
g 2 Roxy's Nightclub
h 3 Amuse

b ▶ Ss take turns to make and respond to suggestions based on the prompts in ex. 3a. Encourage Ss to use different language for suggestions each time.

4a ▶ Ss work alone. They rank the list according to which activity they prefer.

b ▶ Ensure Ss are working with a new partner, not the same one as in ex. 3b. Direct Ss to the example given. Ss compare lists in pairs and discuss their preferences.

5 ▶ Ss work in small groups of four or five. They organise an evening out together, which all members of the group will enjoy. They first agree on an activity and then choose a location in the area. Finally, they agree on a time and place to meet.

OPTIONAL EXTENSION

Ss write an email to a friend with information about the arrangement for tomorrow evening and asking him/her to come.

---

9 Review and practice

1 ▶

Answers
1 taller
2 more handsome
3 fitter
4 fatter
5 happier
6 darker
7 shorter

2 ▶

Answers
2 worse, the worst
3 more beautiful,
   the most beautiful
4 busier, the busiest
5 drier, the driest
6 fitter, the fittest
7 better, the best
8 more informal,
   the most informal
9 noisier, the noisiest
10 more private,
   the most private

3a ▶

Answers
1 f
2 a
3 e
4 g
5 b
6 c
7 h
8 d

b ▶

Answers
2 Kilimanjaro is the highest mountain in Africa.
3 The Great Wall of China is the biggest structure in the world.
4 Edvard Grieg is the most famous Norwegian composer.
5 The Bugatti Veyron is the most expensive car.
6 The Hermitage is the largest museum in the world.
7 Denmark's is the oldest national flag.
8 *Psycho* is the scariest film.

4 ▶

Answers
1 ... prefer watching television
2 ... love reading adventure books
3 ... more than science fiction ones
4 ... hate living in the country
5 ... I prefer driving my car
6 I like playing the guitar more than listening
7 Dario prefers swimming ...
8 ... likes cooking Indian food

5 ▶

Answers
1 a play
2 a painting
3 classical music
4 an opera
5 a horror film
6 a novel
7 a ballet
8 rock music

6 ▶

Answers
1 comedy
2 horror film
3 science fiction
4 action film
5 love story
6 musical

9 Writing bank

1a ▶

Answers
1 when he was four
2 his family travelled a lot; he acted in a TV series from the age of six
3 singer, waiter, salesman, many other jobs, including work in the theatre
4 *LA Confidential*
5 near Sydney, Australia

b ▶

Answer
b

2 ▶

Answers
similar
a paragraph 2
b paragraph 3
c paragraph 1
d paragraph 4

3 ▶

Answers
She also appeared in music videos when she was a teenager should be in paragraph 2.
Other famous films include 'A Mighty Heart' and 'Changeling' should be in paragraph 3.
Jolie also has adopted children from different countries should be in paragraph 4.
Her parents were actors should be in paragraph 1.

4a ▶ Ss' own answers

b ▶ Ss put their notes into the four groups:

– early life

– first acting/sports/music, other jobs

– famous films/songs, achievements

– personal life

▶ *Ss* write their biography.

10 Journeys

Overview

Lead-in	Revision: Means of transport
10.1	Can do: Book a train ticket Grammar: *-ing* form as noun Vocabulary: Transport Speaking and Pronunciation: How to... book a train ticket Roleplay: booking a ticket Listening and Reading: Commuters around the world Listening: Booking a train ticket
10.2	Can do: Describe personal experiences Grammar: Present Perfect with *been*: *I/we/you/they* Speaking and Pronunciation: /ɪ/ *Have you ...* Listening and Reading: An adventure
10.3	Can do: Talk about other people's experiences Grammar: Present Perfect: *he/she/it* Vocabulary: Activities Speaking and Pronunciation: Long and short vowels Personal experiences Listening: A TV chat show
Communication	Give and follow simple directions How to... ask for and give directions
Reference	
Review and Practice	
Writing bank	Write a description of an event How to... join sentences (4): *first, later, in the end*

CEFR Can do objectives
10.1 Book a train ticket
10.2 Describe personal experiences
10.3 Talk about other people's experiences
Communication Give and follow simple directions
Writing bank Write a description of an event

CEFR Portfolio ideas
a) When did you get angry most recently? Write a story explaining why you were angry and saying what you did.
b) A famous adventurer is speaking on the TV/Radio and invites listeners to phone in. Phone the programme and ask your questions or make your comment. Write the dialogue. Record the dialogue with your partner.
c) Write an imaginary short story about an event. Your short story should include:
   i. a mobile telephone
   ii. a piece of food
   iii. a baseball glove
   iv. a woman with brown eyes
   Share your story with the class. Choose the best story.

Lead-in

OPTIONAL WARMER
Write *air travel, rail travel, road travel, sea travel* on the board. Elicit the different modes of transport associated with each (e.g. airplane, helicopter; train, underground, tram; car, bicycle, walking; boat, ferry, etc.) Ss work in pairs. They tell their partner about (1) their journey to class and (2) their journey to visit their parents/ grandparents/relatives. Write the following questions on the board to guide their discussion: *Which mode of transport do you take? How long does it take? How often do you take this journey?*

1 ▶ Ss focus on vocabulary. They match the words 1–5 to their meanings a–e. Explain that *park* is a verb in this exercise. Ss check answers in pairs, then as a whole class.

Answers		
1 b	2 e 3 d	4 c 5 a

2 ▶ Ss look at the four photos and then match them with the captions in pairs.

Answers		
1 B	2 C 3 A	4 D

▶ Ask: *Which commuter has the most pleasant journey, do you think?* Ss give their opinions.

3 ▶ Ss find the forms of transport in the photos. Ss check answers in pairs, then as a whole class.

Answers	
A bicycle	C bus, car, motorbike
B plane	D underground train

▶ Say the words and Ss note the word stress in each word. Focus on the /ʌ/ sound in *suburbs* and *rush hour*.

4 ▶ Ss look at the three headings in the table. They put the words in the box into the correct columns. Some words can go into more than one column.

Answers
Air: flight, journey, passenger, plane, ticket
Rail: journey, passenger, platform, station, ticket, train
Road: car, drive, garage, journey, park, passenger, traffic

5 ▶ Ss tell their partners about their journey to work/ college. Ask: *How many of you travel to work by car/train, etc.?* in feedback

97

10.1 Cycle city

New York is well known for its yellow taxis and London for its black ones, often called taxicabs. Nowadays London cabs are often covered in advertising and can be of different colours. You don't bargain with taxi drivers about the fare, especially once the journey has been completed, but it is customary to tip them. London taxi drivers have to pass a test known as 'the Knowledge' in order to demonstrate that they are familiar with the different areas of the city. A 'For hire' light is visible when a taxi is available for customers and you can hail these cabs from the street by waving or raising your arm. In a taxi rank where customers and taxis queue in line, it is important to wait your turn.

In this lesson, Ss read about and listen to commuters describing their journey to work. They also listen to someone booking a train ticket to Paris. Ss compare different modes of transport in groups and practise booking a train ticket in pairs.

OPTIONAL WARMER

Write *public transport* on the board. Elicit different types of public transport – bus, taxi, tram, etc. Ask Ss: *Do most people use public transport in your country? Why/Why not?* Ss work in pairs and list three reasons why people choose to use public transport and three reasons why they don't. (E.g. *Public transport is cheaper*; *It is better for the environment*; *It can be very slow*, etc.)

Vocabulary | transport

1a ▶ Ss match the mode of transport to the places in pairs. They then find the mode of transport in the photos.

Answers
2 f
3 e
4 a
5 c
6 b

▶ Elicit whether Ss have been to these cities and used these modes of transport.

b ▶ Ss create word maps using the three headings given. Ss can use their dictionaries for this exercise.

Possible answers
Air: plane, hot-air balloon, ...
Water: ferry, boat, gondola, ...
Land: car, bicycle, bus, ...
Ss can choose their own answers.

Reading and listening

2 ▶ Ss focus on photos A and D discuss the questions. Use the photos to teach *rush hour* and *crowded* which come up in the text.

3a ▶ Explain to Ss that they will read the text twice, the first time very quickly and the second time much more slowly. Tell them they have one minute to match the text to two of the photos as quickly as possible. Explain that they do not need to understand the text fully at this point. Stop the activity after one minute and Ss call out the answers.

Answers
D (underground in São Paulo) and B (cycling in Amsterdam)

b ▶ Ss read the texts more slowly, this time focusing on the table. Review *convenient* (easy to use or do) and teach *flat* (no hills or mountains). Ss read through the text and complete the first half of the table. Ss check answers in pairs. Do not give whole-class feedback until Ss have completed the table after the listening exercise.

Answers
Fatima: D; São Paulo; underground/Metro; crowded, often can't find a seat
Jan: B; Amsterdam; cycling; very cheap

4 ▶ 2.28 Teach *Miami* (the pronunciation of this American city might be difficult for Ss) and *rollerblading* (using special shoes with wheels). Play recording 2.28. Ss listen and complete the second half of the table (Julia and Billy). Ss check answers in pairs.

▶ Draw the table on the board, elicit and write in the answers to ex. 3b and 4.

Answers
Julia: small photo at bottom of page; Miami; costs nothing, healthy, enjoyable; dangerous on busy roads, tiring
Billy: C; London; bus; easier than the car, not expensive; sometimes slow, waiting for the bus is boring

Speaking

5 ▶ Ss work in small groups of three or four. They use the questions to talk about different modes of transport and decide which one is the best way of commuting to work.

OPTIONAL EXTENSION

Ss imagine that the government is trying to encourage people not to take their cars to work because of the traffic problems. It would like people to use the bus and metro or to cycle and rollerblade to work instead. Ss work in small groups of three or four. They think of different ways to encourage commuters to use these methods of getting to work by making the four modes of transport safer, faster, more comfortable, etc. Encourage Ss to be imaginative in their ideas. Do not worry about Ss making mistakes during this activity.

Grammar | -ing form as noun

6 ▶ Elicit the four forms of transport from the reading and listening texts, *The bus/The metro/Rollerblading/Cycling*, and write them on the board in a vertical line. Ask: *What kind of words are these, nouns, verbs, adjectives?* (nouns) Use the four words as subject nouns in sentences based on Ss' opinions in ex. 5, e.g. *The bus is the cheapest way to get to work. The metro is the most comfortable way to get to work. Rollerblading is the most enjoyable way to get to work. Cycling is the quickest way to get to work.*

▶ Ss look at the examples in the Active grammar box. They then find and underline two examples in the text. Ss choose the correct word to complete the sentences.

Active grammar

is   Parking

▶ We can use the *-ing* form of the verb as a noun. We don't use the articles (*a/an* or *the*) with this type of noun. *The cycling is the quickest way to get to work* is incorrect. The *-ing* form as a noun is uncountable and takes a singular verb after it. (*Cycling are dangerous* is incorrect.)

▶ When pronouncing these nouns, the *-ing* is always unstressed.

▶ Direct Ss to the Reference section on page 107.

7 ▶ Ss choose the correct word to complete the sentences. Ss check answers in pairs, then as a whole class.

Answers		2	Bicycles	4	Taxis
1	Parking	3	is	5	is

Listening

OPTIONAL LEAD-IN TO THE LISTENING

Teach *standard* (cheapest seats) and *first class* (more expensive seats) on a train. Ask: *Which way do you travel?* Ss work in pairs. They use comparative adjectives to compare the two types of ticket. Write *food, service, seats, facilities, leg room* on the board to prompt points of comparison.

8a ▶ ⬤ 2.29 Ss look at the questions. Play recording 2.29. Ss listen and answer the questions. They check answers in pairs, then as a whole class.

Answers
1 Paris
2 Friday, June 5th
3 £280 for four return tickets
4 £20

b ▶ Ss look at the vocabulary from the listening text and match the words to their meanings. Check answers as a whole class.

Answers		4	g
1	c	5	b
2	f	6	d
3	a	7	e

▶ Ask Ss to identify the word stress in each word/phrase. Point out that the stress falls on the second syllable in both *direct* and *return*; *destination* and *economy* are both four-syllable words but the word stress is different in each.

c ▶ Teach *to book* (to ask someone to keep something for you, e.g. a table in a restaurant, tickets to the theatre). Ss read the audioscript on page 157. Play the recording as they read. Ss read and complete the *How to...* box. Ss check answers in pairs, then as a whole class.

Answers
1 tickets
2 want
3 time
4 direct
5 much
6 like

▶ Ss practise saying the sentences.

▶ Review the use of *would* in *I'd like to go, I'd like four tickets. I like four tickets* is incorrect in this context.

9 ▶ Ss work in pairs. They complete the dialogue by using the vocabulary from ex. 8b and 8c. Check answers as a whole class.

Answers
1 tickets
2 like
3 return
4 class
5 How
6 direct

▶ Ss practise the dialogue in pairs.

10 ▶ Ss conduct the roleplay in pairs. Student A works in a travel agency and Student B is a customer. Student A looks at the information on page 131 and Student B looks at the information on page 101. Give Ss time to read the information and find out what they have to do. Ss work in pairs. Student B finds out about the different options from Student A and decides which train to take.

▶ In feedback, establish which was the most popular train and why.

OPTIONAL EXTENSION

Ask Ss to use the Internet to find the cheapest fare from Dublin to London (Gatwick) return next weekend. Tell them they want to fly to London on Friday afternoon (after 1 p.m.) and return to Dublin on Sunday evening (before 10 p.m.). www.ryanair.com and www.airlingus.com are two websites to check out.

10.2 Experiences

In this lesson, Ss read part of a TV guide and listen to an extract from one of the programmes. This is an interview with four friends who are about to go on an adventure holiday to Australia. Ss ask and answer about activities they have done/not done before.

OPTIONAL WARMER

Ss work in pairs. They decide which is (1) the most exciting sport, (2) the most disgusting food, (3) the most interesting country to visit and (4) the most beautiful place in the world.

Reading and listening

1a ▶ Ss scan through the text to match the TV programmes with the photos. Ss check answers in pairs, then as a whole class.

Answers
The Countryside Today: C and D
The Holiday Show: B
Extreme Sports Challenge: A

b ▶ Elicit Ss' views on the different activities. Ensure Ss know what *a long-haul flight* means. Elicit which of the three programmes Ss would like to watch.

OPTIONAL EXTENSION

Write *negative results*, *experience of a lifetime*, *afraid of heights* on the board. Ss read the TV guide again and try to guess what these words mean in the text.
negative results: bad consequences
experience of a lifetime: something good that will only happen once or twice in your life
afraid of heights: when you find it scary to be high up

2a ▶ ⊕ 2.30 Play recording 2.30. Explain that it is part of one of the TV programmes. Ss listen and decide which one. They check answers in pairs, then as a whole class.

Answer
The Holiday Show

b ▶ Ask: *What words describes how the friends are feeling about the trip to Australia?* (Excited, nervous, etc.) *Why?* (It is new for them. It is the first time for them.) Ss read the sentence and answer the question.

Answer
Yes

▶ Explain that *I haven't been ... before* means that this is his first time.

c ▶ Ss look at the table. Play the recording again. Ss listen and tick the activities which each student has done before. They check answers in pairs, then as a whole class.

Answers
Moira: long-haul flight
Derek: hiking
Todd: horse-riding
Alicia: visit America

Grammar | Present Perfect with *been*:
I/you/we/they

3a ▶ Ss focus on the four sentences from the recording. Ask: *Who said each sentence?* (a Derek; b the interviewer; c Derek; d Todd)

▶ Ss look at the three questions about the sentences and answer them in pairs. Write the answers on the board during feedback and underline the Present Perfect in each one.

Answers
1 d, two years ago
2 a, b, c
3 Present Perfect

b ▶ Ss turn to the audioscript on page 157. Play the recording again. Ss read as they listen and then complete the Active grammar box, starting with the chart. Ss check answers in pairs.

Active grammar
Affirmative: been
Negative: haven't been
Question: you been
Short answers: haven't

▶ Ss choose the correct words to complete the rules in the box. Ss check answers in pairs.

Answers
1 any time up to now
2 past participle

▶ Focus on the first example sentence, *We've been to America.* Ask: *Did they go to America in the past?* (Yes.) *In this sentence do we know when they went to America?* (No.) *Can they go to America again?* (Yes.) Explain that we use the Present Perfect to talk about actions that happened at some point in the past. We don't specify exactly when. *He has been to America last year* is incorrect because *last year* tells us exactly when he went to America.

▶ Stress that it doesn't matter how long ago the action happened (it is not necessarily the recent past), but there must be the possibility of doing it again.

▶ Focus on the weak pronunciation of the contracted form. Explain that we don't use the past participle in the short answer form (*Yes, I have/No, I haven't*, not *Yes, I have been/No, I haven't been*).

▶ Direct Ss to the Reference section on page 107.

OPTIONAL EXTENSION

Write the following time expressions on the board: *two years ago, in my life, when I was 16, yesterday, ever, before*. Ss work in pairs and categorise the expressions into (1) ones we use with the Past Simple and (2) ones we use with the Present Perfect. Ask: *Why?*
Answers:
(1) Past Simple: two years ago, when I was 16, yesterday
(2) Present Perfect: in my life, ever, before
The time expressions in (1) tell us an exact time in the past. The time expressions in (2) do not specify a time in the past but encompass all past time up to now.

4a ▶ Ss complete the questions and answers using the Present Perfect. Ss check answers in pairs, then as a whole class.

Answers
1 been, have
2 Have, haven't
3 Have, went

---

b ▶ Ss find and correct the mistakes with a partner. Check answers.

Answers
1 I haven't been bungee jumping before.
2 They haven't been to Scotland.
3 Have you been to a classical concert?
4 We haven't been on an adventure holiday before.
5 I haven't been to Brazil.
6 Have they been hiking before?

Pronunciation | /ɪ/

5a ▶ ● 2.31 Write *India* and *Greece* on the board. Say the words and write the phonetic symbol /ɪ/ under *India* and the symbol /iː/ under *Greece*. Say the two sounds.

▶ Ss look at the two sentences. Play recording 2.31. Ss listen and identify the sound of the underlined words. Ss check answers in pairs, then as a whole class.

Answer
/iː/

---

b ▶ ● 2.32 Ss look at the four sentences. First they predict where the four /ɪ/ sounds will be in each sentence with a partner. Play recording 2.32. Ss listen and identify where the four /ɪ/ sounds actually are. Check in pairs, then as a whole class.

Answers
1 Have you been to the <u>ci</u>nema <u>in</u> <u>Eng</u>land?
2 I've been to a <u>di</u>sco <u>with</u> <u>him</u>.
3 Have they been to <u>di</u>nner <u>in</u> <u>Fin</u>land?
4 We haven't been to Pa<u>ris</u> <u>in</u> <u>spring</u>.

▶ Direct Ss to the Pronunciation bank on page 148.

6 ▶ Ss look at the photos in ex. 1 again and write questions. Then they take turns to practise asking and answering the questions with a partner. Monitor closely, correcting any errors you hear.

Answers
Have you been bungee jumping?
Have you been on a long-haul flight?
Have you been hiking?
Have you been horse-riding?
Yes, I have./No, I haven't.

Speaking

7 ▶ Divide the class into As, Bs and Cs. As look at page 131, Bs look at page 134 and Cs look at page 103. Each group has a different list of activities. Give Ss time to check the meaning of the activities on their list with other members of their group.

▶ When they are ready, Ss mingle, asking the other Ss if they have been to the places on their list. If the answer is *No*, they move on to the next student but if the answer is *Yes*, they must ask the follow-on question *Did you like it?* Stop the activity when each student has spoken to about five others in the class.

10.3 Adventurers!

Two of the most famous British adventurers are Victorian explorers Dr David Livingstone (1813–1873) and Henry Morton Stanley (1841–1904). Livingstone, a Scottish missionary, was based in Africa but had not been heard of for some time. In 1869, Stanley was commissioned to mount an expedition to find him. Two years later, Stanley eventually found Livingstone in Ujiji, in present-day Tanzania, where he is said to have greeted the missionary with the famous line 'Dr Livingstone, I presume?'.

In this lesson, Ss listen to part of a TV chat show about modern-day adventurers and listen to people talking about unusual experiences. Ss ask and answer about unusual experiences they and their friends/family have had.

OPTIONAL WARMER

Put the following headings on the board: *Sail solo around the world*, *Travel to the South Pole on foot*, *Climb Mt Everest without oxygen*, *Run across the Sahara Desert*. Ss work in pairs. They think of reasons why people choose to do these kind of activities. Ask: *Would you like to do any of these things?* in feedback.

Vocabulary | activities

1a ▶ Ss match the photos to activities in the box.

Answers
flying a small aircraft
flying in a hot-air balloon
walking to the South Pole

b ▶ Ss match the verbs to the phrases. Ss check answers in pairs, then as a whole class.

Answers
1 c
2 e
3 b
4 a
5 d

c ▶ Ss describe their experiences to others in the class.

Listening

2 ▶ 🔘 2.33 Explain to Ss that you will play the recording several times and that it will help to understand if they focus on different questions each time. Ss look at ex. 2. Play recording 2.33. Ss listen and decide what they think an adventurer is.

Suggested answer
someone who chooses to do unusual, exciting activities in exotic locations

3a ▶ Ss look at the list of activities. Play the recording again. Ss listen and note the things Ben Fogle has not done.

Answers
2 and 5

b ▶ Play the recording again. Ss listen and complete the chart.

Answers
Atlantic: 2006, 50 days, 2,500 km
Sahara: 2004, 7 days, 200 km
Monaco: 1993, 9 days
Kilimanjaro: 2006

Grammar | Present Perfect: *he/she/it*

4 ▶ Ss look at the extracts from the interview and match the questions to the answers.

Answers
1 d
2 a
3 c
4 b

5 ▶ Write *He's climbed Kilimanjaro* and *He's taken a trip* on the board. Ask: *What verb forms are these?* (Present Perfect) *Which verb is regular?* (he's climbed – -ed ending) *Which is irregular?* (he's taken – no -ed ending)

▶ Ss focus on verb forms in italics in ex. 4. Direct Ss to the chart in the Active grammar box. Ss add those verb forms to the chart. Ss then complete the sentences in the box. Ss check answers in pairs, then as a whole class.

Active grammar

Regular verbs: rowed, cycled, walked, sailed
Irregular verbs: done, won, run, heard
1 has, have
2 Regular

▶ Explain that most verbs are regular but many commonly used verbs (*eat, sleep, drink*, etc.) are irregular. Some irregular past participles (e.g. *bought, slept*) are the same as the irregular Past Simple forms but others (e.g. *drunk, seen*) are different. Encourage Ss to note down Past Simple and past participle forms of irregular verbs as they learn them.

▶ Point out that the past participle (e.g. *been*) never changes. The auxiliary verb (*to have*) can be *have* (*I/we/you/they*) or *has* (*he/she/it*).

▶ Direct Ss to the Reference section on page 107 and to the Irregular verbs list on page 149.

6 ▶ Ss write the correct form of the verbs in brackets to complete the text. Ss check answers in pairs, then as a whole class.

Answers
2 has climbed
3 has left
4 has lived
5 has crossed
6 has sailed
7 has written

7a ▶ Ss use the prompts to make sentences using the Present Perfect.

Answers
1 Lucinda has not left school.
2 Kathy has won a competition.
3 Sanjeev has visited an African country.
4 Piotr has not stayed in a five-star hotel.

b ▶ Ss use the verbs in ex. 7a to ask and answer questions about themselves. Draw Ss' attention to the sample dialogue before they start.

OPTIONAL EXTENSION
Ss stand up to form a circle. Call out the base form of verbs, both regular and irregular, to Ss in turn. The student immediately responds with the past participle form of the verb (e.g. T: *make*; St: *made*). This should be done in a quick and snappy way. When a student doesn't know the past participle form, he or she sits down and the next student answers. The last student left standing is the Past Participle Champion!

Pronunciation | long and short vowels

8a ▶ 🔊 2.34 Write *ship* and *sheep* on the board. Say the two words and ask Ss *Which sound is longer?* (the /iː/ in *sheep*) Write the short /ɪ/ sound under *ship* and the long /iː/ sound under *sheep* and explain that /ː/ in the symbol tells us that the sound is a long sound. Ss focus on the two lists. Play recording 2.34. Ss listen and repeat the words.

b ▶ 🔊 2.35 Ss look at the six pairs of words. They decide which word has a long vowel sound and which a short vowel sound. Play recording 2.35. Ss listen and underline the word they hear from each pair. Ss check answers in pairs, then as a whole class.

Answers
1 have
2 fit
3 short
4 park
5 bald
6 sleep

▶ Direct Ss to the Pronunciation bank on page 147.

Listening and speaking

9a ▶ 🔊 2.36 Ss look at the list of experiences and guess the missing words. Ss compare with a partner. Play recording 2.36. Ss listen and complete the phrases with a past participle and other information.

Answers
2 stayed, star
3 flown, balloon
4 eaten
5 played, sport

b ▶ Direct Ss to the sample dialogue. Give Ss a few minutes to think of questions to ask their partner, using the verbs in the box to help them. Ss work in pairs. They take turns to ask and answer questions about their experiences.

OPTIONAL VARIATION
Ss work in pairs. They think of six questions about unusual experiences to ask other Ss. Ss re-form into groups of five. Each student from the original pairs should join a different group. Ss ask and answer their questions in groups.

10 Communication

In this lesson, Ss follow directions on a map and practise asking for and giving directions.

OPTIONAL WARMER

Elicit the names of (1) a good place to get a coffee and pastry, (2) the nearest place to buy a newspaper, (3) a place nearby to get money from a cash point, (4) a good place for a romantic dinner, (5) a place that offers good value for lunch and (6) a place nearby to check emails. Do not elicit directions at this point, just the names of the places.

1 ▶ Ss match the directions with the diagrams. Ss check answers in pairs, then as a whole class.

Answers
1 B
2 F
3 C
4 A
5 E
6 D

2a ▶ Ss look at the picture and in pairs decide whether the statements are true or false. They correct the false statements.

Answers
1 T
2 T
3 F – The supermarket is on the right.
4 F – The bus stop is on the left.
5 T
6 F – The cinema is at the end of the road.

b ▶ Ss name other places and people in the picture.

Answers
a man and a woman sitting outside the café
a bank and mobile phone shop on the left
a shopper on the right
two pedestrians and a cyclist at the end of the road, in front of the cinema

3a ▶ 🔘 2.37 Tell Ss they are going to hear Robin speaking to two different people. Play recording 2.37. Ss listen and answer the questions.

Answers
1 Robin has lost his wallet.
2 He wants to go to the police station.
3 No, because she doesn't know this part of town.

b ▶ Ask Ss to look at the places on the map. Ask: *Where is the art gallery?* (on Church Road) *Where is there a café?* (on Mill Street, for example, between the phone shop and the bar) Establish where the library is on the map as this is the starting point for the directions. Play recording 2.37 again. Ss listen and follow the directions on the map. They find the three places on the map. Ss check answers in pairs, then as a whole class.

Answers
1 post office D
2 bookshop B
3 police station A

c ▶ Play the recording again. Ss listen and complete the *How to...* box. They check their answers in the audioscript on page 158.

Answers
1 know
2 Turn
3 into
4 straight
5 along
6 end

▶ Ss practise saying the directions. Help with the pronunciation of *straight* and *right*.

4 ▶ Ss work in pairs. Student A looks at the instructions on page 132 and Student B looks at page 134. Using the map, they ask for and give directions from and to the places listed. Monitor carefully, correcting any errors you hear.

OPTIONAL EXTENSION

Ss think of two places they often go to near the school, e.g. somewhere for lunch, a train station, etc. Ss work in small groups of three or four. Each student gives directions to the places they have thought of without mentioning what the place is. The other Ss try to work out where and what the place is.

10 Review and practice

1 ▶

Answers
1 Paying
2 Swimming
3 Going
4 Driving
5 Taking
6 Commuting

2 ▶

Answers
1 I haven't been on a long-haul flight.
2 Have you been on an adventure holiday?
3 We've been to New York and Boston.
4 She's been horse-riding in Scotland.
5 Have they been bungee jumping in New Zealand?

3 ▶

Answers
Liz: We went last winter.
Sue: I haven't been to Switzerland.
Liz: we went in January
Sue: Have you been there in the summer?

4 ▶

Answers
1 run
3 written
4 played
6 met

5 ▶

Answers
1 have seen
2 has stayed
3 hasn't been
4 haven't won
5 have visited
6 has driven
7 hasn't done
8 have climbed

6 ▶

Answers
1 direct
2 return
3 class
4 platform
5 rush hour
6 passengers

7 ▶

Answers
1 b
2 d
3 e
4 a
5 c

10 Writing bank

1 ▶

Answers
1 Karl
2 It was full of people.
3 ten pounds
4 to get his card from the cash machine
5 He was two hours late for work.

2a ▶

Answers
1 T
2 F
3 T
4 F
5 T
6 F

b ▶

Answers
life
friend
opinions
adjectives
exclamation
forms
interesting

3a ▶

Answers
a T
b F
c T

b ▶

Answers
1 First
2 Later
3 so
4 and
5 In the end

4a ▶ Ss note down key points about something interesting that happened to them recently.

b ▶ Ss write a blog entry.

Overview

Lead-in	Revision: Instructions; school subjects
11.1	Can do: Understand signs and rules Grammar: *can/can't, have to/don't have to* Speaking and Pronunciation: /f/ and /v/ Reading: Traffic school Listening: Driving in Britain Listening: Life in America
11.2	Can do: Talk about your education Grammar: Review of *wh-* questions Vocabulary: Schools and subjects New technology Speaking and Pronunciation: Intonation of *wh-* questions Listening: Schools and educational experiences Reading: Teachers together
11.3	Can do: Give and understand instructions Grammar: The imperative Vocabulary: Education Listening and reading: Lifelong learning Listening: A phone call to enrol on a course
Communication	Check instructions and information How to... check information and ask for repetition
Reference	
Review and Practice	
Writing bank	Write a message for an online message board How to... use pronouns (2)

CEFR Can do objectives
11.1 Understand signs and rules
11.2 Talk about your education
11.3 Give and understand instructions
Communication Check instructions and information
Writing bank Write a message for an online message board

CEFR Portfolio ideas
a) Video/Audio. With a partner, make a recording of the roleplay on page 116.
b) You would like to be able to find some work for one month in a foreign country. Write a question for a message board, explaining this and describing the work you can do.
c) Video/Audio. With a partner role play a customs official inspecting the luggage carried by a tourist visitor to your country. Tell the tourist what he/she cannot bring in to the country [e.g. drugs, food, etc.]
d) On a message board, Tony asks which is the best season to visit your country. He also wants to know about visa requirements. Tony is a Canadian citizen. Write an answer to Tony's question.

Lead-in

1 ▶ Ss identify the four learning situations. They discuss with a partner which courses they have done.

> **Answers**
> A group exercise class
> B classroom learning
> C learning to drive
> D learning to play the piano

2a ▶ Ss look at the eight rules and match them to the learning situation in the photos. Ss check answers in pairs, then as a whole class.

> **Answers**
> | | | | | | | |
> |---|---|---|---|---|---|---|
> | 1 | C | 3 | A | 6 | C, D | |
> | 2 | D | 4 | D | 7 | B | |
> | | | 5 | B | 8 | C | |

b ▶ Ss think about their schooldays. Elicit the types of rules which existed in the schools the Ss went to, e.g. no smoking, no eating in class, etc. Teach *to obey the rules* (to do what you are told) and *punishment* (staying late after school, etc.). Ss work in pairs and discuss the questions. In feedback, elicit some of the types of punishment. Ask: *What was the worst punishment in school?*

3a ▶ Ss look at the words in the box and match three of the subjects to the definitions.

> **Answers**
> | | | | |
> |---|---|---|---|
> | 1 | history | 2 | biology |
> | | | 3 | physics |

b ▶ Ss check the meanings of the other subjects with a partner or with a dictionary. Explain that science usually encompasses biology, chemistry and physics. Ss tend to study science until the senior school cycle.

c ▶ Ss add other school subjects to the list (e.g. art, music, physical education, etc.).

4 ▶ 🔊 2.38 Ss look at the vocabulary items again. In pairs they decide how many syllables each word has. Play recording 2.38. Ss listen to check the number of syllables for each word, twice if necessary.

> **Answers**
> Four: biology
> Three: chemistry, geography, languages, literature
> Two: history, physics, science
> One: maths
> Biology has the most syllables.

EXTEND THE LEAD-IN

Ss categorise the list into (1) subjects they liked in school and (2) subjects they didn't like in school.
They could also think of different types of night class (ballet, yoga, learning the piano ...) and divide them into interesting/enjoyable classes and boring classes.

11.1 Rules of the road

In this lesson, Ss read about driving in the US and what happens to people who break the rules of the road. They listen to a tourist information phone line about driving in Britain and also listen to Steve describing other rules in the US. Ss compare rules and regulations in their own countries.

> **OPTIONAL WARMER**
>
> Write the following on the board: *speeding, parking in front of a car entrance, drink-driving, driving without documents, careless driving, talking on the mobile phone while driving.* Ss work in groups of three or four. They look at the list of driving-related offences and rank them 1–6 in order of seriousness.

Reading

1 ▶ Direct Ss to the questions. Teach *speed limit, fine* (money you have to pay) and *points on their licence* (a system where drivers get points on their licence when they are caught breaking the rules of the road; after a certain number of points they lose their licence). Ss discuss the questions with a partner.

2a ▶ Scanning: Explain to Ss that they will read the text twice, the first time very quickly and the second time much more slowly. Direct Ss to the question and tell them they have one minute to find which country the text is about. Explain that they do not need to understand the text fully at this point. After a minute, Ss call out the answer.

> **Answer**
> the USA

b ▶ Ss read the text more slowly and find the answers. Teach *offenders* (people who break the rules). Check answers.

> **Answers**
> 1   drive faster than the speed limit, park in the wrong place, drive through a red light
> 2   pay a fine, get points on your driving licence, not allowed to drive
> 3   in the classroom, online
> 4   a written examination

c ▶ Ss discuss the questions as a whole class.

Grammar | *can/can't, have to/don't have to*

3a ▶ Ss focus on the extracts from the text. They use the text to fill in the missing words.

> **Answers**
> • can't
> • can, can
> • have to, don't have to

b ▶ Ss work in pairs. They match the verbs to the meanings.

> **Active grammar**
> 1   d
> 2   b
> 3   a
> 4   c

▶ Write *They have to do a course* and *They can do a course* on the board. Ask: *What is the difference between these two sentences?* (*Have to* means there is obligation, they must do it; *can* means it is possible to do it if they want, but it is also possible not to do it.). Explain that *can/can't* and *have to/don't have to* are often used to describe rules, what is compulsory and what is allowed. We use *have to* when there is an obligation and *don't have to* when there is no obligation to do something. We use *can* to say that something is allowed and *can't* when it is not allowed. Note: Focus on the difference in meaning between *can't* and *don't have to*.

▶ Teach the forms of *have to*: *I/you/we/they* <u>have</u> to but *he/she/it* <u>has</u> to do something. The auxiliary *do/does* is used to make negative and question forms.

▶ Direct Ss to the Reference section on page 117.

4 ▶ Ss look at the road signs. Teach *overtake* (to pass another car in front of you). Ss write the rules using *can/can't* and *have to/don't have to* using the words and phrases in the box to help them. Ss check answers in pairs, then as a whole class.

> **Answers**
> 3   You can't go faster than 120 km per hour.
> 4   You can't overtake.
> 5   You have to give way to traffic.
> 6   You can park here.
> 7   You have to turn left.
> 8   You can get petrol here.
> 9   You can't enter here.
> 10   You can go.

5a ▶ 🔵 2.39 Tell Ss they are going to listen to a computer-operated information line. Ss look at the list of options. Play recording 2.39. Ss listen and identify which information is not mentioned. They check answers in pairs, then as a whole class.

> **Answers**
> 4 and 6

b ▶ 🔵 2.40 Ss look at the information box on driving in Britain. Play recording 2.40. Ss listen and complete the information box. Ss check answers in pairs, then as a whole class.

Answers
Visitors to Britain:
* have to
To rent a car:
* have to
* have to
* have to
When driving in Britain:
* don't have to
* can't

c ▶ Ss find the words in the leaflet.

Answers
1 documents
2 regulations
3 valid

6 ▶ Ss write four sentences about Sami, using *can/can't* and *have to/don't have to.*

Possible answers
2 He doesn't have to get a British driving licence.
3 He can drive in Britain without a British licence.
4 He can't turn right at red lights.

OPTIONAL EXTENSION
Write *the ball, your opponent, your team, the goal/net, use feet/hands/head,* etc. on the board. Ss work in pairs and take turns to describe the 'rules' of their favourite team sport, e.g. *you can't touch the ball with your hands, you don't have to exchange jerseys with your opponent after the game,* etc. Monitor closely, correcting any errors you hear.

Pronunciation | /f/ and /v/

7a ▶ ⊕ 2.41 Ss read the sentence. *Have* is underlined twice. Play recording 2.41. Ss listen and decide if the pronunciation of *have* changes.

Answer
No. The ending of *have* sounds different in each case: /f/ and /v/.

b ▶ ⊕ 2.42 Ss look at the pairs of words. Write the phonetic symbols /f/ and /v/ on the board. Play recording 2.42. Ss listen and identify which sound they hear. Ss check answers in pairs, then as a whole class.

Answers
1 leaf
2 few
3 fan
4 V

c ▶ ⊕ 2.43 Ss listen to the sentences in recording 2.43 and practise saying them in pairs.

▶ Direct Ss to the Pronunciation bank on page 147.

Listening and speaking

The age of majority, when you are deemed to be legally an adult, is 18 years old in most English-speaking countries. However, it is 21 in the state of Mississippi in the United States. You can get married at 16 with parental approval in most English-speaking countries (without parental consent in Scotland). The drinking age varies between countries. In the UK, you are allowed to drink alcohol with food in licensed premises from the age of 16 if an adult family member orders for you. In the US, the legal age to drink alcohol is 21 although a few states allow some exceptions, such as drinking with parents or in private clubs.

8a ▶ Teach *military service* (a compulsory year in the army). Explain that Steve is American. Ss look at the prompts in ex. 8b with a partner and guess what Steve will say about these things.

b ▶ ⊕ 2.44 Play recording 2.44. Ss listen and note down what Steve says about the eight topics. Ss then write sentences about the US using *have to/don't have to* and *can/can't.* Ss check answers in pairs, then as a whole class.

Answers
1 Americans don't have to have identity cards.
2 They can drive when they are 16.
3 They can buy guns when they are 21.
4 Americans can get married when they are 18.
5 They can have a bank account when they are 18.
6 Americans have to be 21 to go into bars.
7 They can't smoke in offices, shops or restaurants.
8 Americans have to pay to see a doctor or go to a hospital.

9a ▶ Ss work in pairs. They discuss the rules and regulations in their country in relation to the headings given, e.g. *How old do you have to be to get a passport? Do you need a credit card to rent a car?* etc.

b ▶ Ss re-form into small groups of three or four. They discuss the rules in the US and (1) compare them to rules in their country and (2) give their opinions about the rules. This activity can be usefully done with groups from the same country or groups from different countries, depending on your class context.

OPTIONAL EXTENSION
Ss write up an information leaflet for tourists similar to the one in ex. 5b about their country. They can use the headings in ex. 9a.

11.2 Experiences of learning

In this lesson, Ss listen to four people describing the school system in their countries and read a number of posts on a message board for teachers. Ss talk about their schooldays and give their views on the use of technology in the classroom.

> **OPTIONAL WARMER**
>
> Ss work in small groups. They discuss what they consider to be the five most important qualities of (1) a good teacher and (2) a good student. Encourage Ss to use *have to/don't have to* which they learnt in the previous lesson, e.g. *I think a good teacher has to be patient. He/She doesn't have to be young*, etc.

Listening

1 ▶ Elicit Ss' views on their schooldays. Encourage Ss to give reasons for their answers.

2a ▶ ⬤ 2.45 Tell Ss they are going to hear four people discussing their schooldays. Play recording 2.45. Ss listen and tick the topics mentioned.

> **Answers**
> number of years at school
> favourite subject
> age of leaving school

b ▶ Ss match the education to the person in the photo. Ss check answers in pairs, then as a whole class.

> **Answers**
> 1 Ross   3 Andreas
> 2 Sarah   4 Harumi

c ▶ Ss look at the questions. Play the recording a second time. Ss listen and answer the questions.

> **Answers**
> 1 thirteen years
> 2 at sixteen – but fifteen if your parents agree
> 3 an academic school called a gymnasium
> 4 email, message forums, interactive whiteboard

Vocabulary | schools and subjects

3a ▶ Ss categorise the words from recording 2.45 under the headings given. Ss check answers in pairs, then as a whole class.

> **Answers**
> 1 secondary school, elementary school, high school, gymnasium
> 2 teacher training college
> 3 English, law, politics, economics, maths

b ▶ Ss add words to the categories in pairs.

> **Suggested answers**
> 1 nursery school, junior school, middle school, prep(aratory) school, academy, comprehensive school, grammar school, sixth-form college, etc.
> 2 college of further education, college of art, technical college, etc.
> 3 biology, history, science, business, religious studies, etc.

Grammar | review of *wh-* questions

4a ▶ Direct Ss to the questions in ex. 2c. Elicit the question words used in each question and write them on the board. Elicit the other question words Ss know and write them on the board. Write: *What kind of school did Andreas go to?* and *Did Andreas go to a secondary school?* on the board. Ask: *What is different about the answers to these questions?* (yes/no answers and information answers) *How*, although not technically a *wh-* question word as it begins with the letter *h*, is generally grouped with and follows the same rules as other questions words.

▶ Ss match the words to make up complete questions.

> **Answers**
> 1 d   2 a   4 b
>   3 e   5 c

b ▶ Ss look at the question words and match the words and phrases in the box to the appropriate question word. Ss check answers in pairs, then as a whole class.

> **Answers**
> How long? – periods of time
> Which? – a choice between two (or more) things
> Where? – places
> Whose? – possession
> What? – things and ideas
> Why? – reason
> When? – times
> How much? – prices or cost
> How many? – numbers and quantity
> Who? – people

▶ Review the pronunciation of question words, especially the initial /h/ and /w/ sounds.

▶ Direct Ss to the Reference section on page 117.

Pronunciation | intonation of *wh-* questions

5a ▶ ⬤ 2.46 Play recording 2.46. Ss listen and decide whether the voice goes up or down at the end. Ss check answers in pairs, then as a whole class.

> **Answer**
> down

b ▶ ● 2.47 Play recording 2.47. Ss listen to the intonation. Remind Ss of the different intonation for Yes/No questions (see Lesson 9.3).

> **Answer**
> up

c ▶ Play recording 2.46. again. Ss listen and repeat the questions.

> **OPTIONAL VARIATION**
> Ss write the questions as a dictation exercise before practising saying them.

6a ▶ Ss look at the four answers and write questions for them. More than one question is often possible. Ss check answers in pairs, then as a whole class.

> **Possible answers**
> 1 When did you start studying English?
> 2 Where do you live?
> 3 Have you got pets/a dog?
> 4 Who is your best friend?

b ▶ Ss practise asking and answering the questions with a partner. Monitor closely and correct any mistakes you hear.

▶ Direct Ss to the Pronunciation bank on page 148.

Speaking

7 ▶ Ss prepare five open-ended questions to ask other students about their education, e.g. *When did you start school? Where did you go to secondary school?* etc. Ss work in small groups. They use their questions to discuss their educational backgrounds.

Reading

> **OPTIONAL LEAD-IN TO THE READING**
> Ss work in pairs. They compare a modern education system with that of their parents/grandparents' time. Ask: *What were the main differences between then and now?* Write *subjects, discipline, technology* on the board to guide their discussion. In feedback, focus on the use of technology in the modern classroom. Try to find an opportunity to teach *interactive whiteboard, message board* and *website* during feedback.

8a ▶ Ss read the posts to decide what their main topic is.

> **Answer**
> 3

b ▶ Ss look at the statements, then read the posts again to decide whether they are true or false. Ss check answers in pairs, then as a whole class

> **Answers**
> 1 F
> 2 F
> 3 F
> 4 T

c ▶ Ss match the person to the statements with a partner.

> **Answers**
> 1 B
> 2 R
> 3 A
> 4 S
> 5 S

Vocabulary | new technology

9 ▶ Ss complete the sentences with words from the box. Ss check answers in pairs, then as a whole class.

> **Answers**
> 1 download
> 2 online
> 3 forum
> 4 wiki
> 5 LMS
> 6 podcasts

Speaking

10 ▶ Ss discuss the questions in groups of three or four. Elicit their views in relation to using technology in the language classroom during feedback.

11.3 Lifelong learning

Lifelong learning and adult education have become increasingly popular phenomena in recent years. Many people return to learning later in life for various reasons and most colleges and universities have become much more flexible and accessible in their approach. Many universities have followed the Open University's lead and now offer distance learning courses where students can study from home.

In this lesson, Ss read a number of adverts for educational institutions and listen to people talking about the courses available there. They also listen to a phone conversation about enrolling for one of the courses. Ss discuss different types of learning contexts and practise giving instructions.

Reading and listening

OPTIONAL WARMER

Explain *distance learning* (you don't attend college but you do all the work at home and contact lecturers and other students online) and *evening classes*. Ss work in pairs. They list three reasons why people choose to study this way, e.g. *can't give up job*, *live far away from the university*, *have young children*, etc. Elicit reasons in feedback and write them on the board.

1 ▶ Elicit Ss' responses to the two questions. Make sure Ss have understood what lifelong learning and distance learning are.

2a ▶ Ss look at the four adverts for different courses. Write *retired*, *career prospects*, *gain* on the board. Ss guess what these words mean as they read the adverts (over 60/65 and not working, your job in the future, get). Ss match the adverts to the headings. They check answers in pairs, then as a whole class.

> **Answers**
> 1 D
> 2 C
> 3 B
> 4 A

b ▶ 🔘 2.48 Tell Ss they are going to listen to four people describe the different courses. Teach *extras* (when you have to pay for extra things, e.g. books, photocopying, etc.). Explain that you will play the recording twice. The first time Ss must listen to get the general idea and the second time they must listen to get more detailed information.

▶ Play recording 2.48. Ss listen and put the adverts in the order the speakers talk about them. Ss check answers in pairs, then as a whole class.

> **Answers**
> A 4   C 1
> B 3   D 2

3 ▶ Play the recording again. Ss listen and complete the table. They check answers in pairs, then as a whole class.

> **Answers**
> **Bexley Green College:**
> £800 for most popular course
> 10 hours a week for ten weeks
> languages and business
> **Open University:**
> at home, a few classes during the year, often a summer school
> 12 hours a week
> art history, maths, computing, nursing, ...
> **MicroMatters Ltd:**
> the centre
> £900 for a week's course
> computer skills
> **University of the Third Age:**
> halls or schools all over the country
> around £20 a year
> weekday afternoons

Vocabulary | education

4a ▶ Ss choose five words from the box to match the definitions. Ss check answers in pairs, then as a whole class.

> **Answers**
> 1 full-time
> 2 lecturer
> 3 trainee
> 4 distance learning
> 5 part-time

b ▶ Ss categorise the words in any way they wish. Ss compare categories with a partner.

> **Possible answers**
> learners, teachers, types of learning, people, etc.

c ▶ Ss add words to the categories with a partner. You might like to add the following categories in order to review vocabulary covered in previous lessons: *places to learn* (school, university, etc.), *verbs to learn* (study, listen, learn, etc.), *equipment/technology for learning* (CD player, interactive whiteboard, chalk, etc.)

Speaking

5 ▶ Ss work in small groups. They discuss the four questions in their group. Do not worry about Ss making mistakes during this activity. Note down any obvious errors you hear to deal with later.

OPTIONAL EXTENSION

Ss think of one successful and one unsuccessful learning experience outside of school (e.g. learning to drive, to paint, computer skills, yoga, etc.). In pairs, Ss discuss the two learning experiences and why they think one was successful and one wasn't. (E.g. *I learned to drive last year. My teacher was very patient. I needed to learn for my job so I was very interested in it*, etc.)

Listening

6a ▶ 🔘 2.49 Ask: *Do you prefer online application forms or paper/hard copy application forms? Why?* Elicit Ss' views. Then, direct them to the questions. Explain that they will hear the recording twice: the first time, they must answer the general questions; the second time, in ex. 6b, they must complete the application form. Play recording 2.49. Ss listen and answer the questions. They check answers in pairs, then as a whole class.

> **Answers**
> 1   Bexley Green College
> 2   Moscow, Russia
> 3   can't manage to send the online application form
> 4   Yes; the woman explains how to do it

b ▶ Ss look at the information needed for the application form. Play the recording again. Ss listen and complete the form.

> **Answers**
> Name: Nadia Koparova
> Nationality: Russian
> Course choice: Advanced Improvers' English and Business for Beginners
> Course start date: 22nd June
> Payment: Credit card

Grammar | the imperative

7a ▶ Elicit the missing words from the phone call and write the sentences on the board.

> **Answers**
> 1   Click
> 2   enter
> 3   don't

b ▶ Ss match the columns and complete the rule in the Active grammar box. Ss check answers in pairs, then as a whole class.

> **Active grammar**
> 1   a positive instruction
> 2   a negative instruction
> We *don't usually use* the pronoun *you* before an imperative verb.

▶ Explain that we don't say <u>You</u> enter the start date and <u>You</u> don't do that when giving instructions.

▶ Ask: *Does the instruction change if we are talking to more than one person?* (No, the imperative form never changes; remind Ss that there is no 'polite' form of the verb in English.)

▶ Explain the difference between *You can't take photographs* (covered in Lesson 11.1) and *Don't take photographs*. (The meaning is more or less the same but the structure is different.)

▶ Direct Ss to the Reference section on page 117.

8a ▶ Ss match three of the signs to the instructions. They check answers in pairs, then as a whole class.

> **Answers**
> a   3
> b   2
> c   1

b ▶ Ss write instructions for the other three signs.

> **Suggested answers**
> 4   Don't take photographs here.
> 5   Use the litter bins.
> 6   Don't come in here.

9 ▶ Ss work in pairs. They use the symbols and notes to write instructions for a drinks machine.

> **Answers**
> 2   Choose your drink.
> 3   Pay the correct money/Put the correct coins in the slot.
> 4   Don't use notes.
> 5   Press the button and take your drink.

OPTIONAL EXTENSION

Ss think of signs and notices to put around the classroom. (E.g. *Practise your English every day*; *Don't speak in your own language*; *Guess the meaning of the word*; *Use an English/English dictionary*; *Watch films in English*, etc.)

---

11 Communication

In this lesson, Ss listen to someone asking for information about a course and practise asking for and giving information about courses.

OPTIONAL WARMER

Elicit the types of extracurricular classes which people can do and write them on the board, e.g. cookery, photography, a language, a sport, history and culture, home improvement, yoga and relaxation, beauty, etc. Ss rank the items on the list in order of preference and then compare choices with a partner.

---

1 ▶ Ss discuss the questions in groups.

2a ▶ ⬤ 2.50 Play recording 2.50. Ss listen and tick the topics mentioned in the conversation. Teach *ingredients*.

Answers
start date
times of lessons
ingredients
location of college
price

---

b ▶ Play the recording again. Ss listen and make notes under the five headings. Ss check answers in pairs, then as a whole class.

Answers
start date: 13th September
times of lessons: 7:00 to 9:30 on Wednesday evenings
price: £225
ingredients: students bring their own ingredients
location of college: the annexe to the main building on York Street

---

3a ▶ Ss complete the sentences from the conversation in pairs.

Answers
1 check
2 Can
3 repeat
4 right
5 ask
6 Sorry, that

---

b ▶ Ss check their answers in the audioscript on page 159.

c ▶ Explain the difference between checking information (to make sure you understand) and asking for repetition (you didn't hear properly the first time). Ss look at the sentences in ex. 3a and decide whether they are used to check information or to ask for repetition. They then complete the *How to ...* box. Help Ss with the typical intonation patterns for these expressions.

Answers
Checking information: 1, 2, 4, 5
Asking for repetition: 3, 6

---

4 ▶ Ss conduct two telephone roleplays asking for information about courses. Ss do the first roleplay in pairs and then swap roles and move on to the second roleplay. Student A looks at the information on page 132 and Student B looks at the information on page 116. Tell them to read the information for Roleplay 1. Give them a few minutes to read the information before starting the roleplay.

▶ When Ss have finished, they swap roles and move on to the second roleplay. Ss read the information for Roleplay 2 before starting the second roleplay.

OPTIONAL EXTENSION

Elicit other reasons Ss have to make phone calls asking for information, e.g. train times and schedules, doctor's appointments, information about museums, exam results, etc. Ss work in pairs. They discuss (1) whether they prefer to telephone, ask in person or check out information online. They speak about (2) times when they have had to make these kind of calls in English or another foreign language and (3) whether they would make these calls themselves in English or ask someone else to do it for them.

---

11 Review and practice

1 ▶

Answers
1 You can't park here.
2 You don't have to be a hotel guest.
3 You can find a restaurant here.
4 You have to show your passport.

2 ▶

Answers
1 can't   5 has to
2 can't   6 can't
3 doesn't have to 7 can't
4 can   8 doesn't have to
                9 can

3 ▶

Answers
1 e
2 When – c
3 How – g
4 What – a
5 How long – d
6 Who – h
7 Why – b
8 How much – f

4 ▶

Answers
2 Be friendly to the other children.
3 Don't eat and drink in the classroom.
4 Don't run in the school buildings.
5 Don't shout.
6 Stand up when the teacher comes in.

5 ▶

Answers
1 distance learning
2 trainee
3 literature
4 primary school
5 part-time course
6 maths

6 ▶

Answers
1 college (isn't a subject)
2 trainee (isn't a teacher)
3 high school (isn't for young children)
4 primary school (isn't education for older students)
5 petrol (isn't a punishment)
6 driving licence (isn't a motorist's action)
7 sport (isn't technology)
8 driving test (isn't used online)

11 Writing bank

1 ▶ Ss' own answers

2 ▶

Answers
1 students and tutors from the University of Gresham
2 Craig
3 He wants to find out about the media studies course.
4 No.
5 He asks Colin not to make comments about tutors on the message board.

3

Answers
I love it (the media studies course), watching them (films), it's interesting (the course), what can you do with it (media studies), even good ones (tutors)
the trouble with that (changing to media studies now)

4a ▶

Answer
He wants to know other people's opinions about whether he should continue to learn English at university or start a new language instead.

b ▶ Ss' own answers

5 ▶ Ss reply to Selim on the message board.

Overview

Lead-in	**Revision:** Extreme challenges
12.1	**Can do:** Talk about intentions
	Grammar: *be going to*
	Vocabulary: Geography
	Future time
	Speaking and Pronunciation: Sentence stress, /ə/
	Find someone who's going to …
	Reading: No more continents?
	Listening: Planning a trip
12.2	**Can do:** Explain the reasons for your actions/plans
	Grammar: Infinitive of purpose
	Revision of *be going to*
	Speaking and Pronunciation: Rhymes
	Listening: Everyone wants to be famous
	Listening: Fame
12.3	**Can do:** Talk about likes, dislikes and ambitions
	Grammar: *like* and *would like*
	Pronunciation: /aɪ/ and /eɪ/
	Listening and Reading: Charity Champions
Communication	Ask about and discuss plans
	How to… ask about and talk about plans and ambitions
Reference	
Review and Practice	
Writing bank	Write a thank you letter
	How to… use punctuation (4): apostrophes

CEFR Can do objectives
12.1 Talk about intentions
12.2 Explain the reasons for your actions/plans
12.3 Talk about likes, dislikes and ambitions
Communication Ask about and discuss plans
Writing bank Write a thank you letter

CEFR Portfolio ideas
a) Write an advertisement for a course for learning an extreme sport in your country. Invent any details you need.
b) Video. Make a short video for your teacher. Say thank you for the lessons. Tell your teacher the things which you liked best in the course.
c) Write a letter to your neighbour, Mrs Hanson. She is 95 years old. She sent you a nice blue scarf for your birthday.
d) Look carefully at the layout of an informal letter in English. Compare it with the layout of letters in your language. What is the same? What is different?

Lead-in

OPTIONAL WARMER
Write *adventure holiday* on the board. Elicit the activities people do on adventure holidays in summer and winter (e.g. canoeing, surfing, horse-riding, rock climbing, etc.; downhill skiing, snowboarding, tobogganing, etc.). Ss work in pairs. They tell each other which type of activity holiday they would like best: (1) a winter or summer adventure holiday, (2) which adventure sport they would choose and (3) which country/area they would go to.

1 ▶ Ss look at the four photos of various adventure sports. They choose one word or phrase from box A and from box B and write a label to match each of the pictures. Ss check answers in pairs, then as a whole class.

Answers
B   sailing under a bridge
C   cycling in a tunnel
D   trekking in a canyon

2 ▶ Ss discuss the questions in small groups. Elicit their views in feedback. Review *bungee jumping* which comes up in the listening.

3a ▶ 🔵 2.51 Tell Ss that some of the photos are from Paul and Mia's holiday last summer. Play recording 2.51. Ss listen and identify which photos are described. Ss check answers in pairs, then as a whole class.

Answers
A, C and D

b ▶ Ss look at the four questions. Play the recording again. Ss listen and answer the questions. Ss check answers in pairs, then as a whole class.

Answers
1   white-water rafting
2   horse-riding
3   horse-riding
4   to go bungee jumping in New Zealand

4 ▶ Ss work in pairs. They ask and answer the questions about the four activities in the photos and their ambitions for the future.

OPTIONAL EXTENSION
Ss write a short advert for an adventure holiday in their country/region. Put the adverts around the room. Ss circulate reading the adverts. Each student chooses a holiday to go on.

12.1 One world

Isambard Kingdom Brunel (1806–1859) was a major figure in the history of British engineering, famous for his innovative, influential ideas in the construction of bridges, tunnels and railways. He is particularly associated with the construction of the first British railway, the Great Western Railway. In 2002, Brunel came second only to Winston Churchill in the major BBC series called *Great Britons*, which sought to identify and rank by public poll the 100 greatest Britons of all time.

In this lesson, Ss read about various engineering projects which seek to link together different places in the world by tunnel or bridge. They listen to someone planning a trip and ask and answer each other about their own future intentions.

OPTIONAL WARMER

Write *tunnels* and *bridges* on the board. Elicit any famous tunnels or bridges Ss know (e.g. the Mont Blanc tunnel, the Golden Bridge in San Francisco, etc.). Ss discuss how they feel crossing very high bridges and going through very long tunnels (scared, excited, etc.).

Reading and vocabulary

1 ▶ Ss look at the map of the world. They name the continents and ways of travelling between continents.

Answers
1 six: Africa, America, Antarctica, Asia, Australia, Europe
2 by sea, by air, by land

2a ▶ Explain to Ss that they will read the text twice, the first time very quickly and the second time much more slowly. Direct them to the questions in this exercise and tell them they have one minute to find the answers. Explain they do not need to understand the text fully at this point. Stop the activity after a minute. Ss choose the right option.

Answer
2

b ▶ Ss read the text more slowly and match the places 1–6 with the places a–f. Ss check answers with a partner and match the pairs to the pictures A–F on the map. Check answers as a whole class.

Answers
2 a – D on map
3 c – E on map
4 f – F on map
5 b – A on map
6 e – C on map

c ▶ Ss discuss the questions in pairs. Do not worry about Ss making mistakes. Elicit their views in feedback.

3a ▶ Ss look at the words in the box and find them in the text. They answer the questions. Ss check answers in pairs, then as a whole class.

Answers
1 connect, join, link
2 continent, island, mainland

b ▶ Ss complete the questions with the words and write the answers.

Answers
1 connect (1994)
2 island (a bridge)
4 continent (Asia)

c ▶ Ss think of three more questions to ask about the text. Ss take turns to ask and answer the questions in pairs. Invite five or six Ss to put their questions to the whole class during feedback.

Grammar | *be going to*

OPTIONAL GRAMMAR LEAD-IN

Ss look at the answers to ex. 2b and the map again. Ask them to categorise the projects into (1) finished projects and (2) future projects. Ss can check answers in the text. (finished projects: Channel Tunnel, Oresund Bridge and Tunnel; future projects: Sicily/Italian mainland, Sunda Strait Bridge, Europe/Africa, Alaska/Siberia).

4 ▶ Ss look at the sentences and tick the correct explanation. Ss check answers in pairs, then as a whole class.

Answer
1 intentions

5 ▶ Ss complete the Active grammar box in their books.

Active grammar
Affirmative: are, is
Negative: is not
Questions: Are, Is

▶ Write *They + are + going to + build* ... on the board. Explain that the *going to* future is formed with *to be* (Present Simple) + *going to* + infinitive of the verb.

▶ Help Ss with the contracted forms.

▶ Write *I'd like to visit Spain next year* and *I'm going to visit Spain next year*. Ask: *What is the difference?* (*I'd like to visit Spain* is a desire, something that would be nice to do in the future. We use the *going to* future to describe intentions and plans about the future: *I'm going to visit Spain* expresses my intention, a definite plan.)

▶ Direct Ss to the Reference section on page 127.

6 ▶ Ss work in pairs. They use the prompts to write sentences using *going to*. Check answers.

> **Answers**
> 1 Britain isn't going to build any more airports.
> 2 Are the Americans going to build a tunnel?
> 3 They are going to open a new bridge in 2030.
> 4 I'm going to start a new course in September.
> 5 My parents are going to retire next year.
> 6 We're not going to have a holiday next summer.

Listening

7a ▶ 🌐 2.52 Tell Ss that Julie is in England and is going to Belgium. Elicit ways of getting to Belgium from England (e.g. fly, take a ferry, drive or take a train through the Channel Tunnel). Ss look at the questions. Play recording 2.52. Ss listen and answer the questions.

> **Answers**
> 1 the start of the summer
> 2 by car and train, through the Channel Tunnel

b ▶ Ss look at the sentences. Play the recording again. Ss listen and complete the sentences. They check answers in pairs, then as a whole class.

> **Answers**
> 1 is going to visit   3 isn't going to
> 2 are going to move   4 is going to drive
>   5 isn't going to go

c ▶ Ss discuss the questions with a partner. Elicit plans and intentions from individual Ss during feedback.

Pronunciation | sentence stress, /ə/

8a ▶ 🌐 2.53 Direct Ss to the *going to* sentence. Play recording 2.53. Ss listen and note the sentence stress. Ask: *What do you notice about the pronunciation of* to? Ss compare answers in pairs, then as a whole class. Ss practise saying the sentence.

> **Answer**
> *to* is pronounced /tə/

b ▶ 🌐 2.54 Play recording 2.54. Ss listen and repeat the sentences, then mark the sentence stress. Ss check answers in pairs, then as a whole class.

> **Answers**
> 1 She's going to get fit.
> 2 They're going to sell their car.
> 3 We're going to learn French.
> 4 I'm going to buy a laptop.

▶ Ask: *Which type of words are stressed?* (main verbs and nouns, but not pronouns, prepositions, suffix endings or auxiliary verbs)

▶ Direct Ss to the Pronunciation bank on page 148.

Vocabulary | future time

9a ▶ Ss listen to the conversation from ex. 7 again and tick the time expressions they hear.

> **Answers**
> next week, later this year, the week after next, last year

b ▶ Ss look at the time expressions and put them in chronological order. Ss check answers in pairs, then as a whole class.

> **Answers**
> 1 last year
> 2 today
> 3 tomorrow
> 4 the day after tomorrow
> 5 by Saturday
> 6 next week
> 7 the week after next
> 8 later this year
> 9 next year
> 10 next summer
> 11 in two years' time
> 12 three years from now

c ▶ Ss work in pairs. They take it in turns to ask each other about their future intentions using the time expressions from ex. 9a.

Speaking

10 ▶ Ss work in groups of four. Nominate each student as A, B, C or D. As look at page 130, Bs at page 132, Cs at page 133 and Ds at page 121. Ss ask the others in their group about their future intentions until they find someone who corresponds to the information in their brief. Encourage them to use time expressions in their questions and answers, e.g. *Are you going to get married in the next two years? Are you going to move house soon?* etc.

▶ In feedback, ask: *How many of you are going to visit another country? How many of you are going to get a pet soon?* etc.

> **OPTIONAL EXTENSION**
> Ss work in groups of three or four. They imagine that student elections are going to be held in the school. Each group represents a party and prepares an election manifesto describing their intentions to the voters. Elicit one or two suggestions before Ss start, e.g. *We are going to introduce coffee during the lessons*, *We are going to provide free books*, etc. The suggestions do not need to be serious ones. Each group prepares four points for their manifesto and then presents it to the class.

12.2 Fame and fortune

The early years of the 21st century have been notable for promoting the so-called 'celebrity culture', where fame is seen as the ultimate aspiration. Famous people are often categorised into 'A-list' or 'B-list' celebrities (or 'celebs') and are followed, adored or vilified by fans and the media simply because of their fame rather than their talent or achievements. Reality TV shows such as *Big Brother* and *Survivor* and talent competitions such as *The X Factor* and *American Idol* continue to be extremely popular and create fame and fortune for their contestants, often ordinary people who have become household names almost overnight, usually for only a very short time. The Andy Warhol phrase '15 minutes of fame' is often used to describe such short-lived celebrity status.

In this lesson, Ss listen to a poem and to three people who would like to be famous one day and who talk about their plans for the future. Ss plan various ways of becoming rich and famous themselves.

OPTIONAL WARMER

Ss work in small groups. They list three good things and three bad things about being very famous (e.g. good: lots of money; bad: no privacy, etc.). Elicit the advantages and disadvantages on the board during feedback.

Listening

1a ▶ Elicit different ways people can become famous. Accept all suggestions and write them on the board.

b ▶ Ss discuss the questions with a partner. In feedback, ask: *Would you like to enter a competition like this on TV? Why/Why not?*

2a ▶ 🔊 2.55 Ss look at the two statements. Play recording 2.55. Ss listen and decide which of the statements is true.

Answer
2

b ▶ Ss read the poem and check their answer in pairs, then as a whole class.

c ▶ Do this as a whole-class discussion. Encourage Ss to explain the reasons for their answers as fully as possible.

Pronunciation | rhymes

3a ▶ 🔊 2.56 Ss focus on the final words in each line from the poem. Elicit answers to the question.

Answer
The final word in each pair of lines have the same sound.

▶ Help Ss with the pronunciation of the word *rhyme*. Ask: *What rhymes with* rhyme? (*time, I'm, climb*)

b ▶ 🔊 2.57 Play recording 2.57. Ss listen and circle the word which doesn't rhyme.

Answer	
1	being
2	stay
3	there
4	am
5	drive

OPTIONAL VARIATION

For stronger Ss, ask Ss to close their books for this exercise. Ss listen and write the words they hear, then circle the odd word out in each group of words.

4a ▶ Ss use the words in ex. 3b to complete the lines from a song with a partner. Explain that each pair of lines rhyme.

Answers
cry
clever
forever
name
fame
see
free

b ▶ Elicit the names and some of the lines of Ss' favourite songs in English.

Listening

5a ▶ Ss look at the photos A–C. Elicit ways for the people in the photos to become famous. Accept all suggestions.

b ▶ In pairs, Ss look at the vocabulary in the box and match four of the words or phrases to each photo. Ss can use dictionaries for this activity.

Answers	
A	ball control skills, football team, reserve team, training session
B	election, politician, politics, vote
C	acting, drama, perform, a play

6a ▶ 🔊 2.58 Play recording 2.58. Ss listen and match the speakers to the photos. Ss check answers in pairs, then as a whole class.

Answers	
1	C
2	B
3	A

b ▶ Ss look at the statements. Play the recording again. Ss listen and choose an answer. Ss check answers in pairs, then as a whole class.

Answers
1 university student
2 student
3 reserve team

c ▶ Ss listen again and write sentences about what each speaker is going to do. Ss look at the reasons a–c and match them to the sentences.

Answers
Victoria is going to learn how to sing and dance – b
Helena is going to work for a politician next summer – c
Lewis is going to practise with the reserve team twice a week – a

Grammar | infinitive of purpose

7 ▶ Ss read the two statements made by Lewis and decide which is the correct purpose of the underlined phrases. Ss check answers in pairs, then as a whole class.

Active grammar
1

▶ Write *Lewis is working hard because he wants a place in the first team*. Explain that we can replace the *because …* clause with *to get a place in the first team*. Write *Lewis is working hard to get a place in the first team*.

▶ Make sure students understand that we use the infinitive to explain the reason we do something or the purpose of something, e.g. *Helena is working for a politician to learn about elections. Victoria is going to drama school to become a famous performer.*

▶ Direct Ss to the Reference section on page 127.

8 ▶ Ss put the words in the correct order to make sentences. Ss check answers with a partner, then as a whole class.

Answers
1 Marcie's going to take an exam to become a lawyer.
2 Karl goes to the gym to get fit.
3 My friend reads magazines to improve his English.
4 I play the lottery to win lots of money.

9 ▶ Ss look at the five statements and decide whether they agree with the reasons given or not. If Ss don't agree, they re-write the sentence with a reason which is true for them.

OPTIONAL EXTENSION
Elicit reasons why people want to become famous (money, meet other famous people, etc.). Ss make sentences using the infinitive of purpose to explain the reasons (e.g. *They want to be famous to meet other famous people, They want to be famous to make a lot of money*, etc.).

Speaking

10a ▶ Ss work in groups of four or five. They decide which of the ideas listed would be the best way to become rich and famous. Encourage Ss to give reasons for their opinions.

b ▶ Each group chooses one of the ideas from ex. 10a and plans exactly how they will achieve fame and fortune in this way. Write *Step 1 …, Step 2 …, Step 3 …* on three different lines on the board to guide their discussion.

▶ When Ss are ready, invite one student from each group to describe their plan to the rest of the class.

▶ Do not worry about Ss making mistakes during this activity but encourage them to express their ideas as best they can.

OPTIONAL EXTENSION
Write the following on the board: *career prospects, interest, something to do, pass an exam, travel, communication with others, need it for my job, other reason*. Ss work in small groups of three or four. They discuss their reasons for learning English. Ask *Which are the most important/least important reasons for you?*

12.3 Extreme challenges

Red Nose Day is a charity event which takes place every second year in the UK. On that day, people in schools and workplaces throughout the country organise fund-raising activities for the British charity organisation Comic Relief. Many people wear red plastic or foam noses, which they are given in exchange for a donation. The main event of the day is a live telethon lasting right through the TV schedules, where actors, singers and other celebrities give of their time and present a variety of special performances for the charity. The event generates huge TV ratings and viewers phone in to donate money. In 2009, the event raised over £80 million.

In this lesson, Ss read part of a website for Charity Champions, an organisation which helps people raise money for charity. They listen to a telephone call where several questions about the organisation are answered and then read the 'summary of expeditions' webpage for Charity Champions. Ss discuss their own personal ambitions in small groups.

Reading

OPTIONAL WARMER

Teach *charity* (an organisation which gives money or other help to people in need, e.g. Oxfam). Ss work in pairs. They list all the ways they can think of to raise money for charity, e.g. raffle tickets, charity shops, street collection, etc. Put the suggestions on the board in feedback.

1 ▶ Teach *challenge* (something very difficult to do). Explain to Ss that they will read the text three times, the first time very quickly, and then more slowly. Tell Ss that after the first reading, they have one minute to answer the two questions. Explain they do not need to understand the text fully at this point. Stop the activity after a minute. Ss check answers in pairs, then as a whole class.

Answers
1   a
2   a

2a ▶ Ss now read the text a second time, slowly, and focus on new vocabulary in the text. They look at the words and match them to the definitions. Ss check answers in pairs, then as a whole class.

Answers
1   e
2   f
3   a
4   c
5   b
6   d

b ▶ Ss read the text a third time and decide whether the five statements are true or false. They correct the false statements. Ss check answers in pairs, then as a whole class.

Answers
1   F – The text describes challenge expeditions to raise money for charity.
2   F – There are three levels of difficulty but always a challenge.
3   T
4   T
5   F – There are more than thirty different challenges to choose from.

3 ▶ Teach *fit/fitness* (when your body is in a good condition) and *sponsor* (to give you some money to do the trip). Ss work in pairs. As turn to page 132 and Bs turn to page 134. Ss read the information and ask and answer each other's questions. Ss check answers with another pair, then as a whole class.

Answers
Student A's questions
1   You pay for yourself.
2   You choose the charity yourself.
3   find people to sponsor your trip and other ways like walking other people's dogs or selling your old things
Student B's questions
1   yes
2   half an hour three or four days a week at the start
3   give advice and help at training weekends

Listening

OPTIONAL LEAD-IN TO THE LISTENING

Ss close their books. Tell Ss they are going to listen to someone asking questions about Charity Champions. Ss work in pairs and predict the questions David might ask. Elicit the questions in feedback and write them on the board.

4a ▶ ⏺ 2.59 Tell Ss they are going to hear a phone call between David and one of the workers in Charity Champions. Ss look at the questions which David asks. Play recording 2.59. Ss listen and put the questions in the correct order.

Answers
1   b
2   f
3   a
4   d
5   e
6   c

b ▶ Ss answer the questions with a partner.

Answers
1 all over the world
2 hiking, cycling, sailing, rafting, mountain climbing, horse-riding
3 You have to have a good level of fitness.
4 You pay yourself.
5 working for people, e.g. charity dog walking, doing people's gardens
6 You choose your own charity.

5 ▶ Play the recording again. Ss listen and complete the chart. Ss check answers in pairs, then as a whole class.

Answers
likes/loves: cycling
would like/love to: climb a mountain, try rafting
doesn't like: sailing
wouldn't like to: walk dogs

Grammar | *like* and *would like*

6 ▶ Write *He likes cycling. He would like to climb a mountain* on the board. Ss focus on the verb endings after *like*. Ask Ss *Which form of the verb goes after* likes? (the -*ing* form) Ask Ss *Which form of the verb goes after* would like? (the infinitive)

▶ Ss complete the rules in the Active grammar box with a partner. Ss check answers in pairs, then as a whole class.

Active grammar

like (love, etc.)
would like (love, etc.)
would like (love, etc.)
like (love, etc.)

▶ Explain the difference in meaning between *I like …* and *I'd like …*: *I like playing tennis* (now, in general) but *I'd like to play tennis tomorrow* (a specific choice for the future).

▶ Direct Ss to the Reference section on page 127.

7 ▶ Ss choose the correct form of the verb to complete the sentences in pairs. Check answers.

Answers
1 dancing, to be
2 learning, to leave
3 to travel, flying
4 living, to leave
5 staying, to get
6 to visit, to stay

8 ▶ Ss look at the summary of expeditions list from the Charity Champions website. Review the use of the Present Perfect to talk about past experiences quickly before Ss start (see Lesson 10.2). Ss work in small groups of three or four. They discuss the questions together, e.g. *I've never been to China. Have you? I'd love to do that expedition because I really enjoy trekking and I'd love to go to China*, etc.

OPTIONAL EXTENSION

Ask Ss to imagine they are going on one of the Charity Champions expeditions. Elicit a few different well-known charities. Ss discuss in pairs which charity they would choose to support and why.

Pronunciation | /ɑɪ/ and /eɪ/

9a ▶ 🔘 2.60 Ss look at the sentence. They listen to recording 2.60 to determine if the pronunciation of the vowel sound in the underlined words is the same or different. Ss check answers in pairs, then as a whole class.

Answer
No. The vowel sound in *like* is /ɑɪ/. The vowel sound in *play* is /eɪ/.

b ▶ 🔘 2.61 Ss look at the pairs of words. Play recording 2.61. Ss listen and underline the words they hear on the recording. Ss check answers in pairs, then as a whole class.

Answers
1 white
2 Dave
3 late
4 mine
5 lake

▶ Ss practise saying the words in pairs.

OPTIONAL EXTENSION

Dictate the following sentences to Ss: (1) *I hate waiting for the train in the rain.* (2) *Mike likes riding his bike but he hates playing games.* Ss underline the /ɑɪ/ and /eɪ/ sounds they hear.

Speaking and writing

10a ▶ Give an example of a personal ambition of your own, e.g. take a year off work and travel around the world. Elicit one or two other ideas of things people have never done but would really like to do one day, e.g. write a book, go scuba diving on a coral reef, etc. Ss write down four or five personal ambitions.

b ▶ Ss work in small groups. They compare ambitions and whether they would like to do similar things or not. In whole-class feedback, elicit the different ambitions and establish what the most popular ambition is.

c ▶ Direct Ss to the example in their books. Ss use the verbs in ex. 6 to write a similar short paragraph describing their ambitions.

12 Communication

In this lesson, Ss listen to four people speaking about their plans for the coming months and the future. Ss discuss their own plans and ambitions in small groups.

OPTIONAL WARMER

Ask: *How much time off work/studies do you usually have during the summer?* Elicit the kind of things Ss usually do during the summer months. Ask: *Do you usually go away on holiday? Do you usually stay at home with your family? Do you usually work?* etc.

1 ▶ Ss look at the photos with a partner and answer the questions.

Answers
They are young people doing different things in their holidays.

2a ▶ ⬤ 2.62 Play recording 2.62. Ss listen and identify each speaker in the photos. Ss check answers in pairs, then as a whole class.

Answers
1   A
2   D
3   B
4   C

b ▶ Play the recording again. Ss listen and complete the chart.

Answers
Martina:
Plans: to go home and relax
Ambitions: would like to work for two months
Jacques:
Plans: to take part in a summer camp for children
Ambitions: would like to work with children, start a teaching course
Hiroshi:
Plans: to travel in Europe, to practise his English
Ambitions: would like to get a place in a university in England next year
Silvia:
Plans: to study all summer
Ambitions: would like to go to medical school

3 ▶ Play the recording again. Ss listen and complete the *How to...* box. They read the audioscript on page 160, then check answers in pairs and as a whole class.

Answers
1   going to
2   going to
3   planning to
4   like
5   want
6   hope

▶ Focus on the different forms used to express plans and ambitions. Help Ss with the intonation patterns for these expressions.

4a ▶ Go through the list of ideas for things to do in the summer. Then, invite Ss to think about their own plans for the summer and choose three or four things they would like to do. They can use their own ideas or the ideas mentioned in the lesson.

b ▶ Ss work in pairs and agree on two or three things they might do together during the summer. Ss share their ideas with the other Ss in whole-class feedback.

5 ▶ Ss work in small groups of four. They tell each other (1) about their immediate plans for the future and (2) their longer-term ambitions and plans.

OPTIONAL EXTENSION

Ss work in small groups. They tell the others in their group how they see themselves (1) in one year's time, (2) in five years' time and (3) by the time they have retired. Put the following headings on the board to guide the discussion: *family, work/career/studies, home, travel, money.*

12 Review and practice

1 ▶

> **Answers**
> 1 They are/They're going to build an old people's home in the suburbs.
> 2 They are/They're going to open a local history museum in the town centre.
> 3 Our town is going to close the swimming pool in Rectory Road.
> 4 Our town is going to introduce a 35 km per hour speed limit in the central area.
> 5 Our town is going to start a new 24-hour telephone information line.

2 ▶

> **Answers**
> 1 Toyota isn't going to build new factories in Europe.
> 2 Are you going to have a holiday this summer?
> 3 Is Tom going to buy a new mobile phone?
> 4 My parents aren't going to sell their house.
> 5 Is your father going to retire next year?
> 6 Your friends aren't going to stay here tonight.

3 ▶

> **Answers**
> 1 I am/I'm going
> 2 The children are going
> 3 we're going to go back
> 4 to meet
> 5 She isn't going to

4 ▶

> **Answers**
> 1 to see the Acropolis
> 2 to use the Internet
> 3 to meet new people
> 4 to commute to work
> 5 to send text messages

5 ▶

> **Answers**
> 1 studying, to go
> 2 flying, to travel
> 3 eating, to work
> 4 smoking, to marry
> 5 feeling, to live

6 ▶

> **Answers**
> 1 rafting
> 2 driving
> 3 horse-riding
> 4 mountain biking
> 5 kayaking
> 6 cycling
> 7 mountain climbing
> 8 surfing
> Activity X = trekking

12 Writing bank

1 ▶ Ss' own answers

2a ▶

> **Answer**
> a thank you letter for a present

b ▶

> **Answers**
> 1 Carrie
> 2 He sent her a present in the post.
> 3 something you can wear every day, e.g. a bracelet or a watch
> 4 She's looking forward to seeing Uncle Harold at her mother's birthday party next month.
> 5 contractions, as it is an informal letter

c ▶ Ss' own answers

3a ▶

> **Answers**
> 1 B
> 2 F
> 3 C
> 4 G
> 5 A
> 6 D
> 7 E

b ▶

> **Answers**
> 1 closing sentence
> 2 main paragraph
> 3 opening sentence

4 ▶

> **Answers**
> a Mum's
> b It's, I'm
> 1 They're very excited about Jane's wedding.
> 2 I don't like Michael's new girlfriend.

5 ▶

> **Answers**
> I'm really sorry to hear that you're not feeling well. I hope that you're not going to stay in hospital very long and that you'll soon get better.
> I'm going to send you some roses because I know you're very fond of flowers. They're from Dad's garden.

6a ▶ Ss plan what they will say in their thank you letter.

b ▶ Ss write a thank you letter.

Audioscripts

Do you know...?

Track 1.01
a b c d e f g h i j k l m n o p q r s t u v w x y z

Track 1.02
a h j k b c d e g p t v f l m n s x z i y o q u w r

Track 1.03
oh/zero, one, two, three, four, five, six, seven, eight, nine, ten

Track 1.04
eleven, twelve, thirteen, fourteen, fifteen, sixteen, seventeen, eighteen, nineteen, twenty, twenty-one, twenty-two, thirty, forty, fifty, sixty, seventy, eighty, ninety, a hundred

Track 1.05
1 Listen.
2 Look at page ...
3 Ask and answer.
4 Read.
5 Write.
6 Complete.
7 Match.
8 Repeat.
9 Correct.
10 Check your answers.
11 Read the tip.

Track 1.06
M = Man, W = Woman
M: How do you say *coche* in English?
W: Car.
M: How do you spell that?
W: C–A–R.
M: And what does *grandmother* mean?
W: She's your mother or father's mother.
M: I don't understand. Can you repeat that?
W: Yes. She's your mother or father's mother.
M: Oh. OK. Thanks.

Unit 1

Track 1.07
M = Man, W = Woman
1
W: Hi, I'm Silvia. What's your name?
M: Hi, Silvia. My name's Pedro.
2
M: What's your name, please?
W: It's Caroline Stacey.
M: How do you spell that?
W: It's C–A–R–O–L–I–N–E S–T–A–C–E–Y.
3
M: Hello. My name's John Logan.
W: Hello. I'm Maria Burton. Nice to meet you.

Track 1.08
020 651 3472

Track 1.09
M = Man, W = Woman
1
M: What's your number?
W: It's 01452 946 713.
2
W: What's your phone number, please?
M: 02096 659 248.
3
M: Is your mobile phone number 951 327 946?
W: Yes, that's right.
4
W: Excuse me. Can you tell me your phone number?
M: Of course. It's 02096 639 247.
W: Thanks.

5
M: Can you give me your mobile number, please?
W: It's 01542 984 731.
M: 01542 984 731?
W: Yes. That's right.

Track 1.10
1 Australian 2 Argentinian
3 Brazilian 4 Italian 5 Germany
6 Iranian 7 Spain 8 Polish
9 English 10 Chinese 11 France
12 Greece

Track 1.11
Australia	Australian
Argentina	Argentinian
United States of America	American
Brazil	Brazilian
Italy	Italian
Germany	German
Iran	Iranian
Russia	Russian
Spain	Spanish
Poland	Polish
England	English
Turkey	Turkish
China	Chinese
Japan	Japanese
France	French
Czech Republic	Czech
Greece	Greek

Track 1.12
I'm Brazilian. I'm from São Paulo.
1 Jennifer López is American. She's from New York.
2 We're Polish. We're from Warsaw.
3 A: Excuse me, where are you from?
   B: I'm from Colombia.
4 A: What is it?
   B: I think it's a Japanese car.
5 A: Who are they?
   B: They're students in my class. They're from Brazil.

Track 1.13
This is a picture of my wedding. This is me and this is my husband Rafael. Rafael's sisters' names are Nathalia and Alessandra. They're from Brazil. Rafael's mother is Nilza and his father is Almir. This is my brother, he's called Connor. Our parents are called Kim and Steve. My grandparents, my mother's mother and father, are called Eileen and Seamus.

Track 1.14
This is a picture of my family from Canada. This is my mom and this is my dad and this is my brother, Ben. His wife is Sheri and these are their two daughters, Julia and Erica. This is my grandmother, Margaret and my grandpa, Jack. They live in southern Ontario. This is my sister, Emily. Her husband's name is Tom and their son's name is James. This is my uncle, Jay. His wife's name is Shelley. And this is their dog. His name is Shadow.

Track 1.15
Mike
Let's see, interesting jobs in my family. Well, erm, my parents are retired, so that isn't very interesting. My sister, my sister's in marketing – she's a marketing director, and, oh yes, her husband, my brother-in-law, is a television producer. Um, my sister-in-law is a lawyer, and, who else? Oh, my uncle. My uncle's a farmer.
Helen
My family's jobs? Well, yes, there are some interesting jobs in my family ... my parents

are landlords in a restaurant, and my brother is a chef there, so that's a real family business. My other brother's an engineer and my sister's in computing – she's a computer programmer. Um, let's see, who else? Well, my cousin's a teacher – not very interesting, erm, oh, I know, her father – my uncle – is a sea captain – a captain of a very big ship. Now, that's different!

Track 1.16
a an

Track 1.17
an actor an architect a chef
a computer programmer a dentist
a doctor an engineer a farmer
a lawyer a sea captain
a shop assistant a TV producer

Track 1.18
1
A: Open your mouth, please. Say Aah.
B: Unnngh.
A: That's good. Thank you.
2
Stop ... Stop now. Good boy! OK, now come here, here boy. Good dog!
3
A: Look at these plans. They aren't correct, are they?
B: No, I think you're right.
A: OK. Let's think. What ...
4
Number 3 is ready. Jane, where are you? Number 3 to table, please. Quick!

Track 1.19
M = Man, W = Woman
1
W: Good morning.
M: Hi.
W: Are you a new student?
M: Yes, I'm in the elementary class.
2
W: No, she's his girlfriend.
M: Oh, OK. Well, see you later.
W: Bye.
3
W: Excuse me.
M: Yes?
W: Are you the teacher?
M: No, I'm a student in the ...
4
W: Great. Thanks for your help ...
M: OK. Bye.
W: Goodbye.
5
W: Good evening.
M: Hello. We've got a reservation for dinner at 8 o'clock.
W: Yes, come this way ...
6
M: Great party!
W: Yes. See you at the next one!
M: Yes. See you soon.

Track 1.20
1
M = Maria, C = Clara
M: Hello, I'm Maria.
C: Hello Maria, I'm Clara.
M: Pleased to meet you. Where are you from?
C: I'm from Alicante.
M: Oh! Do you work there?
C: No, I'm a student.
2
J = Jordi, K = Krystof
J: Excuse me, are you Krystof?
K: Yes, I am. What's your name?

J: My name's Jordi. Are you Polish?
K: Yes, I am. I'm from Warsaw.
J: What do you do?
K: I'm a teacher.

Unit 2

Track 1.21

What time is it?
1 It's six o'clock.
2 It's ten past two.
3 It's quarter past eight.
4 It's twenty past three.
5 It's half past seven.
6 It's twenty-five to two.
7 It's quarter to four.
8 It's five to five.

Track 1.22

1 I get home late at night, at about quarter to twelve.
2 We leave work at ten past five in the afternoon.
3 I get up at quarter past seven in the morning.
4 We have dinner at half past six in the evening.

Track 1.23

M = Man, W = Woman
W: When do you get up?
M: At ten in the evening.
W: Do you work at night?
M: Yes, I do.
W: What do you do in the afternoon?
M: I sleep.
W: When do you have dinner?
M: I have dinner at about eleven in the morning.
W: Do you work in an office?
M: No, I don't.
W: Where do you work?
M: I work in a hospital.
W: So, what do you do?
M: I'm a doctor.

Track 1.24

walks, listens, organises

Track 1.25

cleans, talks, washes, likes, goes, watches

Track 1.26

1 The teacher talks in English in class.
2 Jake washes his hair every morning.
3 Matt likes his new job – it's very interesting.
4 Tracy goes to work at 9:00 in the morning.
5 My brother watches football on TV every evening.
6 Patrick plays games on the computer at work.

Track 1.27

M = Man, W = Woman
W: Does Jeanette like her work?
M: Yes, she does. She loves it.
W: Does she clean the shark tank?
M: Yes, she does. And she feeds the sharks.
W: Do the sharks eat every day?
M: No, they don't. They eat three times a week.
W: So... does Jeanette work every day?
M: No, she doesn't. She works five days a week.

Track 1.28

Hi, I'm Jodie and this is Hell's Kitchen, New York City. It's the home of a famous flea market, you know, where people sell old things, things they don't want any more. It's right in the centre of the city, so it's very busy. The market is open Saturday and Sunday from 9:00 in the morning to 6:00 in the evening, and people come here every weekend to buy and sell all kinds of things. My brother Karl and I come here every weekend, too. We have a stall and I sell old clothes, shoes, bags, scarves and things like that. Karl doesn't sell clothes – he sells things like mobile phones, laptop computers and digital cameras. Our things are all useful, or beautiful, and they're quite cheap, but some people sell really expensive, useless things! We love it here – it's really good fun!

Track 1.29

K = Karl, J = Jodie
K: Hey, Jodie. You're here already.
J: Hey, Karl. Yeah, I'm early today.
K: So, everything's ready.
J: That's right. Here are all my clothes – my bags, shoes and scarves, oh, and I have some watches today, too – they're nice, don't you think?
K: Yeah, they're great! What are those books?
J: Oh, a friend has a book store. He wants to sell some of these old books.
K: OK. What's the time?
J: Quarter to nine. Do you have your things?
K: Yeah, here they are – some fantastic mobile phones today, and these two laptops.
J: Oh, they're good. Listen, do you want a coffee before we start?

Track 1.30

K = Karl, J = Jodie, Ja = Jane
J: It isn't very busy today, is it? I know, let's go and have a look at Jane's clothes stall.
K: OK. ... Hi, Jane! Only us! Oh, look – this is horrible! What is it?
J: I'm not sure ... is it a belt?
K: I really don't know, and look over there. Now that's really ugly!
J: Oh, it is. What is it?
K: I think it's a coat. But she has some nice scarves. Look.
J: Oh, yeah, these are pretty. ... Jane, hi, I want one of these scarves. OK?
Ja: Sure. Put it over there and come back later.
J: OK, thanks. Karl, just look at those shoes, they're so old-fashioned!
K: Yeah, but that bag is really useful – I like that.
J: Come on Karl, there are some people at our stall.

Track 1.31

this   these

Track 1.32

big, clean, green, listen, niece, read, sister, swim, teacher, think

Track 1.33

Matt
On holidays I like to go on city breaks, erm, I go with my girlfriend and we like to walk around the city and look at the sights. We get up at about nine o'clock and don't go to bed until quite late. We take with us our camera because I like taking photographs of the buildings, erm, and we also take a guidebook so we can find our way around.

Wendy
When I go on holiday, I love to go to Thailand, because my brother lives there and I can visit him and spend some time with my nephews and nieces. I love to go to the beach, er, I always get up early and get a book and take it down to the beach with me, and I take my brother's children with me, um, I always take some presents with me when I go, to give to the children, er, they love presents from England, particularly from London. In the evening I usually spend some time with my brother, in his house, talking, and maybe eat another meal and get some good sleep, and then the next day back to the beach!

Gareth
I go on holiday with my family, er, we usually go skiing in Italy or Austria. We like that, er, all of us, the kids, too. So we get up quite early, er, at about eight o'clock, so that we can start skiing in the morning, then we ski all day. Boring, isn't it? But we love it! We come back to the apartment at about four o'clock and have a big meal, then we play games with the children. Um, when they go to bed we just read books or play more games, but we go to bed early, too because we're always tired. Oh, we always take sunscreen with us, um, because it's often hot and sunny, and of course we take games and books for the evenings.

Unit 3

Track 1.34

Stig
In my lunch break, I usually have lunch at my desk and at the same time I check my email and read the news. Er, when I finish my lunch I usually go for a walk. Sometimes I go to the park, sometimes I go to the shops, er, but I always leave my desk at least for fifteen to twenty minutes at lunchtime.

Amber
Um, at lunchtime, I, um, sometimes go into town, um, and go shopping, um, but I don't always take a lunch break and I quite often sit at my desk, um, and carry on working. Um, occasionally I surf the Internet, um, but usually I work through my lunch break.

Matt
In my lunch break I usually surf the Internet but sometimes I go to the gym or walk through the park. Occasionally I visit a café and I sit and have lunch and read my book.

Ailsa
Um, I usually go up to the canteen to have lunch with some colleagues and sometimes when I'm busy, I stay at my desk and have a sandwich. There's a bus into the town centre, so I often take the bus into town to do some shopping or go to the bank. I never go to the gym at lunchtime.

Track 1.35

W1 = Woman 1, W2 = Woman 2
W1: Hello, Mrs Smith. How's your Susie?
W2: She's fine, thank you, Mrs Jones. And how's Jonny?
W1: He's OK, thanks. He can play the guitar now, you know.
W2: Oh, Susie can play the guitar, and she can play the piano, too.
W1: Well, Jonny can't play the piano but he can sing.
W2: Oh, can he? Susie can sing ...
W1: Can Susie dance?
W2: Yes, she can. Can Jonny dance?
W1: No, he can't. He doesn't have time to dance. He can play football – he's in the school team, and he can play tennis, and ...
W2: Susie can't play football – she doesn't like it. It's not a nice game for a girl. But she can play tennis, and she can ski, of course. Tell me, can Jonny ski?
W1: No, but he can speak French, you know ...

Audioscripts

W2: Oh, of course Susie can speak French, and she can speak Spanish, too, and she can …
W1: Jonny can ride a bike and he …
W2: Susie can't ride a bike but she can drive a car. Can Jonny drive?
W1: Of course he can't drive. He's only ten!

Track 1.36
Can you dance? Yes, I can. No, I can't.

Track 1.37
six
sixteen
sixty
six hundred
six hundred and one
six hundred and sixty
six thousand
six thousand, six hundred and sixteen
sixty thousand
six hundred thousand
six million
six billion

Track 1.38
sixteen sixty fourteen forty

Track 1.39
1 forty 2 eighty 3 seventeen
4 thirteen 5 ninety 6 sixteen

Track 1.40
1
T = Tony, J = Jane
T: This is 054 898 4567. Please leave a message after the tone.
J: Hi, Tony, it's Jane. Let's meet outside the cinema at ten to eight. See you there, OK? Bye.

2
M = Mandy, S = Steve
M: Hello, this is Mandy and John's phone. We're not here right now so please leave a message with your name and number and the time of your call. Thank you.
S: Mandy, it's Steve Henshaw here. It's twenty past three on Wednesday. Can you call me? My number's 068 919 0752. Thanks.

3
M = Michael, C = Carol
M: This is Michael Brown's voicemail. Please leave a message now.
C: Good morning, Mr Brown. This is Carol at Benson Cameras. Your new camera is here. Can you come to the shop and get it this week? We are open from nine o'clock until half past six every day.

4
J = Judy, D = Damian
J: Hi, I'm not here right now so please leave a message after the beep. Thanks.
D: Judy, it's Damian. Why don't we meet for dinner this evening? How about the Italian restaurant in Green Street at twenty-five past eight? Give me a call. I'm in the office all afternoon.

5
R = Reception, M = Mary
R: Good morning. Brandon Travel Agency.
M: Hello. Can I speak to David Renton?
R: I'm afraid he isn't in this morning. Can I take a message?
M: Yes, can you ask him to call Mary Wilde?
R: Of course. What's your telephone number?
M: It's 713 391 8834.
R: Sorry? Can you repeat that?
M: 713 391 8834.
R: Fine.
M: Thanks. Bye.

Track 1.41
M = Man, W = Woman
W: Hello.
M: Hello, can I speak to Laura, please?
W: She isn't here right now. Can I take a message?
M: Yes, please ask her to phone Jeffrey.
W: OK. What's your number?
M: It's 011 908 5561.
W: OK. Bye.

Track 1.42
I = Interviewer, D = Dario, L = Lizzie
I: Dario, what's your phone number?
D: It's 887 715 992.
I: Do you have any special abilities?
D: Well, I can play the piano and the guitar, and I can drive. I love driving.
I: Can you speak any foreign languages?
D: No, I can't. Only English!
I: Can you use computers at all?
D: Yes, but I only use them to play games!
I: And what do you need?
D: Well, it's my sister's wedding next month. We need a photographer; we want good photos.
I: OK.
I: Lizzie, what about you? Do you have any special abilities?
L: I can play a lot of different sports.
I: Really? Which ones?
L: Football, basketball and tennis.
I: What about practical skills?
L: Well, I'm a good cook. And I like cleaning and housework.
I: What about computers?
L: Oh, I really don't understand computers! Actually, that's what I need. Can someone repair my new laptop?
I: I see. And what's your phone number, Lizzie?
L: My mobile number is 0777 334 898.
I: Right.

Unit 4

Track 1.43
1
Well, my husband's from Brazil so we eat a lot of Brazilian food. My favourite is a dish called *feijoada*, made from black beans, and rice and meat. We eat that quite a lot because it's very cheap to make. We don't eat much fast food, except sometimes on the weekends and we also eat lots of seafood.

2
Oh, in Canada we eat a lot of seafood, especially lobster and scallops, anything that comes from the sea. But we don't eat much lamb or duck and we don't eat many takeaways. But my favourite food is maple syrup and I usually have it twice a week on pancakes.

3
My family's from Iran. We eat a lot of rice and stews. The stews are made with meats and lots of dried fruits and lots of delicious spices. I think my favourite food is a dish called *fesenjan*, made with nuts and fruits and spices, and my children love it and, best of all, it's really easy to cook. We don't eat any pork or ham, and Iranians don't eat much seafood.

Track 1.44
Hello and welcome to *In The Rubbish Bin*, the show where we look at people's lives by looking at their rubbish. I'm Laurence Redburn.
Today we look at the diets of two very different families. I have their rubbish bins in

the studio, with a typical day's rubbish, so, let's start with rubbish bin 1. What does this family eat and drink? We have some cans … cola cans – not very healthy. Mmm, instant coffee. Some boxes … cheese and tomato pizza, burgers. Some biscuits, and … crisp packets – all fast food, and not very healthy. Do they eat any vegetables or fruit? I don't think so. Oh dear, not a healthy diet. A lot of this food is bad for you, so this family is probably not very healthy.
Now let's look at rubbish bin 2. This is very different – it's good. This family eats a lot of fruit and vegetables … some potatoes, carrots … bananas and apples. What do they drink? We have a juice carton, a milk carton and we have a water bottle – very good, all very healthy so far. Tea bags … well, OK. They eat some pasta, and fish – that's good. I can't see any fast food here. I think this is a very healthy family.

Track 1.45
W = Woman, L = Laurence
W: But Laurence, that's really not fair!
L: What do you mean?
W: Well, this bin doesn't really show our diet.
L: Go on.
W: OK, we eat a pizza once a week – I don't think that's bad – and the children eat some burgers. And, yes, we sometimes drink some coffee, and the children drink a can of cola once or twice a week, but we don't drink any tea, and we drink a lot of water – about ten litres a week. We also eat a lot of vegetables every day, and we eat some meat and chicken. We don't eat any sweets or chocolate – that's good, isn't it?
L: Well, yes, but where are the water bottles and vegetables in your bin?
W: We recycle them, of course!

Track 1.46
pasta, some

Track 1.47
salad, butter, lamb, apple, lunch, carrot

Track 1.48
W = Waitress, S = Sam, J = Jenny
W: Hi. What can I get you today?
S: Hi. I'd like a cheese sandwich, please.
W: On white or brown bread?
S: On brown, please.
W: Would you like fries?
S: Yes.
W: Regular or large size?
S: Large.
W: And your friend?
S: Jenny, what would you like?
J: Do you have salads?
W: Yes. Small, medium or large?
J: Can I have a medium salad?
W: Sure. Anything to drink?
J: Sam, do you want some juice?
S: No, thanks. I'll have a coffee.
J: OK, a small cup of coffee for …
S: No, no, a large one.
J: OK. A large cup of coffee for him and a small glass of mineral water for me.
W: Fine. Coming right up!

Track 1.49
W = Waitress, S = Sam, J = Jenny
W: OK, here we are. Two vegetarian pizzas.
S: No, they're not for us. Our order is a sandwich with fries and a salad.
W: Oh, sorry, that's the wrong order. Just a moment.
J: Two vegetarian pizzas? I really like them! Can we change our order?
S: Of course not.

W: OK. I think this is your order. A medium salad for you, sir.

S: Oh no, the salad's for her.

W: OK. Right. A medium salad and a small glass of mineral water for you, madam; and a cheese sandwich on brown bread with large fries and a large cup of coffee for you, sir.

S: Yes. Thanks. Can we pay now?

W: Sure.

S: How much is that?

W: That's sixteen dollars and seventy cents, please.

S: Can I pay by credit card?

W: Of course.

Track 1.50

W1 = Woman 1, M1 = Man 1, W2 = Woman 2, M2 = Man 2

W1: Hello.

M1: Good morning to you! Can I help you?

W1: Yes, I need some fruit. I'd like three bananas, a kilo of apples and a melon, please.

M1: We don't have any melons today. Sorry.

W1: OK, just the bananas and apples then, please.

M1: A kilo of apples – they're two euros a kilo, and three bananas. Here you are.

W1: Thank you. How much is that?

M1: That's three euros and fifty cents, please.

W1: Three euros, fifty. Here you are. Thank you. Bye.

M1: Bye.

W2: Can I help you?

W1: Yes, I'd like 500 grammes of beef, 400 grammes of this fish, and a chicken, please.

W2: Um, I don't have any chickens left, I'm afraid.

W1: Oh dear. OK.

W2: That's 500 grammes of beef and 400 grammes of fish. That's eighteen euros altogether. Thank you.

W1: Hello.

M2: Hello there. What can I do for you?

W1: I'd like some cheese, please.

M2: Certainly. Which cheese?

W1: Umm, can I have 200 grammes of that one, please?

M2: Of course. Is that it?

W1: No, do you sell milk?

M2: Yes, it's in the fridge.

W1: Ah, can I have two litres, please?

M2: Yes. Right, that's two euros eighty.

Unit 5

Track 1.51

A = Estate agent, J = Jon

A: Unusual Homes. Good afternoon. Can I help you?

J: Yes. I'm interested in the house in Italy with the unusual roof.

A: Oh, yes, I know it.

J: Can I ask you a few questions about it?

A: Of course.

J: Well, first, how many bedrooms does it have?

A: Umm, let me see. It has five bedrooms.

J: Oh, good. And is there only one bathroom?

A: No, there are two bathrooms.

J: Excellent. Is there air conditioning?

A: No, you don't need air conditioning in a house of that type. But there is central heating.

J: Mmm, OK. Is there a garden?

A: Yes, there's a large, sunny garden; it has a lot of outside space.

J: OK, good. Is the house near a village?

A: Yes, it is. The village is one kilometre away.

J: Oh, good. So are there many shops in the village?

A: I'm afraid I don't know. There's a cash machine in the village, so there are probably shops.

J: Are there any schools in the area?

A: Well, yes, there's a school in the village.

J: Oh, that's good. OK. Now, can I check, how much is the house?

A: It's 300,000 euros.

J: Oh, that's not bad. Can I see it?

A: Yes, of course. Tell me when you can get to Italy, and then I can call the owners and …

Track 1.52

A = Insurance agent, P = Pete

A: Allied Insurance. Can I help you?

P: Yes. I need some home insurance.

A: OK. Can you answer a few questions?

P: Sure.

A: What's your full name?

P: It's Peter Morgan.

A: Are you married?

P: Yes. But we haven't got any children.

A: OK, Mr Morgan. Have you got your own house?

P: No, I haven't. I've got a modern studio apartment in the centre of town, but it's rented.

A: Has it got a garden?

P: No, it hasn't got a garden, but it's got a small terrace.

A: Is there a kitchen in the apartment?

P: Not a big one, but there's a kitchen area with a fridge, a microwave and a sink. But I haven't got a cooker.

A: What about furniture?

P: We've got a coffee table. It's valuable because it's very old. And there are two chairs, they're made of wood. And we've got a sofa.

A: No dining table?

P: No, we always eat on the sofa!

A: OK. Now, electrical equipment. Is there a TV?

P: Yes, of course. And we've got a music system.

A: Any computers?

P: Yes, I've got a laptop computer – I use the Internet a lot.

A: And have you got a mobile phone?

P: Yes, I have.

Track 1.53

A: OK, Mr Morgan. Have you got your own house?

P: No, I haven't. I've got a modern studio apartment in the centre of town, but it's rented.

A: Has it got a garden?

P: No, it hasn't got a garden, but it's got a small terrace.

Track 1.54

He's got a laptop, a cat and a watch.

Track 1.55

1 hat 2 on 3 top 4 packet

Track 1.56

Ana

I'm Ana. I'm from Spain and I love this country – in Spain there are so many places and things to see. There's even a famous desert in Spain – it's true – the Almeria Desert. It's in the south of Spain. They make a lot of films in this desert because it's really hot and dry. There are also a lot of beautiful beaches in Spain.

Marcin

My name's Marcin and my home is in Poland, in the east of the country. There are some beautiful lakes in the east of Poland – it's a lovely area. A lot of Polish people take their holidays here. In fact, it's quite popular now with people from other countries, too.

Costas

I'm Costas. I live in Greece, on the island of Kefalonia. People don't think that Greece is a green country, with a lot of trees, but Kefalonia is a very green island. There's a lovely forest in the north of the island. Of course, there are also beaches on Kefalonia – it's a very popular holiday island.

Yumiko

My name's Yumiko. I come from Japan, from a city called Osaka. It's a huge city in the west of Japan, and it's very busy and noisy, and it's not very friendly. There are a lot of shops and offices in the city, and people are always in a hurry. I don't like it here – I like the mountains.

Track 1.57

river desert

Track 1.58

river desert detached famous luxurious noisy popular

Track 1.59

1 It's really hot and dry.

2 It's quite popular now with people from other countries, too.

3 Kefalonia is a very green island.

4 It's very busy and noisy, and it's not very friendly.

Track 1.60

Hello. My name's Megan, and I come from Wales. I don't live there now; I live in England, but Wales is still my home. I come from the south of Wales, a village near Cardiff, the main city in Wales. My parents still live there. Wales is a lovely country. It has mountains in the north and hills in the south, and there are a lot of beautiful beaches in the west. There are also a lot of rivers in Wales – our word for them is 'aber' – yes, we have our own language! I like Wales because it's very beautiful and because the people are really friendly.

Unit 6

Track 1.61

art gallery, bank, bar, bus station, café, cinema, factory, hospital, library, museum, post office, restaurant, school, train station

Track 1.62

A = Angeles, J = Jason

A: Oh, that's an interesting building. What is it?

J: The Hoover Building? Oh, that's a supermarket.

A: A supermarket? You have lovely supermarkets here, Jason!

J: Well, they planned it as a factory in the 1930s. So it was a factory for years before it was a supermarket.

A: Oh, I see.

J: Yes, in fact, my grandfather worked there in the 1960s, after he married my grandmother. But he stopped working there a long time ago. He produced electrical equipment.

A: Really?

J: Yes, it only opened as a supermarket about 30 years ago.

A: That's interesting. You know, there's a building in Madrid like that, I mean, it

Audioscripts

changed from one thing to another – the Reina Sofia. It's an art gallery now.
J: Oh, yes. I know it. I visited it when I was in Madrid last year. It's fantastic! It's all 20th century art, isn't it?
A: That's right. It's my favourite gallery – you know I studied modern art – I often go there. I love *Guernica*, you know, the famous painting by Picasso.
J: Of course. What was it before, then?
A: It was a hospital – doctors and nurses lived and worked there, and looked after sick people. They started changing it into a gallery in 1980, then the gallery opened in 1992.

Track 1.63
worked, opened, started

Track 1.64
changed, lived, looked, planned, produced, studied, visited

Track 1.65
I = Interviewer, S = Sean, M = Meera
1
I: Sean, can I ask you some questions for our series on immigrants?
S: Sure.
I: Are you Irish or American?
S: Well, I'm a New Yorker! No, that's a joke. I'm American, of course. Well, that's what my passport says! But my family were Irish, so I'm Irish-American.
I: Did you grow up in the USA?
S: Yes, I did. I was born in New York and I went to school in Brooklyn – that's a suburb of New York. And I still live there.
I: Where did your family come from?
S: My great-great grandparents came from Waterford. That's a city on the south coast of Ireland.
I: Why did so many Irish people go to the USA?
S: Well, life was very difficult in Ireland. There wasn't enough food or work for all the people in the 1840s and 50s, so poor people came to America to look for jobs and a better life.
2
I: Why are there so many Indian people in England, Meera?
M: Well, for hundreds of years India and Pakistan were part of the British empire. So there were a lot of connections between the countries. Rich Indians sent their children to school in England and poor people came here as servants.
I: Were you born in London?
M: No, I was born in Mumbai, in India. But my family came to the UK in the 1980s. My father worked as a teacher and my mother worked in a restaurant. There were lots of jobs for Indians in Britain in those days.
I: Did you go to school in India?
M: No, I didn't. I didn't go to school there because my parents moved here when I was five, so I went to school in England.
I: Do you ever go to India?
M: Yes, I went there last year – for my cousin's wedding. It was fantastic. The people were so friendly! But it was very hot. I was happy to come home to London!

Track 1.66
Heather
I was born in Canada and my family lives in Canada. I grew up in New Brunswick and I went to French school in New Brunswick. I left home in 2005 and went travelling overseas. I went to all sorts of different countries and I met my partner overseas in 2006. I came to England in September 2007.

Stig
I was born in Norway but I didn't grow up there. We moved to England when I was five. So I didn't go to school in Norway, I went to school in England. I went to university in London. I studied economics but I didn't get a job in economics, I became an English teacher instead.

Track 1.67
1
Were you born in London?
No, I was born in Mumbai.
2
Did you visit Venice?
No, we visited Rome.
3
Was it nice?
No, it was horrible.

Track 1.68
C1 = Customer 1, S = Shop assistant,
C2 = Customer 2, C3 = Customer 3
C1: Excuse me. Where can I find men's shoes?
S: Men's shoes. That's on the top floor.
C1: Where are the stairs?
S: There are escalators on your right.
C1: Right. And have you got any maps of London?
S: No, we haven't. Sorry.
C1: OK. Thanks.
S: Can I help you?
C2: Yes. I'd like a laptop computer.
S: You need the computer department.
C2: Where's that?
S: In the basement. There are stairs on your right.
C2: Thanks very much. Oh, and I need a present for my son. Do you sell CDs?
S: Yes, we've got a music department on the ground floor.
C2: Great.
C3: Hello, is this the information point?
S: Yes. How can I help you?
C3: Where can I find dining tables and chairs?
S: That's in the furniture department on the top floor.
C3: Is there a lift?
S: Yes. Go to the end of the beauty hall and turn left.
C3: I need some other things. Have you got a store guide?
S: Yes. They're just here.
C3: Can I have a copy, please?
S: Of course.
C3: How much is that?
S: It's free.

Unit 7

Track 2.01
1 G has got blue eyes.
2 B has got long fair hair.
3 F has got dark skin.
4 G has got short grey hair.
5 F has got a beard.
6 B is slim.
7 C is young.
8 F is bald.
9 A is tall.
10 C is short.
11 E wears glasses.
12 F has got a moustache.

Track 2.02
C = Carol, M = Marianne
C: So, Marianne. What's your news?
M: Something exciting happened yesterday.
C: What?
M: Do you remember that man on the beach – the one I told you about in my email?
C: Er, yes.
M: He spoke to me! He's really friendly. He's Brazilian. He works in one of the big hotels on the beach, so he speaks good English.
C: What does he look like?
M: Well, he's very handsome, and tanned of course. About 22 or 23 I think. He's slim and he's got dark hair.
C: Long or short?
M: Short. And he's got a little beard.
C: What's his name?
M: Luis.
C: And has he got a wife or girlfriend?
M: No, he's single at the moment …
C: So, do you think he likes you?

Track 2.03
In Canada we celebrate Canada Day on July the first. This is basically Canada's birthday and the day that united Canada as a single country. The first Canada Day was in July 1867. On July the first we celebrate, everyone has the day off work and we have festivals, parties, there's usually a parade – just general celebration for everyone.
We celebrate Halloween on October the thirty-first and this is a day when people of all ages celebrate, dress up in costumes, children go around in their neighbourhood from door to door collecting candy and yelling 'trick or treat!'. If you're at home you have candy and treats by the door to give to everyone that comes by. They also usually carry a charity box and collect donations from people as well as the candy.

Track 2.04
first second third fourth fifth sixth
seventh eighth ninth tenth eleventh
twelfth thirteenth fourteenth fifteenth
twentieth twenty-second thirtieth thirty-first

Track 2.05
M = Mike, J = Jane
M: Hi, Jane, it's me.
J: Oh, hello, Mike. What's the problem?
M: You didn't write the names or addresses on those presents. I want to wrap them and take them to the post office. Who are they for?
J: Sorry.
M: The DVDs. Are they for Gordon?
J: Yes, they're his.
M: What about the trainers … are they Davy's?
J: Yes, the trainers are his.
M: What about the clock? Who is that for?
J: That's for my mum and dad.
M: OK, so the clock's theirs. And the handbag? Is that for Tara?
J: The handbag? Of course not. That's mine!
M: It's yours? Oh. So what did you get for Tara? I know it's her birthday next week.
J: The diary, that's hers.
M: Right. OK. Well, what about the umbrella?
J: The umbrella?
M: Yes, there's an umbrella on the table.
J: A black one?
M: Yes.
J: That belongs to us. It's ours!
M: Is it? Oh yes. Of course …

Track 2.06
birthday, brother, bathroom

Track 2.07
1 free 2 think 3 thick 4 thirst
5 three

Track 2.08
1 sixth 2 eighth 3 eat 4 hate
5 thin 6 three 7 lift 8 fifth

Track 2.09

G = Geoff, I = Isabel

G: What's wrong, Isabel?
I: I don't believe it. It's my computer. Look – nothing!
G: Phone the computer department then. They can repair it.
I: That's not the problem. I need to finish writing up the sales information for the meeting this afternoon.
G: So? You've got time.
I: No, I haven't. I also need to meet Mr Schäfer at the airport before the meeting. He arrives in half an hour.
G: Oh, I see … . Look, I can meet him. I've got time.
I: Oh, can you, Geoff? That's really nice of you. He's on flight …
G: Wait a minute! I don't know Mr Schäfer – do you?
I: Well, I met him about three years ago.
G: So what does he look like?
I: He's quite tall, about two metres, I think.
G: How old is he?
I: He's middle-aged. I think he's in his forties, his late forties now.
G: OK. What colour is his hair?
I: Well, he had brown hair when I met him, dark brown hair, but maybe he's grey now.
G: Oh, this isn't easy. Does he have long or short hair?
I: Short, I think, yes, quite short.
G: Right. Let's think, what's his body type?
I: Pardon?
G: Is he fat, thin … ?
I: Oh, slim, quite slim, I think.
G: What colour is his skin? Dark, fair … ?
I: He was very pale when I met him – yes, I remember that. Very pale.
G: And what colour are his eyes?
I: Oh, come on, Geoff! I can't remember that! I didn't look into his eyes, you know!
G: OK, OK. Is there anything else you can remember? Any other features I can look out for?
I: Um, yes. He had a beard, quite a short beard, and he had glasses. Does that help?
G: Yes, it does. What's he like?
I: Oh, he's nice. He's very friendly.
G: OK, that's fine. Well, see you later with Mr Schäfer. Good luck with your computer.
I: Oh, Geoff, wait a minute.
G: Yes?
I: Why don't you just hold up a card with his name on?

Unit 8

Track 2.10

M = Man, W = Woman

M: I want to go shopping at lunch time, I really need some new clothes. Are there any good clothes shops around here?
W: Well, there's a shop that sells nice jeans on the main road.
M: Oh, I think jeans are uncomfortable. I never wear them.
W: Really? I wear jeans all the time, even to work.
M: But jeans are very casual. You can't wear jeans to a formal business meeting!
W: That's true, but I never go to formal meetings. Now, what about shirts and pullovers? Tight shirts and pullovers look good.
M: Actually, I prefer loose shirts. And I don't wear pullovers very often. I prefer smart jackets.
W: Even in the winter?

M: Yes. But I usually wear a coat. Winter coats are usually warm and comfortable.
W: Really? I think winter coats are too heavy. I hate them!

Track 2.11

J = Jools, A = Anna, W = Whitney
Ju = Justin, P = Pam, M = Mika

J: Hello there, everyone! It's festival time here in the UK and today we're bringing you some pictures and information about late summer festivals around the world. Let's start in the US. Our reporter Anna Lindstrom is at the Boston Carnival right now. How's it going, Anna?
A: Hi, Jools. It's great. It's a really hot, late August day. I'm having a good time – everyone is having a good time.
J: What's happening right now?
A: Well, I'm standing in the street and I'm watching some fantastic dancers. They're moving slowly towards me. They're wearing really colourful costumes and they're dancing really well.
J: Sounds good.
A: Yes, and I'm with Whitney, who makes food for all the partygoers here. Whitney, what are you doing?
W: Well, I'm cooking some lovely Caribbean chicken curry.
A: Mmm, it smells wonderful.
J: Thank you, Anna. Now, Boston isn't the only place having a party at this time of year. Our reporter Justin Leonard is at the Mariachi festival in Guadalajara, Mexico. Justin, how's it going over there?
Ju: Hi, Jools. It's great here. I'm sitting in the town square and I'm listening to some fantastic mariachi music. In this band the guitarists are all playing together; it's lovely.
J: It sounds noisy there.
Ju: It is! The spectators aren't just listening, they're clapping and shouting and singing with the music.
J: Thank you, Justin. And in Helsinki, Finland, Pam Sykes is reporting on the Helsinki Festival.
P: Hello, Jools. Well, it's quiet here – it's not like Mexico. This is an arts festival, so it's all in cinemas, theatres and concert halls. Some people are queuing behind me to go into a theatre. I have Mika here with me. Mika, what are you queuing for today?
M: I'm not queuing for the theatre – I'm with my children – they're over there; they're waiting to see some funny films, some old films with Charlie Chaplin.
P: That sounds like fun! Thank you, Mika. Back to you, Jools.
J: Thanks, Pam. Now, in the studio this afternoon …

Track 2.12

1 She's dancing.
2 They're talking.
3 Are you listening?
4 We aren't leaving.

Track 2.13

OK, I'm looking at a picture of a street scene. It's a festival, I think. At the front of the picture two women are dancing. They're enjoying it! They're wearing really colourful costumes. On the left there are some people watching the dancers, and at the back of the picture there are some buildings, shops, and maybe houses, I think. There are musicians playing on the right of the picture – they're all wearing black so they're all together; they're part of the festival. I think everyone's having a good time!

Track 2.14

1
Woman: Ailsa, what's the weather like in Scotland right now?
Ailsa: In the south of Scotland it's quite warm and sunny but in the north, in the highlands, there's still snow on the mountains.

2
Woman: What's the weather like in Canada at the moment?
Heather: Well its summertime in Canada right now, but it's actually not that warm. It's 15 degrees and really foggy today.

3
Woman: Hi, Stig. What's the weather like over there?
Stig: At the moment in Norway it's late summer and today it's warm and sunny.

4
Woman: Amber, what's the weather like in Brazil now?
Amber: Well, this morning it was really hot and sunny but now it's raining.

Track 2.15

cold, hot, foggy, snowing

Track 2.16

1	cold	gold
2	top	told
3	snow	hot
4	not	lot

Track 2.17

old, clock, cost, note, hotel, not, on, wrote, own, bottle

Track 2.18

J = Jan, L = Luke

J: Hello.
L: Jan? It's Luke.
J: Luke? You don't usually call at this time. You always phone in the evenings.
L: I know. But I'm not at work. I'm at home.
J: Oh. Are you sick?
L: No, but I can't get into the office. The underground isn't working today.
J: Really? Why?
L: It's snowing here.
J: Snowing! So what?
L: Well, it's really snowing a lot. So the trains and buses aren't running. People can't get to work and lots of people are staying at home.
J: But it snows all through the winter in New York. Nothing stops because of that!
L: I know. But it hardly ever snows in London. It's a shock for us.
J: That's crazy!
L: Well, at least it isn't raining!
J: Yes, I hate rainy weather. I always feel sad and depressed when the sky is grey and there's no sun.
L: I know what you mean. London's always dark in December and January.
J: Yeah, I prefer snow really. Everything looks so beautiful …
L: Mm. I suppose so …

Track 2.19

1
R = Receptionist, W = Woman

R: Can I help you, madam?
W: Yes, I'm calling from room 342.
R: Yes, madam.
W: Well, it's very hot in here. I think there's a problem with the air conditioning.
R: Oh, I am sorry, madam. Is the air conditioner turned on?

W: Yes, it is. But it isn't working. Can you send somebody to repair it?

R: Of course. I'll ask the engineer to go to your room.

2

S = Shop assistant, M = Man

S: Can I help you?

M: Yes. I bought this DVD player from you, but it isn't working.

S: I see. Have you got your receipt?

M: Yes, I have. Can I exchange it for another one?

S: Of course. Just a moment. Here you are.

M: Thanks very much.

3

S = Shop assistant, W = Woman

W: Excuse me. Can you help me?

S: Yes, madam?

W: I bought this pullover yesterday and it doesn't fit.

S: Do you want to try a different size?

W: No, I'd like a refund.

S: Have you got your receipt?

W: Yes. Here it is.

S: OK. So that's 150 euros. Here you are.

Unit 9

Track 2.20

Ai = Ailsa, Am = Amber

Ai: Um, what have you got under painting?

Am: Um, I put cartoon under painting.

Ai: Yes.

Am: What about you?

Ai: Yes, I've, I've got cartoon as well, and I also put modern art under painting.

Am: Oh, yes, of course. And literature?

Ai: Um, I've got three things under literature: horror, novels and poetry.

Am: Oh, I put horror under film.

Ai: Yes, I think it can go there, too.

Am: Um, what about music?

Ai: Under music I've got classical music ...

Am: Yep, me too.

Ai: Um, opera ...

Am: Yeah ...

Ai: And rock music.

Am: And opera can also perhaps be classed under theatre?

Ai: Yeah, I agree.

Am: With dance and ballet.

Ai: Yeah. Under, so what have you got under theatre?

Am: Um, dance, ballet, and I think that's all I had.

Ai: OK, I also put comedy and plays.

Am: Oh, comedy can also go under literature, can't it?

Ai: Yeah, and film.

Am: Yeah.

Track 2.21

1 easier than
2 faster than
3 colder than
4 healthier than

Track 2.22

P = Petra, N = Nick

P: It says here that 70 percent of Americans got news about the election on the Internet. I think that's amazing.

N: Amazing? I don't find it surprising at all. I mean, with an election, people want to find out news very quickly, and it's faster on the Internet than on TV. How many Americans use the Internet for news every day?

P: Erm, well, it says 37 percent here.

N: Well, there you are, about half of the first number.

P: Mmm, do you think the number is the same here?

N: I think that it's probably the same. I think a lot of younger people use the Internet for news stories, but older people are more traditional – they read newspapers or watch the news on TV.

P: I don't think that it's just older people. I believe that newspapers are still better than other news sources because you can read them anywhere – on the train, in a restaurant, even in front of the TV!

N: Yes, I suppose so. What do you think of getting news on your mobile phone, then?

P: Well, it's OK, but in my opinion, it's better to read a newspaper or watch TV for news, to get more information and other people's opinions.

Track 2.23

P = Presenter, M = Mariela

P: Good evening. Tonight we've got Mariela Dolcino with us to talk about her favourite films from the last ten years. As you know, Mariela is the film critic for *The Sunday Reporter*. Welcome to the show, Mariela.

M: It's good to be here, Neil.

P: OK. Let's start with the best. Mariela, what do you think is the best film of the last ten years?

M: Well, there's no competition for me. I know a lot of people think it was the films in the *Lord of the Rings* series, and they were good, but for me the best film in the last ten years was *Slumdog Millionaire* – it was so different, very clever, and it had the best photography, I think.

P: I think a lot of people agree with you. What's the most exciting film of the last ten years, do you think?

M: That's easy – *Casino Royale*. I think it's the best James Bond film – Daniel Craig was fantastic in the character of James Bond – he's by far the best Bond in my opinion.

P: OK. Were there any surprises for you in the last ten years?

M: Surprises? Let me see ... well, yes. I think the biggest surprise was *An Inconvenient Truth* – you know, the Al Gore documentary about the environment. It was really interesting, and I think a lot of people understood the problem better when they watched it.

P: What about foreign language films? Any good ones there?

M: Well, lots, of course, but the one that I think was best was *The Lives of Others*, the German film. It was a lovely film, very sad, but the most interesting foreign language film of the last ten years, and for me the most successful winner of the Oscar for the best foreign language film.

P: Mmm, I liked that one, too. You don't like violent films, do you?

M: No, I don't, but there's one violent film that I want to talk about – *No Country for Old Men*. That was very violent, possibly the most violent film of the ten years, but it was very good – and the actor Javier Bardem was really fantastic as the bad guy – it's not usually the kind of part he plays, but you can believe that he's a real villain in this film!

P: And any good comedies?

M: Oh, yes, my favourite was *Little Miss Sunshine* – it really was the funniest film of the last ten years for me, especially the scene when the little girl is at the Little Miss Sunshine competition, but it's also quite sad in places.

P: Well, I think that's all we have time for ...

M: No, wait a moment. There's one more film I really want to mention, and that's *Chicago*. I don't usually like musicals at the cinema, but it really was the freshest musical for a long time – it was really good.

P: OK. Thank you very much, Mariela, and now we turn to ...

Track 2.24

J = Jenny, S = Serge

J: I'm going to the Banksy exhibition. Do you want to come?

S: Is it expensive?

J: No, it's free.

S: Er, no thanks. I don't like going to exhibitions really. They're boring.

J: But Banksy's really good. I love his work.

S: Who's Banksy? Is he famous?

J: Yes. He's a really famous modern artist. He paints graffiti on the sides of buildings.

S: That sounds stupid. I prefer traditional paintings to modern ones. Anyway, I want to stay at home. It's the final of *Pop Star Search* on TV this evening.

J: Oh no. I hate listening to those stupid kids singing.

S: Well, I love it. It's so exciting.

J: It's rubbish.

S: Oh, you hate everything on TV.

J: No, I don't! But I like serious programmes more than talent shows. I prefer watching films or documentaries. Programmes that make you think.

S: But I don't want to think when I watch TV. I just want to relax.

Track 2.25

1 Is it expensive?   2 Is he famous?

Track 2.26

1 Is it nice?
2 It's lovely.
3 Is it interesting?
4 It's boring.
5 Are we late?
6 Does she know?

Track 2.27

M = Matt, W = Wendy, G = Gavin

M: What shall we do this weekend?

W: Oh, I don't know.

G: How about going to the cinema?

M: Ooh, what's on?

W: Ahh, I think there's a new *Harry Potter* ...

M: Oh no, I don't like that.

W: Oh, don't you? I love that!

M: I, I saw the last one and it was really boring.

W: Oh, it was great! I read the book. I loved it.

G: I don't think so.

W: Oh, it's two against *Harry Potter*. OK, OK, not *Harry Potter*.

M: What about going out for dinner?

W: Mmm ... yeah ... Thai food – anybody like Thai food?

G: It's OK.

M: I don't really like Thai food.

W: How can you not like Thai food? I love Thai food.

M: And restaurants are quite expensive. Um, there's a football match on Saturday, why don't we go and watch that?

G: I think that's a great idea.

W: Ahhh ... mmm ... OK, I do quite like football. Yeah, ah, hang on though, because football could be a bit expensive.

M: My brother's band, they're on at the local club this weekend. Why don't we go and see them?

W: Ah, yeah, that'd be great.

G: That sounds good.

W: I'd love it.

M: Let's meet at the station.
W: Good idea. What time?
M: About seven?
W: Seven's good.
G: Seven's fine.
W: Fantastic, seven o'clock at the station.
M: See you there.
W: Yeah.

Unit 10

Track 2.28

Julia

The way I commute to work is probably quite unusual! I rollerblade! I live in Surfside, a suburb in the north of Miami and I work at a hotel on Miami beach. It takes about twenty-five minutes to get to work. And of course it costs nothing. It's usually warm and sunny in Miami and rollerblading is very healthy – I really enjoy it. But rollerblading is a bit dangerous when you cross busy roads. And it's tiring!

Billy

Commuting is really difficult in London. It's a huge city and there's a lot of traffic. You can't really commute by car because it's impossible to park in the centre of London. There's a good underground system but there aren't any stations near my house so I get the bus to work. It isn't expensive but it's sometimes quite slow because of all the traffic. And I hate waiting at the bus stop in the winter, it's very boring!

Track 2.29

B = Brendan, T = Travel agent
B: Good morning. Do you sell tickets for Eurostar trains?
T: Yes. What's your destination?
B: Paris.
T: And when do you want to go?
B: I'd like to go on Friday the fifth of June.
T: Return or one-way?
B: I'd like return tickets, please. We want to come back three days later. And I'd like four tickets.
T: OK. I'll just check. OK, do you want first or standard class?
B: Oh, first class is expensive. I'd like standard class. How much is that?
T: Let me see. Four return tickets in standard class, and your departure date is the fifth. That's £280.
B: Right. What time does the train leave London?
T: At ten thirty in the morning.
B: Is it a direct train?
T: Yes. There are no stops.
B: And can we take our bikes on the train?
T: Yes, but it costs an extra £20 for each bike.
B: Fine. I'd like four tickets then, please. Can I pay by credit card?
T: Sure. Put your card in the slot ...

Track 2.30

J = Jason, D = Derek, A = Alicia, M = Moira, T = Todd
J: I'm here at Heathrow Airport with a group of friends from Lancaster University: Derek, Moira, Todd and Alicia. Today's the start of an amazing adventure for them. In half an hour they get on a plane to begin the holiday of a lifetime. Derek, how are you feeling right now?
D: To be honest, Jason, I'm feeling quite nervous ... nervous but excited.
J: Why are you nervous?
D: Well, this is my first long plane journey. I haven't been on a long-haul flight before so it's my first time ... and Australia is a long way away.

J: Are the rest of you experienced travellers?
A: We've been to America!
M: Yes, the three of us have been on a long-haul flight before. I went to Florida last year with Todd and Alicia.
J: Have you been to Australia?
M: No, we haven't.
D, A, T: No, we haven't been to Australia.
J: So I guess you're all very excited about those activities in Australia? Have you been horse-riding, hiking or bungee jumping before?
T: Alicia and I have been horse-riding. We went when we were in Scotland two years ago. But Derek and Moira stayed in the hotel! So they haven't been horse-riding before.
M: It was cold!
D: But we've all been hiking. We went last year.
J: And have you ever been bungee jumping?
D: Oh no. We haven't been bungee jumping. It's the first time for all of us.
M: I'm very nervous about it!

Track 2.31

1 Have you been to Australia?
2 No, we haven't been to Australia before.

Track 2.32

1 Have you been to the cinema in England?
2 I've been to a disco with him.
3 Have they been to dinner in Finland?
4 We haven't been to Paris in spring.

Track 2.33

P = Presenter, A = Author
P: Let's talk about your new book now. It's called *Modern-day Adventurers*. What exactly do you mean by 'adventurer'?
A: Mmm, that isn't an easy question. It's probably best to give you some examples of adventurers.
P: OK ...
A: Take Jessica Watson.
P: I've heard the name. What's she done exactly?
A: She's sailed solo around the world, you know, on her own, and she's only sixteen. And then there's Ramona Cox.
P: I haven't heard of her.
A: She's done lots of solo flying – long flights in small aircraft. But perhaps the most remarkable adventurer is Ben Fogle, the TV presenter. He's cycled across Europe, he's walked, and run across the desert, he's ...
P: Hold on ... what hasn't he done?
A: I don't know! His most famous adventure was crossing the Antarctic; it was a race actually – a race of over 500 kilometres to the South Pole. He and James Cracknell did it in January 2009, and it took seventeen days.
P: James Cracknell ... now what has he done?
A: He's won two Olympic gold medals in rowing – that's how you know him, but he's also rowed across the Atlantic, with Ben Fogle – that's over 2,500 kilometres; they did that in 2006, again in a race. It took them fifty days and they came fourth.
P: Very impressive! And you mentioned the desert.
A: Oh, yes. Ben Fogle has done the Sand Marathon – that was in 2004; it's a race across 200 kilometres of the Sahara Desert. That took him seven days. And he's also cycled across Europe – that was when he was much younger. He cycled to Monaco with a group of friends in 1993, and they did it in nine days.
P: What about mountains? Has he ever climbed a mountain?

A: Yes, he has. He's climbed several! He climbed Kilimanjaro in 2006 – that was his fourth peak of over 6,000 metres ...
P: This is amazing ...
A: Yes, well, now you know what I mean by adventurer!

Track 2.34

parked, had, walked, got, seen, written

Track 2.35

1 have 2 fit 3 short 4 park
5 bald 6 sleep

Track 2.36

1
Matt: Have you ever met anyone famous?
Amber: No, I haven't, but my brother has. He works in the film industry so he meets famous people all the time.

2
G = Gavin, W = Wendy
G: Have you ever stayed in a five-star hotel?
W: Yes I have, ah ...
G: You have?
W: Yeah in, um, Venezuela, in, ah, the capital city of Caracas, I stayed in the Hilton there and I think that's a five-star.

3
A = Amber, M = Matt
A: Have you ever flown in a hot-air balloon?
M: I haven't. Have you?
A: Yes, I have. It was a birthday present from my husband. It was amazing.

4
W = Wendy, G = Gavin
W: Have you ever eaten insects?
G: No, I haven't. I have a friend who has ...
W: Really?
G: ... but I don't think it's a good idea.
W: Why not?
G: I don't like the idea of eating insects.
W: Ah. I've, I've eaten insects in Thailand on holiday.
G: You have?
W: Mmm, it wasn't very nice.

5
A = Amber, M = Matt
A: Have you ever played any unusual sports?
M: Well, I don't really play it, but I like to go rock climbing.
A: Oh, wow, that is quite unusual.

Track 2.37

R = Robin, W = Woman, M = Man
R: Excuse me. I've lost my wallet. I think somebody has stolen it. Is there a police station near here?
W: I'm afraid I don't know. I haven't been to this part of town before. Why don't you ask in the library over there?
R: OK. Thanks. ... Excuse me. Do you know the way to the police station?
M: The police station. Yes, it's easy. You turn left at the next road, Mill Street ...
R: Turn left, OK ...
M: Then go straight on for about 200 metres. Then you get to the post office.
R: The post office.
M: Yes, it's on the right.
R: On the right, OK.
M: Next to the post office, turn right into Beech Road.
R: Beech Road. OK.
M: Go along the road, then turn left at the bookshop, into Lime Avenue.
R: Yes, OK.
M: The police station is in Lime Avenue. It's at the end of the street, on the left.
R: OK, thanks very much.

Audioscripts

Unit 11

Track 2.38
biology, chemistry, geography, history, languages, literature, maths, physics, science

Track 2.39
Welcome to the free Tourist Information Line for visitors to Great Britain. For information on visas and immigration, please press one. For information on driving in Britain, please press two. For information on hotels, please press three. For information on public transport in Britain, please press four. To return to this menu at any time press the star key.
You have chosen option two: driving in Britain.

Track 2.40
If you have a valid driving licence from your own country, you can drive in Britain without a British licence for six months. After six months, you have to get a British driving licence. To get a British licence you have to take a driving test. You can find information about the British driving test on our website. To rent a car in Britain you have to have a valid driving licence from your country and a credit card. Drivers under the age of eighteen can't rent cars in Britain.
When you are driving in Britain, you don't have to keep your documents with you. The British drive on the left side of the road and, unlike the United States, you can't turn right at a red traffic light.
For more information on British driving regulations, please look at our website. That is the end of the driving section. To return to the main menu press the star key.

Track 2.41
You don't have to be a British citizen to take a British driving test but you have to have a valid British visa.

Track 2.42
1 leaf 2 few 3 fan 4 V

Track 2.43
1 Philip finds French films very violent.
2 Very few fines feel fair.
3 Fiona Philips never gives fitness advice to fresh fruit fanatics.

Track 2.44
We don't have a lot of rules in the United States really. I mean we don't have to do military service and we don't have to have identity cards. You can drive when you're sixteen and you can even buy a gun when you're twenty-one! And in most states you can get married and have your own bank account or credit card when you're eighteen. Actually, you can usually get married when you're sixteen, but you have to have permission from your parents.
But some things aren't so easy. You have to be twenty-one to go into a bar or a nightclub, and smoking is difficult – you can't smoke in offices, shops or restaurants. And of course we have to pay when we see a doctor or go to hospital, which is pretty expensive.

Track 2.45
P = Presenter, S = Sarah, H = Harumi,
R = Ross, A = Andreas
P: Now, as you know, the government is thinking of making the school-leaving age eighteen, up from sixteen, and of course there was a report recently which suggested that children should start serious learning at six, not four or five. In the studio we've got four people from different educational backgrounds: Sarah, from England; Harumi, from Japan; Andreas from Germany, and Ross, from New Zealand. Good morning all.
All: Hi/Hello.
P: Sarah, let's start with you. Where did you go to school?
S: Mmm, my primary school was in a little village in the west of England ... then I went to the secondary school in the local town when I was eleven. I left when I was sixteen to start work. I trained to be an electrician.
P: So you had, what, eleven, twelve years at school. Harumi, you went to school in Japan. How long did you spend at school?
H: Well, I went to elementary school then high school in Kyoto – for about thirteen years, yes, six to eighteen. Then I went to university and studied English.
P: That's why your English is so good. Ross, when did you leave school?
R: I left at eighteen too – though you can leave at sixteen, or even fifteen in New Zealand if your parents agree. I went from high school to a teacher training college and studied sport – that's what I teach now.
P: What about you, Andreas? Did you leave school at eighteen?
A: At nineteen actually. Then I went on to university and studied law – that was another seven years after about fourteen years at school!
P: What a punishment! What was your favourite subject at school? Law?
A: No, come on! I went to a gymnasium, which is an academic school, but they don't do law, even there. No, I really liked politics and economics, and maths, surprisingly.
P: OK, one other thing. Another current topic is the use of new technology in schools – how much to have in schools and so on. Which kinds of new technology did you use? Sarah?
S: Hah! New technology – you're joking, aren't you? When I was at school a CD player was new technology!
P: Ross, I think you're the youngest here. Did you use much new technology at school?
R: Yeah, we used email at school and we also had forums, you know, where you can send messages to whole groups, like the history forum, the sports forum. And in my last year, we had interactive whiteboards, you know, so the teacher had the whole book up on the board. That was cool!

Track 2.46
1 Where did you go to school?
2 What was your favourite subject?
3 How long did you spend at school?
4 When did you leave school?
5 Which kinds of new technology did you use?

Track 2.47
Did you leave school at eighteen?

Track 2.48
H = Host, C = College, OU = Open University,
MM = MicroMatters, U3A = University of the Third Age
H: Good afternoon. Welcome to *Live to Learn*. People today often want to continue learning throughout their lives, but what are their choices? First, let's talk to Aileen Murphy, head of Bexley Green Language and Business College.
C: Good afternoon. Well, at Bexley Green College, we offer a range of languages and business topics, so it's a good place to get more skills.
H: Which languages do you teach at the college?
C: Well, English, of course – we have a lot of students from overseas, all over the world really, who take English and perhaps a business course, too – we have very well-qualified business tutors. But we also offer French, Spanish, German, Russian and Chinese for English speakers. A lot of our students are business people who want to learn another language.
H: How much do the courses cost?
C: It depends. Our most popular course is a ten-week part-time language course of about ten hours a week, and that costs about £800.
H: And your classes are all at your college?
C: No, most of our classes are at the college, but we have evening classes at the local university buildings, too.
H: Thank you, Aileen. Now we have Graham Knight, from the Open University.
OU: Well, the Open University is a distance learning university – that is, you study at home, using books, CD-ROMs, the Internet. There are a few classes during the year, and there are often summer schools. Our students have to study for about twelve hours a week.
H: And what subjects do you offer?
OU: Almost everything! You can study academic subjects like art history or maths, or subjects like computing or nursing.
H: Thank you, Graham. Oh, what about cost?
OU: Most of our courses are about £600 a year, at the moment.
H: Thanks. Now, Beth Anderson works for a professional training company, MicroMatters Ltd.
MM: Right. We offer training courses in computer skills for people who are actually working with computers.
H: Do you offer courses to people who aren't working?
MM: Oh, yes. Most of our courses last two or three days, for people in work, but we also have full-time courses for a week or two weeks, and evening courses.
H: And the cost?
MM: A week's course costs about £900. Of course, we provide everything – the trainers, the training room at our centre, the computers – the trainees don't have to pay for any extras, so we aren't cheap.
H: Thank you. Now, finally, James Beecham, to tell us about the University of the Third Age.
U3A: Good afternoon. The University of the Third Age is for retired people, so it's mostly older people. We have groups across the country, and each group organises its own courses. Usually, the group uses a hall in its town, or a local school, and lecturers come to speak to the group on weekday afternoons. We try to make our type of learning very cheap. The membership cost is different in different groups, but most are around £20 a year – so it's very cheap.
H: Yes, I see. And what kind of courses or subjects do you offer?
U3A: Well, the speakers talk about their special subjects or their interests, so we have a lot of different topics, but it's not usually very academic.

H: Right. Thank you, everyone, for coming. Now, let's move on to …

Track 2.49

S = Secretary, N = Nadia

S: Good morning. Bexley Green College. Can I help you?

N: Hello, yes. I'm calling from Moscow, Russia. I want to enrol for one of your courses online, but I'm having problems. I tried to send the application through, but I don't think it went.

S: OK. What's your name?

N: Koparova, Nadia Koparova.

S: Could you spell your last name for me?

N: Yes, it's K–O–P–A–R–O–V–A.

S: Thank you. Ummm, no, I don't have a form from you.

N: Oh, what did I do wrong?

S: OK, let's see. Is your computer on?

N: Yes.

S: Do you have the application form on the screen?

N: No, I've got your home page, with phone numbers.

S: Right, click on 'apply now' at the top of the page.

N: OK. Now I've got the application form.

S: OK. Let's go through it together.

N: I don't have a problem with the personal information, but I'm not sure if I filled in the rest correctly.

S: OK, so you've got your personal details. What about the course?

N: I want to do two courses at the same time.

S: That's fine. There are three lines under 'course choice', you just put your two choices on the first two lines. What are they?

N: I want to do 'Advanced Improvers' English' …

S: That's code 30755 – put that in now.

N: OK, and 'Business for Beginners'.

S: That's code 72592 – put that on the second line.

N: Right.

S: Now enter the start date for the courses.

N: That's 22nd June. OK.

S: And choose how you want to pay.

N: Um, credit card. My number is …

S: Don't give me the details now; it isn't necessary.

N: OK. Now I click 'send' …

S: No, don't do that! You have to read and accept the conditions first.

N: Oh, I didn't do that before. So, I read those … and I click here … OK.

S: When you click 'accept the conditions', a 'send' box appears.

N: I see. Yes, it's there.

S: Now you click on that and the form comes to us. OK, do that now.

N: Right. Oh, that's OK now.

S: Yes, I can see your form on my screen now. That's all fine, Ms Koparova, you can expect to hear from us in two or three days …

Track 2.50

R = Receptionist, P = Peter

R: Hello, Windham Catering College.

P: Oh, hello. I'm phoning about the Italian cookery course. I'd like to enrol for it. Can I do that on the phone?

R: No, I'm afraid not. You can enrol by post or online.

P: Oh, I don't have a computer here. How do I enrol by post?

R: Let me take a few details and I can get a form to you. Then you just fill it in and send it back to us with your payment.

P: Oh, let me check – you send the form to me?

R: That's right.

P: Can I ask some questions first?

R: Of course. What would you like to know?

P: Can I just check the date it starts?

R: Yes. All our courses start in the week of 13ᵗʰ September, with a break of one week in the week of 23ʳᵈ October and …

P: Can you repeat that, please? A break in …

R: A break in the week starting 23ʳᵈ October.

P: OK, and it's on a Wednesday evening, is that right?

R: Yes.

P: Can I ask what time the lessons start?

R: They start at 7:00 and finish at 9:30.

P: That's OK, good. And the price is about £220, I think.

R: Yes, £225 exactly.

P: Does that include the ingredients?

R: No, it doesn't. You have to bring the ingredients – you get a list each week for the next week.

P: Oh, I see. I think that's everything.

R: You know that you have to come to the other building in the evening, don't you?

P: Sorry, what was that?

R: Evening classes aren't in the main building; they're in the annexe. Come to the main building and then take the first road on the left – York Street.

P: Oh, OK. Thanks.

R: Right, your name is …

Unit 12

Track 2.51

P = Paul, M = Mia

P: Look, here's the photo of us rafting on the Colorado River last summer.

M: Oh, yes. That was so frightening. I didn't really enjoy that – the raft went so fast! It was really dangerous.

P: Well, I thought it was fantastic.

M: I preferred trekking in the Grand Canyon really.

P: Yes, that was fun. But a bit slow. And do you remember when we went on those bikes in the hills behind San Francisco?

M: Yes. I remember cycling up the hills and through all those tunnels!

P: Yes, that was great.

M: Mm, I really enjoyed that. Do you think that was the best part of our trip?

P: No, horse-riding was the best. That was really exciting.

M: Yeah, you're right. I think horse-riding was my favourite, too. It was a lot of fun.

P: Next year I want to try something different.

M: What?

P: Bungee jumping in New Zealand.

M: Wow. That sounds great!

Track 2.52

O = Omar, J = Julie

O: So, Julie. It's the start of the summer holiday next week. What are your plans?

J: Oh, we're going to visit my grandparents in Belgium.

O: Are you going to take the children?

J: Yes. My grandparents are going to move to a small flat later this year, so this is our last chance to stay with them.

O: Are you going to fly there?

J: No, we're going to take the train the week after next.

O: So you're going to go through the Channel Tunnel?

J: Yes. I'm going to drive the car to the station at Ashford and put it on the train. It's really exciting. What about you, Omar?

O: Well, I haven't got much money at the moment, so I'm not going to go away. I'm going to stay at home …

J: But that's what you did last year!

O: I know. My life's really boring!

Track 2.53

We're going to take the train.

Track 2.54

1 She's going to get fit.
2 They're going to sell their car.
3 We're going to learn French.
4 I'm going to buy a laptop.

Track 2.55

Everyone Wants To Be Famous

Everyone wants to be famous,
To be someone everyone knows.
To live in a mansion with servants,
And star in the best TV shows.

A sports star, an actor, a winner,
Whatever it takes to get fame.
A model, a dancer, a singer,
So people remember your name.

But when you're alone
In a hotel or home
The night is so cold
And there's no one to hold.
When life seems so blue
Just who do you talk to?

Because when you're a star
Everyone knows who you are.
They know what you do,
But do they really know <u>you</u>?

Track 2.56

Because when you're a star
Everyone knows who you are.
They know what you do,
But do they really know <u>you</u>?

Track 2.57

1 me being see free tree
2 fly high stay cry my
3 together there never forever clever
4 fame same name game am
5 nice price advice drive rice

Track 2.58

Victoria

I've joined the drama group at university because I really love performing. I'm going to learn how to sing and dance. I want to act in plays and musicals and of course I'd like to be famous one day. Sometimes TV producers watch our student shows so anything is possible!

Helena

My ambition is to become a famous politician, perhaps a minister in the government. At the moment I'm just a student – I'm studying politics at college. But I'm going to work for a politician next summer. I want to learn more about elections and voting. I'm really excited about it.

Lewis

That was my first training session with the team, so I'm a bit tired. It's only the reserve team but I'm going to practise with them twice a week to improve my physical fitness and ball control skills. I'm going to work really hard to get into the first team. I know I'm a good footballer and I'm sure I'm good enough to get a place in a professional team. These days footballers are the biggest stars in the world, and I'd really like to be rich and famous.

Track 2.59

A = Andi, D = David

A: Good morning. *Charity Champions*, Andi speaking. How can I help you?

D: Oh, hello. My name's David MacMahon. I'm thinking of doing one of your

Audioscripts

challenges, but I want to ask a few questions first.

A: That's fine, David. Please go ahead.

D: Well, first question, where exactly do the challenges take place?

A: All over the world; in Africa, Latin America, and the Caribbean, Asia, the Middle East and Europe.

D: Oh, I see. And what kind of challenges are they? I mean, what kind of activities are they?

A: Well, we have hiking, cycling, sailing, rafting, mountain climbing and horse-riding.

D: Oh good. I like hiking and I love cycling – I use my bike every day – but I don't like horses. And I don't like sailing much.

A: Well, there are quite a few there that you like. What about rafting and mountain climbing?

D: I'm not sure. I mean, I'd like to climb a mountain one day. I haven't done any rafting, but I'd love to try it. Do you have to be very fit?

A: Well, yes, you have to be quite fit. Our expeditions are difficult and you have to have a good level of fitness. Erm, really, you need to choose an activity you know you can do and start training early. We have training weekends, too. People find them very useful.

D: Oh, that sounds good. Er, ... who pays for the expedition?

A: Um, you do. Well, you pay for the expedition, or you raise money to pay for it.

D: And how do I raise money for the expedition?

A: Well, there are several things you can do, for example, you can do a charity dog walk to get money.

D: Oh, I'm not sure about that. I mean, I like dogs but I wouldn't like to walk them.

A: Well, there are other ways. How about working for people, you know, doing their gardens? Anyway, we also ask you to raise money for your charity.

D: Oh, yes, of course. Erm, who chooses the charity?

A: You do. Do you have any other questions, David?

D: Yes, how do I raise money for the charity?

A: The same as for the expedition, or you ask people to sponsor you, you know, a pound for each kilometre on a trek. So do you want to join one of our expeditions, David?

D: I'm not really sure. Can you send me some information?

A: Certainly. I can send you a brochure. Let me take your details and ...

Track 2.60

I'd really like to play the classical guitar.

Track 2.61

1 white 2 Dave 3 late 4 mine
5 lake

Track 2.62

M = Martina, S = Silvia, J = Jacques,
H = Hiroshi

M: Oh, I'm so glad the exam's over. Now we can relax a bit.

S: What are you all going to do for the summer, then? What about you, Martina?

M: I'm going home to Krakow next week, and I'm certainly going to spend two or three weeks at home, just relaxing, perhaps sitting in the garden if the weather's good enough.

S: Isn't that going to get boring?

M: Yes, probably. I'd like to work for two months, but it's difficult to get summer jobs at home at the moment.

J: I've got a job.

H: Really, Jacques. What are you going to do?

J: I'm going to take part in a summer camp for young children in Canada, so I can work and make some money, and continue to speak English.

S: Aren't you going to go back to France for the summer?

J: No, I'm planning to go back in September. You know I really want to work with children – I hope to start a course on teaching in primary schools in September.

S: Oh, that sounds lovely. What are you going to do, Hiroshi?

H: Me? I'm going to travel.

M: Travel? Why?

H: Well, I'm a long way from home, so it makes sense to travel in Europe while I'm here. I'm going to go to Paris next week – by Eurostar – and then I'm just going to go where I want. I'm not going to make any arrangements.

J: It sounds fantastic! I'd like to come with you!

H: But you've got a job! No, I want to practise my English. I hope to get a place in a university here next year.

S: You're all so lucky – doing interesting things. I'm going to study all summer.

M: Study – why?

S: I really want to go to medical school and it's very difficult to get a place.

J: Well, good luck!

ActiveBook and ActiveTeach contents

The ActiveBook component features the Students' Book pages in digital format and includes integrated audio and video as well as interactive exercises for students to do in class or at home. The ActiveTeach component will help you get the most out of the course with its range of interactive whiteboard software tools and extra resources.

ActiveBook

Students' Book pages and interactive activities

Audio bank (Class CD material)

Video clips

Interactive video activities

Phonetic chart and dictionary

Video clips to play on DVD player

ActiveTeach

Students' Book pages and interactive activities

Interactive whiteboard tools with save functionality

Audio bank (Class CD material)

Video clips

Interactive video activities

Phonetic chart and dictionary

Extra resources for the teacher:
- class photocopiables
- video photocopiables
- printable audio and video scripts
- editable tests

Video clips to play on DVD player

Pearson Education Limited
Edinburgh Gate
Harlow
Essex CM20 2JE
England
and Associated Companies throughout the world.

www.pearsonlongman.com

First published 2011
Second impression 2011

ISBNs:
**New Total English Elementary Teacher's Book and
Teacher's Resource Disc Pack**
9781408267264

Set in Meta Plus Book-Roman
Printed in Spain by Graficas Estella